Scenic Driving MONTANA

S.A. Snyder

HELENA, MONTANA

A FALCON GUIDE®

Falcon® Publishing is continually expanding its list of recreational guidebooks. All books include detailed descriptions, accurate maps, and all the information necessary for enjoyable trips. You can order extra copies of this book and get information and prices for other Falcon® guidebooks by writing Falcon, P.O. Box 1718, Helena, MT 59624 or calling toll-free 1-800-582-2665. Also, please ask for a free copy of our current catalog. Visit our website at www.FalconOutdoors.com or contact us by e-mail at falcon@falcon.com.

Printed in the United States of America.

3 4 5 6 7 8 9 10 MG 04 03 02 01 00 99

All black and white photos by author unless noted otherwise.
Front cover: Many Glacier Road, Glacier National Park, *Michael S. Sample*
Back cover: Two Bears Lake, Beartooth Pass, *John Reddy*

Cataloging-in-Publication data is on file at the Library of Congress.

CAUTION

Outdoor recreation activities are by their very nature potentially hazardous. All participants in such activities must assume the responsibility for their own actions and safety. The information contained in this guidebook cannot replace sound judgment and good decision-making skills, which help reduce risk exposure, nor does the scope of this book allow for disclosure of all the potential hazards and risks involved in such activities.

Learn as much as possible about the outdoor recreation activities you participate in, prepare for the unexpected, and be safe and cautious. The reward will be a safer and more enjoyable experience.

 Text pages printed on recycled paper

CONTENTS

ACKNOWLEDGMENTS

Biggest thanks go to Paul, my chauffeur and companion, who helped me keep a level head while trying to navigate the unmarked backwaters of these drives. I could not have done this book without his help and his senses of humor and adventure that made exploring in bad weather more tolerable. For their patience, thanks to P. D. and Sophie, priceless friends who didn't always get to join us at historical sites and monuments, since most don't allow dogs.

Thanks go to my parents, veterans of cross-country camping trips (and either saints or lunatics for bringing along five kids), without whom I might never have known the joys of travel. Thanks also to my ancestors who brought me to Montana and keep me grounded here.

Thank you to those who reviewed sections of this book for accuracy—Dave Walter of the Montana Historical Society and Shelly McKamey of the Museum of the Rockies. And thank you Randall Green, editor, who gave me the opportunity to write about *Montana Scenic Drives.*

Quaking aspen in autumn splendor along the Beartooth Highway. Photo by Michael S. Sample

For my friend, Bill
1899-1991

LOCATOR MAP

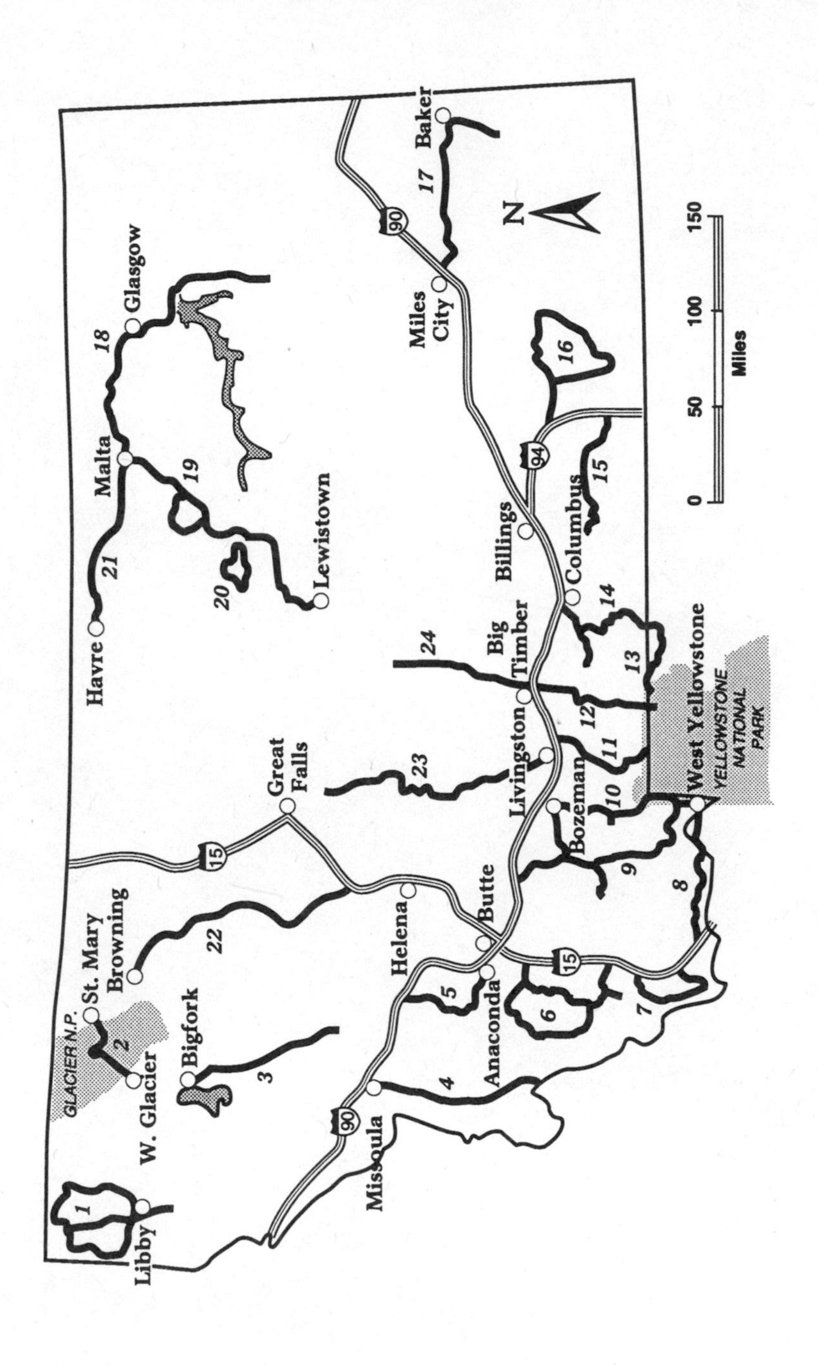

Libby
1
W. Glacier
GLACIER N.P.
2
St. Mary
Browning
Bigfork
3
22
Missoula
90
4
Anaconda
5
Helena
Butte
15
6
7
8
9
Great Falls
15
23
Livingston
Bozeman
10
11
12
West Yellowstone
YELLOWSTONE NATIONAL PARK
Big Timber
24
13
14
Columbus
Billings
15
94
16
Havre
21
Malta
19
20
Lewistown
18
Glasgow
Miles City
90
17
Baker
N
0
50
100
150
Miles

LEGEND

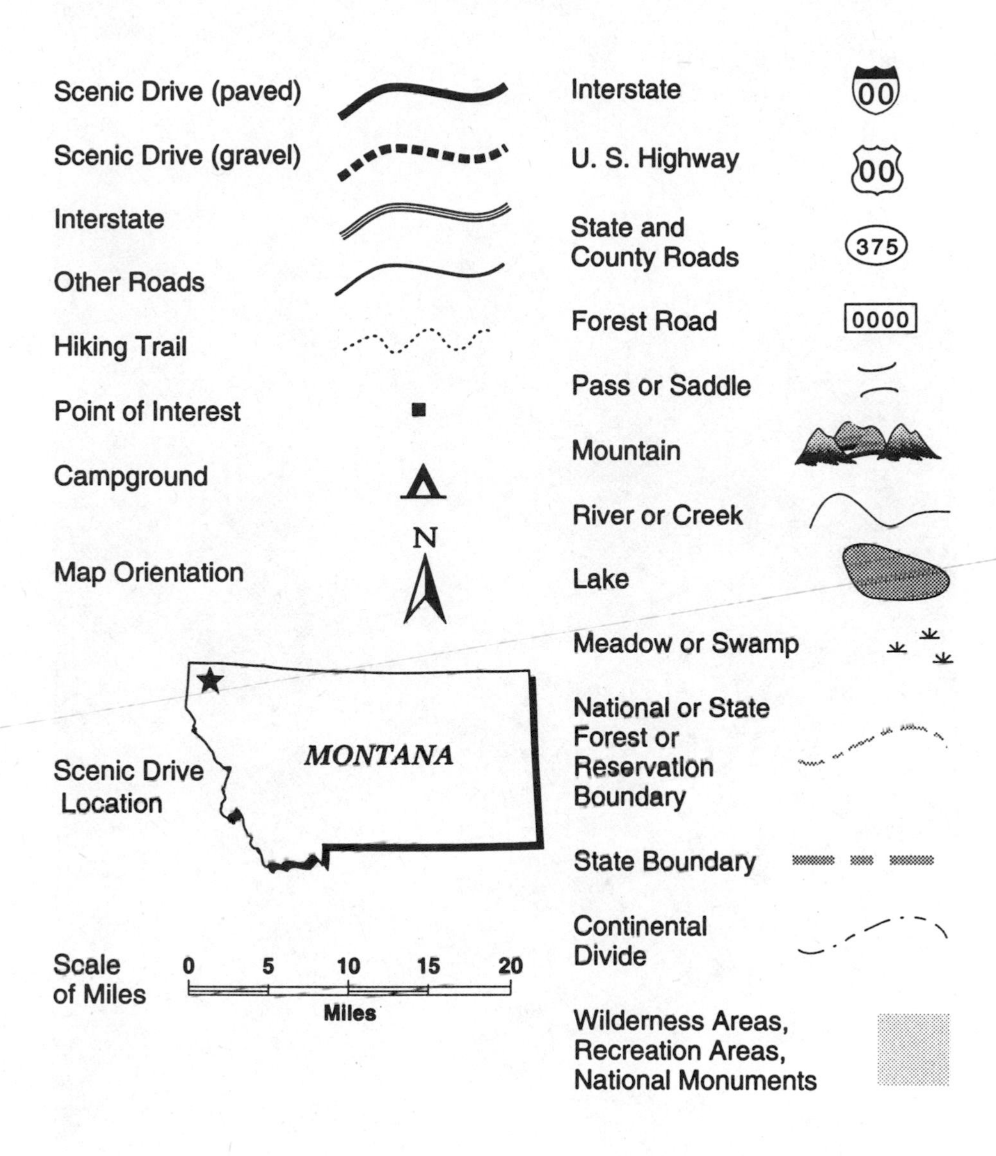

Scenic Drive (paved)
Scenic Drive (gravel)
Interstate
Other Roads
Hiking Trail
Point of Interest
Campground
N
Map Orientation
MONTANA
Scenic Drive Location
Scale of Miles
0
5
10
15
20
Miles
Interstate
00
U. S. Highway
00
State and County Roads
375
Forest Road
0000
Pass or Saddle
Mountain
River or Creek
Lake
Meadow or Swamp
National or State Forest or Reservation Boundary
State Boundary
Continental Divide
Wilderness Areas, Recreation Areas, National Monuments

Rock Creek Canyon on the hairpin descent into Red Lodge on the Beartooth Highway.

INTRODUCTION

> What we [Montanans] are *not* is often more compelling than what we are. The fact of our emptiness is in itself immensely significant.
>
> — K. Ross Toole,
> *Montana, An Uncommon Land*

Few western states conjure up images of leathery cowboys, unscrupulous outlaws, Native Americans, dusty trails, unforgiving mountains, endless wilderness, and old-fashioned lawlessness like Montana does. Throw in a few explorers, trappers, settlers, lots of wild animals, and some cattle and sheep, and you have the state as it once was. This young state, which joined the union in 1889, couldn't have a richer history if it were left to simmer for a few hundred more years.

Montana is the fourth largest state, after Alaska, Texas, and California, and its more than 147,000 square miles are still sparsely populated in relation to the rest of the country. Census estimates for 1994 showed Montana's population has surged to 856,000 in the past decade. Still, cattle outnumber people in the state, three to one. Of all the states, Montana ranks forty-eighth in population density, with between five and six people per square mile, if they were spread out evenly. But most people live in the western part of the state; in eastern Montana, the roughly two-thirds of the state on the Great Plains, many neighboring towns are separated by 2-hour drives.

In such communities, the land's presence overshadows the people. Montana has more than 22 million acres of forest. The rest of its acreage is taken up by grasslands, badlands, croplands, rocky terrain, sagebrush flats, glaciers, or water. The state is huge and diverse. Montana borders three Canadian provinces and four states. Within its boundaries lie two national parks, ten national forests, seven Indian reservations (representing eleven tribes), more than forty state parks, nearly a dozen wilderness areas, more than fifteen national wildlife refuges, dozens more state-owned wildlife management areas, and several national monuments and historic sites.

The name "Montana" was derived from either the French or Spanish word for mountain, although only the western third of the state is mountainous. The eastern part, with scattered bumps, bulges, and canyons, is relatively flat. Agricultural plains and grasslands are dominant features. "Island" mountain ranges add relief to Montana's wide spaces, rising in great lumps, seemingly out of nowhere. Perhaps no other state in the union possesses such dramatic differences in landscape.

This variable landscape is one cause of Montana's weather extremes. Many of these are record breaking. The lowest recorded temperature in the lower forty-eight states was registered at Rogers Pass, north of Helena, in 1954—a cool -70 degrees Fahrenheit. The largest temperature drop was 100 degrees in twenty-four hours near Browning in 1916. Montana has the lowest average monthly temperatures in the contiguous United States for six months of the year, including the month of August, which has seen a low of 5 degrees. West Yellowstone, on Montana's southern border, is consistently the nation's cold spot year-round. Conversely, the state's hot, dry summers can bake the life right out of the land. Medicine Lake, in northeastern Montana, holds the state's record for the highest recorded temperature—117 degrees.

Montana Past and Present

Some anthropologists believe the Kootenai Indians were the first native inhabitants of Montana; their oral traditions say they have been here for several thousand years. The arrival of these first people was followed by that of the Salish, Crow, and Pend d'Oreille Indians, who arrived a few hundred years ago and shortly thereafter were joined by the Blackfeet, Sioux, Assiniboine, Gros Ventre, Cheyenne, Chipewyan, and Cree peoples.

The first whites to come to the region were probably French trappers, but close on their heels were Meriwether Lewis, William Clark, and the other members of the Lewis and Clark Expedition. When the United States bought the city of New Orleans and environs in 1803, the French government threw in an extra chunk of land—the Louisiana Purchase—totaling 838,000 square miles of what is now the American West. Anticipating this acquisition, President Thomas Jefferson planned to send a corps of discovery into the

Bannack remains one of Montana's best preserved ghost towns.

region and asked Congress for money to fund it, even before its purchase was finalized. Upon congressional approval, the expedition set out from Saint Louis in 1804 with orders to map the United States' new holdings and record its plants, animals, and minerals. The explorers were also to make contact with its human inhabitants and make celestial observations. Most importantly, they were to get through to the West Coast; the government wanted to find a northwest passage to the Pacific Ocean.

The expedition covered more than 8,000 miles in two years, four months, and nine days, and the journals that the team kept remain some of the world's most detailed and meticulous. The leader of the expedition, Meriwether Lewis, was only twenty-nine years old at its start (and four years younger than Clark). Lewis made scientific observations and kept records while Clark acted as diplomat and negotiator with the Indians. Only one of the expeditionary party died on the whole trip, reportedly from a ruptured appendix, and there was only one violent, fatal encounter with Indians, in which two Blackfeet were killed. The expedition was considered a grand success by Jefferson and other officials. Montana historian K. Ross Toole attributed the success to Lewis's and Clark's intelligence and ability to command.

The explorers initially made their way across what would later become Montana by following the Missouri River. In the 1840s and 1850s, this wide waterway became Montana Territory's first "road" of sorts, bringing more trappers and explorers such as John Colter (who had accompanied Lewis and Clark), Jim Bridger, and Manuel Lisa (who established the first fur-trading post) into this area. Jesuit priests, called "black robes" by the Indians, arrived at the same time and tried to convert native peoples to Christianity.

This relatively quiet period in Montana's history came to an end when gold was discovered in the early 1860s. Strikes in Grasshopper Creek (Bannack), Alder Gulch (Virginia City), and Last Chance Gulch (Helena) made news back East, and the rush to Montana was on. Trappers and explorers were joined by miners, enterprising settlers, and merchants who served their needs. Steamers and keelboats brought more gold seekers up the Missouri as wagons streamed across the continent in long trains, bringing dreamers and hopefuls to a seemingly endless land.

The stream of Montana's agricultural pioneers began flowing during the 1880s, although the peak of the homestead era came in the dryland farming days from 1914 to 1918. The Homestead Act of 1862 entitled a man who could make a go of it to 160 acres for a ten-dollar filing fee. More land was homesteaded in Montana than in any other state. Although many of the dryland farmers were seasoned, determined, and tenacious, most were nevertheless defeated by geography—Montana's dry and severe climate combined with natural disasters eventually broke their spirits.

With the arrival of European peoples to Montana Territory, Native Americans and their traditional lifeways were threatened. Long-used hunting grounds and sacred sites meant nothing to some land-hungry settlers or gold-greedy miners who believed they had a "Manifest Destiny" to use the

Bighorn Canyon above Yellowtail Dam near Fort Smith.

western spaces. Increasing settlement caused more and more conflicts with native peoples. Miners wanted access to tribal lands, under which lay vast mineral riches. Settlers demanded land and water rights, and sought protection from the U.S. Army, especially in the days following the Civil War. Bison, on which the Indian tribes depended for food, shelter, and clothing, were exterminated by the millions by commercial hunters. Many native people starved. In an effort to control "unruly" Indians and "civilize" them, the government decided to move them onto reservations—lands often deemed unsuitable for crops, livestock, or mining, or whose boundaries were drawn over if minerals proved to be rich there.

The history of the relationship between the U.S. government and Native Americans was one of broken promises. As K. Ross Toole wrote in *Montana, An Uncommon Land*:

> Our "policy" toward the Indian has been no policy at all. It has run an extraordinary gamut from extermination to impractical Christian humanitarianism, but has always been a "policy" which ignored the Indian himself and his peculiar heritage.

Conflict was inevitable when two cultures clashed. The most famous battle between the U.S. Army and Indian tribes in Montana took place on the Little Bighorn River in 1876. The bloody fight killed many on both sides and brought General George Armstrong Custer to his end. Just days before the confrontation, Sioux and Cheyenne warriors had defeated General George

Crook at Rosebud Creek, an event that affected the outcome of the Battle of the Little Bighorn.

Another series of battles, a year later, involved the Nez Perce tribe. Gold was discovered on the Nez Perce reservation in Idaho in 1860, and for several years the Indians had lived in peace with the miners. But when the U.S. government drew up new boundaries for the reservation, shrinking it to about one-tenth of its original size, five bands of Nez Perce refused to sign any more treaties. These bands were considered hostile and ordered onto their new reservation nevertheless. Somewhere in the course of the story, a Nez Perce warrior was killed; his friends retaliated by killing some whites, and the saga of the 1,170-mile Nez Perce march began.

The non-treaty Indians, under the leadership of five chiefs, fled their homeland in search of a new home free from U.S. government interference. Chief Joseph, the Nez Perce spiritual leader, led the entire crew of 800 people, including only 125 warriors, and 2,000 horses. During their four-month journey across Montana, Idaho, and Wyoming, the Indians entered from Lolo Creek, went south up the Bitterroot Valley, crossed into the Big Hole, headed south again into Idaho, went east cutting through Yellowstone Park, then entered Montana again, passing west of Billings, and headed north toward Canada, where they surrendered just shy of the border. In all, nine skirmishes were fought between Nez Perce and U.S. military forces before Chief Joseph's poignant surrender in the Bears Paw Mountains. Scenic Drives 4, 6, 13, 20, 21, and 24 in this book pass by parts of the Nez Perce National Historic Trail (Nee-Me-Poo Trail).

A "victim" of the 1959 earthquake along the Madison River on the shores of Quake Lake.

Index and Pilot peaks in the Shoshone National Forest, Wyoming on the Beartooth Highway.

As Montana's Native Americans were driven onto reservations, the tide of miners, loggers, and agricultural settlers continued to advance. It wasn't long before railroads crisscrossed the state, hauling livestock, minerals, wool, grains, and furs from the commodity-rich West to population centers in the East. Many boomtowns choked and died after just a few short years of prosperity; many others sprang up to take their places. One of the more successful towns was Butte, atop "the richest hill on earth," considered the copper-mining capital of the world. Its mines yielded gold, silver, copper, and abundant minerals.

Two figures in Montana's history, Marcus Daly and William Clark, are synonymous with mining. Known as the "copper kings," both Daly and Clark owned extensive mining claims, mills, and smelters in Butte and Anaconda, as well as their own newspapers. After falling out over territorial delegate elections, Daly and Clark saw fit to destroy each other through slander and dirty tricks. They fought over the designation of the newly created state capital: Clark won with his pick of Helena. Later, he also won the race for U.S. Senate, but Daly's relentless pursuit to get him evicted over allegations of bribery proved fruitful. Clark was forced to resign from the Senate, although he later served a full term. The "war of the copper kings" became worldwide news.

Butte's streets witnessed other kinds of mining wars. Horrible working conditions in Montana mines motivated laborers to form unions, among the first workers' unions ever created in this country. Violent and bloody clashes between union members and anti-unionists were frequent in Butte during the latter part of the nineteenth century and the early days of the twentieth.

Not all of Montana's history was violent. In fact, one of its more famous legislators was known for her pacifism. Jeannette Rankin became the first woman elected to the U.S. Congress—in 1916, before most women in the United States could vote. She served two separate terms, and was the only member to vote against entry into both world wars. In 1941 she announced, "As a woman, I can't go to war, and I refuse to send anyone else." Her congressional career ended after she refused to declare war on Japan, but that didn't stop her from promoting peace. She died in 1973, but the Jeannette Rankin Peace Resource Center in Missoula still carries out her mission.

Montana's present is deeply ingrained with mythic cowboys and Indians, cattle drovers, miners, vigilantes, and mountain men, but its future will most likely be marked by tourists and small-business owners who need only facsimile machines and computers to function. Today, the state's "gold" lies in its scenery, wildlife, and vastness. Towns are booming once again, but not from people coming to seek the mother lode. Instead, most newcomers arrive seeking quieter, slower lifestyles in safer, more friendly communities. Montana's wild and scenic landscapes are icing on the cake.

Yet many native Montanans have soured on the arrival of too many neo-Westerners, many of whom are perceived to threaten the values and lifestyles from which Montana has evolved. Like Montana's Native Americans, cowboys, miners, and loggers feel as if they are targets of Montana's latest heritage assault. Battles are fought over how much wilderness is necessary, how many trees can be cut before destroying habitat and watersheds, how much land should be grazed by cattle, and how many mountains should be bulldozed for gold. Montana is still thought by some to be full of limitless natural resources for the taking. Battles over the consequences of such harvests have been waged in courtrooms and in Congress. Their outcomes may change Montana by a magnitude that it hasn't seen in more than one hundred years.

Natural History

Most of Montana's native trees are conifers, and many of its native hardwoods are only shrubs. Forest types vary from wet to arid and comprise pines, spruces, firs, larches, hemlocks, cedars, Douglas-firs, and junipers. Cottonwoods, aspens, box elders, ashes, and elms are dominant along Montana's rivers and streams. Native herbs, grasses, and shrubs number more than three hundred. Montana is home to 107 native mammals, from the tiny shrew to the awesome grizzly bear. All of our nation's native large hoofed mammals, except caribou, can be found roaming Montana's mountains or eastern prairies. Mountain lions prowl the forests and, lately, with increased numbers, have often found themselves in urban areas. The endangered black-footed ferret was recently reintroduced to Montana, and wolves, once exterminated from the state, have made a dramatic comeback in the last decade in Glacier National Park and along the Rocky Mountain Front.

Nearly 380 bird species have been recorded in Montana, and about 250 of those nest here or are year-round residents. The largest bird in Montana is the trumpeter swan, weighing in at 40 pounds; the smallest is the calliope hummingbird, a whopping 0.1 ounce. Reptiles and amphibians are few in Montana because of the cold climate, although thirty-three species (seventeen reptiles and sixteen amphibians) live in the state's forests, water sources, and arid plains. Montana lakes, rivers, and streams harbor more than eighty fish species. About fifty-five are native, while thirty-two have been introduced.

Hidden in Montana's bowels are the remains of much earlier flora and fauna. Montana is one gigantic dinosaur and fossil bed, where some of the world's most important—and only—finds have been made. Most of the world's *Tyrannosaurus rex* skeletons have been unearthed in Montana, the first discovered in 1902 and the most complete dug up in 1990. One of the world's few discovered dinosaur nesting colonies was found along the Rocky Mountain Front as recently as the 1970s. And one species of dinosaur uncovered in eastern Montana is the only specimen of its kind.

Fossils of marine plants and animals tell us that a much different landscape once existed in what is now eastern Montana. A gargantuan Cretaceous-era sea covered this portion of the state about 75 million years ago. Montana's rich coal deposits and scattered oil finds are the biggest legacies left by these ancient creatures.

Scenic Driving Montana gives you just a taste of what the Big Sky has to offer. You are encouraged to explore the regions not mentioned in this book and meet Montana's people. Montanans are not ostentatious. They do not hide behind veils of secrecy or make apologies for who they are. They are proud to be hard-working and grounded to the land, and are painfully honest about the way life is. The best way to get to know Montanans is to go to county fairs, rodeos, powwows, and museums; hire guides for fishing, hunting, or backpacking; or hang out in local cafes and bars. More often than not a saloon was the first establishment to be erected in every boomtown and the last to close its doors when a town went bust. Even today, Montana bars are gathering places for members of small communities, of all ages. I once saw a hand-printed sign hanging behind the bar in a small-town saloon in western Montana. It read, "Please watch your language. This is a family bar." Considerate, unapologetic, and honest. Welcome to Montana.

BEFORE YOU BEGIN

From east to west and north to south, Montana's highways are dotted with white metal crosses. These sad reminders of lives lost on the road are also warnings to others: slow down, be watchful of wildlife and other users of the road (not just high-speed motorized vehicles), and use common sense, no matter what the driving conditions. Most Montana roads are unimproved gravel or dirt tracks, which are rarely or never maintained. In many counties, even secondary paved roads receive little attention. If a driver has an accident in such rural country, help might not arrive for several hours—if at all, in the most remote places. Many steep, narrow mountain roads have no guardrails, so take it easy on those turns.

Some visible victims of the highway are wildlife of every species, from small reptiles warming themselves on pavement to huge moose crossing the road. Collisions with large mammals have killed motorists; in most cases cars are severely damaged and animals die. Please be alert for wildlife near any Montana road during all seasons and at all times of the day, but especially from dusk to dawn. Slow down whenever you see animals near the road.

Winter can occur during any month of the year in Montana, and severe conditions can pop up faster than a tick in a frying pan. Be prepared for all driving conditions, regardless of geography and season. Winter is a spectacu-

A sad reminder for users of Montana's highways to drive safely.

lar time in Montana, but if you venture into the Treasure State then, it is best to check travel conditions before heading out on any long-distance drive. For a road report, call the Montana Highway Department at 1-800-332-6171, or listen to local weather radio.

Both private property and tribal lands can be found on Montana Indian reservations; ask permission before using these lands. Some tribal lands are off-limits to nontribal members, while other lands are open for hiking, fishing, or certain types of hunting. Permits may be required for these activities. Regulations for each reservation differ, so contact tribal headquarters for details. The appendix of this book lists sources to contact for more information.

Although Montana no longer has a daytime speed limit on federal and state highways, please remember that's not a license to drive foolishly. You can still be ticketed for driving in an "impudent manner." Besides, you can hardly enjoy Montana's awesome scenery when it is nothing but a blur out the window.

Enjoy your travels, drive safely, take only memories away with you—and please don't litter. Thanks!

1 YAAK RIVER COUNTRY
U.S. Highway 2, County Road 508, Montana Highway 37

General description: This 175-mile drive passes through the rainy pine, spruce, and fir forests of northwest Montana. It winds along rivers, over a steep mountain pass, and along the shores of narrow Lake Koocanusa.
Special attractions: Kootenai Falls County Park, Yaak River Falls, Lake Koocanusa, Libby Dam, Cabinet Mountains Wilderness; museums; skiing, snowmobiling, hiking, backpacking, boating, fishing, wildlife viewing, camping.
Location: The extreme northwest corner of Montana, between the Idaho and British Columbia borders. The drive begins and ends in Libby, on U.S. Highway 2.
Drive route numbers: US 2, County Road 508 (Yaak River Road), Montana Highway 37.
Travel season: Year-round. The road from Yaak to Libby Dam along the west shore of Lake Koocanusa is open only as weather permits and is sometimes closed in winter. Snow and ice conditions make travel hazardous. Log truck traffic along the entire route can be heavy at times.
Camping: There are several Forest Service campgrounds along the route, in Kootenai National Forest. Five campgrounds border Lake Koocanusa, with nearly two hundred camping sites.
Services: Full services in Libby and Eureka. Limited services in Troy, Yaak, and Rexford.
For more information: Kootenai National Forest; Libby Chamber of Commerce; Troy Chamber of Commerce; Eureka Chamber of Commerce (see Appendix).

The drive:

> I would only approach the mountain now, and inspect it, creep about its flanks, learn what I could of its history, holding myself ready to flee on the approach of the first storm cloud. But we little know until tried how much of the uncontrollable there is in us, urging over glaciers and torrents, and up perilous heights, let the judgment forbid as it may.
>
> — John Muir,
> *Wilderness Essays*

This scenic drive is one of two that wind their way through Montana's western rain forests. Hundreds of square miles of hiking trails make Kootenai National Forest a great place for those seeking solitude.

The drive begins in the town of Libby on US 2. Originally a gold-mining camp, Libby was founded in 1886. When word reached the miners that a

1 YAAK RIVER COUNTRY

U.S. Highway 2, County Road 508, Montana Highway 37

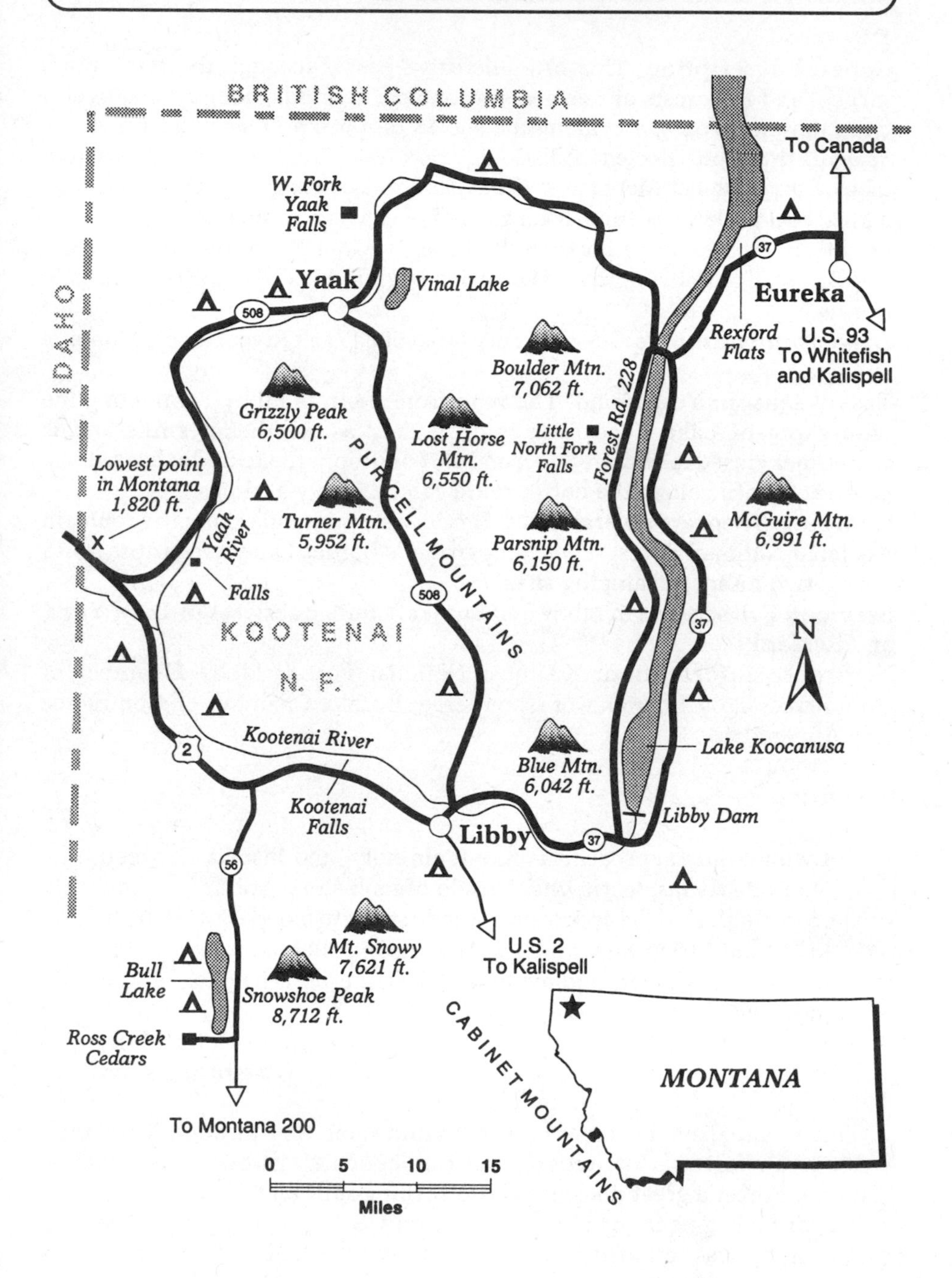

railroad had been proposed for the area, the tent camp on Libby Creek began building a real town in earnest. The abundance of timber in the area allowed pioneers to construct as many buildings as they needed. In 1906, however, a fire destroyed a whole business block in Libby and damaged several others. You can take a historic walking tour of the town; a pamphlet available from the chamber of commerce lists when the town's buildings were erected and describes the original businesses they housed. An Amish auction in June draws people from all over the West to buy handmade goods put on the block. If you're in town the third weekend in July, you can experience Logger Days. Nordicfest, in September, wraps up summer. Just east of Libby on US 2 is the Heritage Museum, open summers only, exhibiting artifacts and relating the history of the people who lived in the area: miners, loggers, trappers, and Native Americans. You can tour several buildings on the grounds, such as a miner's cabin, forestry cookhouse, and wagon barn.

Scenic Drive 1 goes west of town. Take US 2 about 10 miles west to reach Libby-Kootenai Falls County Park, which overlooks the vertical bluffs of the Kootenai River. Named for the Kootenai Indians, who were probably Montana's first native people, Kootenai Falls are considered to be a sacred place, traditionally used for meditation and vision quests. They are also the largest undammed falls in the Northern Rockies. Park in the wide area between the road and the river and take the short, paved trail through a copse of western red cedar and grand fir, where you'll find picnic tables and barbeque pits. The trail continues over the railroad tracks and to the river. The walking is easy, although to get to the falls you do have to go along a rocky

Kootenai Falls roils over rocks as the river cuts a narrow gorge through northwestern Montana.

Libby Dam backs up Lake Koocanusa for 90 miles. Photo by Randall Green.

terrace. There is a series of falls on the river, about 2 miles long, which you can also view from a suspended bridge downstream. Signs will direct you to both bridge and falls.

US 2 meets Montana Highway 56 in another 5 miles (about 15 miles west of Libby). Take MT 56 south about 17 miles to Ross Creek Scenic Area, a 100-acre preserve of giant western red cedars. Turn right (west) onto the road going into the site, which is paved for another 4 miles, and follow it to the parking lot at the trailhead. The winding, narrow road has some turnouts, but be sure to take corners slowly to avoid oncoming traffic. You can camp a few miles from the scenic area on the south end of Bull Lake. Signs will direct you.

Ross Creek Scenic Area was set aside in 1960 to preserve these rare, old-growth cedars. The larger trees are up to 8 feet in diameter and as tall as 175 feet. A 1-mile loop trail leads you on a self-guided nature tour, complete with interpretive signs. Another trail follows Ross Creek up to Sawtooth Mountain. Take time to stand inside the cavity of one of the dead cedars; it can be a humbling experience. Understory plant species you will find here are wild ginger, trillium, queen's cup bead lily, devil's club, Rocky Mountain maple, and several species of fern. Western white pines and grand firs mix with red cedars to complete this dark forest lit only by filtered sunlight. Take a deep breath and smell the richness of the soil. You can picnic in the lush green array along Ross Creek, which tumbles over moss-covered rocks in moist years but is bone dry in times of drought.

Other recreation along MT 56 includes camping, fishing, and boating on Bull and Spar lakes or boating and fishing on Savage Lake. To the east of the highway is the 94,000-acre Cabinet Mountains Wilderness, which you can access via trails along the highway. Check a Kootenai National Forest map for more details.

To continue Scenic Drive 1, retrace your route back to US 2, then turn left (west) and pass through the mining and timber town of Troy. Troy was once a base for railroaders and freight trains on the Great Northern Railway, as well as headquarters for silver miners working in the Cabinet Mountains. A small museum and visitor center relates local history.

About 14 miles past Troy, the Yaak River Road (County Road 508) heads northeast. Turn right here. About 6 miles after the turnoff is a small set of falls on the Yaak River, just above a campground. Though much smaller than the ones on the Kootenai River, Yaak River Falls, like most waterfalls, are worth a stop. The next 73 miles through "the Yaak," as locals call it, is heavily forested and, in places, heavily clearcut. The road twists wildly for much of the drive, but you needn't go fast through here anyway. There are dozens of side roads you can turn off to mountain bike, hike, or cross-country ski. There are also several Forest Service campgrounds. The road is narrow with no shoulder, but the surface is in good shape. Use caution, though, since logging traffic gets heavy. Log truck drivers seem to pay little attention to other traffic.

Why call this a scenic drive, since it crosses thousands of acres of clearcuts scarred by hundreds of miles of timber roads? You can't see most of the roads and clearcuts until you approach the top of the pass northeast of Yaak. Because of high precipitation, this rich logging area also has dense, wet forests. Travelers can explore the hundreds of trails and dozen or more lookout towers here. Plus, those who experience places like the Yaak can encourage ecologically sound forest practices on public lands. As you gaze across the clearcuts, keep in mind that some cutting is necessary to thwart the spread of mountain pine beetle, which would otherwise munch its way through doghair thickets of lodgepole.

For most of the drive the road follows the Yaak River corridor. After skirting Abe Lincoln Mountain, where Seventeenmile Creek spills into the Yaak, you will come to the tiny community of Sylvanite. There is a Forest Service ranger station here now, but this town was once a small gold-mining community (Sylvanite is the name of the gold-bearing ore found here) complete with a grocery, hotel, and newspaper. Those who bothered to bathe could do so three nights a week, but they had to give the barber shop/ bathhouse advance notice. When massive forest fires blazed through Idaho and Montana in 1910, Sylvanite was destroyed and, except for a few buildings, has never been rebuilt.

Watch for moose as you approach the town of Yaak, about 30 miles up the Yaak River Rd. Named for an Indian word meaning "arrow," Yaak is made up of just a few houses and a bar. It is the most northwest town in Montana.

Just before mile marker 30, in the center of town, is the turnoff to a road along the South Fork of the Yaak River, which cuts right through the Purcell Mountains. Take this route for an interesting side trip. The rounded hills you see were sculpted by glaciers moving in from the area that is now British

Awarded for its design and appearance, this is the only bridge that spans Lake Koocanusa on the American side.

Columbia. The sharp-hewn peaks of the Cabinet Mountains are made of the same Precambrian sediments, but were spared complete suffocation by ice and so appear vastly different. The South Fork road also has a maddening twist as it makes its way to Libby, about 38 miles south. Several small lakes and trailheads provide ample recreation along the way, and Turner Mountain serves those who like to downhill ski.

The main loop of the scenic drive continues on the main Yaak River Rd. As you go northeast from Yaak, pay attention to road signs directing you to Lake Koocanusa and the town of Rexford. If you take this drive in autumn, you can see the cottonwoods, aspens, and larches turn gold against the dark green forest backdrop. Drive with the window down and listen to the fallen leaves blow across the road. Smell the spruce trees, a hint of the holiday season to come, their fragrant scent mixed with that of rotting leaves.

About 9 miles beyond Yaak, take a right at the "Y" in the road, going toward Rexford. (If you go left at the "Y" you can view both the upper and lower West Fork Falls.) From this point, the road winds around many curves, and the dense forest on either side adds to the feeling of being in a maze. There are a few small lakes to the east, which you can access by trail from Vinal Lake Road, about 6 miles after the "Y." Vinal Creek Trail will take you to Turner Falls and Fish Lakes. There is also a wildlife viewing area here. Keep on the lookout for pileated woodpeckers, barred owls, goshawks, common loons, and blue herons, as well as moose in the bottoms and pikas on the rocky slopes. You can access Vinal Lake more quickly from Forest Road 746 just northeast of Yaak on the other side of the river. Refer to a more detailed Kootenai National Forest map for more information and directions to specific trails.

At about mile marker 43, the road begins to climb to a pass. If you follow the signs to Boyd Mill Cemetery, you will find that chainsaws replace the usual cherubs on stone markers here, attesting to the livelihood of the men they remember. At this point, you are only about 3 miles from the Canadian border, as the crow flies. The main road climbs along the edge of one of the clearcuts, and the others stand out like giant sores. Take a good look, for the environment's sake. The rainy climate can aid the healing process here, and it can cause more erosion.

At Porcupine Creek, you reach the top of the pass and begin to head down into spruce forest. This is Forest Road 92, also known as Sullivan Creek Road. Keep following the signs to Rexford and Lake Koocanusa. The 90-mile-long lake, a dammed portion of the Kootenai River, got its name from combining "Kootenai" with "Canada" and "U.S.A." It is a popular fishing spot for catching kokanee salmon. Other popular species include westslope cutthroat, rainbow, and Dolly Varden trout. Fishing is open year-round, but check regulations first.

At the lake, the road intersects with West Kootenai Road. Turn here and cross the only bridge across Lake Koocanusa. Once across the bridge, head right (south) to continue on the scenic drive loop. Or you can turn north and head toward the town of Eureka or to recreation areas with campgrounds and boat launches along the eastern shore of the lake at Rexford Flats.

The town of Rexford is now about 2 miles from its original location along the Kootenai River. Since it did not have flood insurance, the two-block town had to pick up and move when Libby Dam was built.

Eureka is built on a little hill along the banks of the Tobacco River. The Pioneer Village Museum has displays depicting early life on the Tobacco Plains. The surrounding country is open, with the Whitefish Range holding the valley on the northeast and the Salish Mountains bordering it on the southwest. South of town and near Lake Koocanusa are several small lakes along the Tobacco River. Many offer fishing, and a few have campgrounds. You can enter Canada just north of Eureka, although there are not many towns near the border and the scenery is similar.

To continue this scenic drive, go south from the Lake Koocanusa bridge, following MT 37 around the lake for 53 miles to Libby Dam. The road winds along rock cliffs and the east shore. Watch for bighorn sheep in late fall and winter.

Evidence of human habitation in the Kootenai River valley dates from as long ago as eight thousand years. Then, the Kootenai River flowed at a higher elevation and had a wider channel. Archaeological digs in the area have produced spear points and evidence of campsites along what would have been the banks of the river at that time.

South of Sutton Creek, Peck Gulch Campground has a boat launch. The next nearest boat launch is Koocanusa Marina and Resort, about 22 miles south; the resort includes a restaurant and fuel station, as well as cabins and a campground. There is also a recreation area below Libby Dam, 17 miles north of Libby. At the dam, you can take tours and stop at the visitor center. The 420-foot-high dam, which created the 370-foot-deep lake, was completed in 1975. It took workers nine years to build it. Displays at the visitor center walk you through the dam's construction and operation. A 1-hour guided tour of the powerhouse completes the picture.

At the south end of the lake, you can either drive across the dam or access the other shore a few miles south of the dam. A paved road along the west shore of Lake Koocanusa offers access to more camping, boat launching, and wildlife viewing. A barrier-free trail to Little North Fork Falls is located 11 miles south of the bridge on the west shore of the lake. Follow signs to the trailhead on Forest Road 336. You may see bald eagles near the lake and Alexander Mountain from October through the first half of December. Cross the bridge over the Kootenai River and head north on Forest Road 228 for about 7 miles to the Alexander Creek Picnic Area, where eagle viewing is best.

Take MT 37 back to Libby to complete this scenic drive.

2 GLACIER NATIONAL PARK

Going-to-the-Sun Road

General description: This spectacular 48-mile mountain drive switchbacks up and over the Continental Divide, following glacial river canyons and crossing an alpine mountain pass.

Special attractions: Glacier National Park, Logan Pass; bald eagle migration during early winter, mountain goats, mountain chalets, glacial lakes and rivers; hiking, boating, fishing, camping, wildlife viewing.

Location: Glacier National Park, in northwest Montana. The drive begins at the park entrance in West Glacier, off U.S. Highway 2, and ends on the eastern side, at Saint Mary, on U.S. Highway 89

Drive route number: None; the drive is known as Going-to-the-Sun Road or the Logan Pass road.

Travel season: From late spring or early summer to snow season. In spring and fall, check with Glacier National Park offices to see if the road is open.

Camping: There are several campgrounds in and around Glacier National Park, but these fill up early in the day. You may need to make reservations for some of these.

Services: Full services in West Glacier, at Lake McDonald Lodge, and in Saint Mary. Full services are also available outside the park in Columbia Falls, Kalispell, and Browning. Limited services in Apgar, Babb, and Kiowa.

For more information: Glacier National Park (see Appendix).

2 GLACIER NATIONAL PARK

Going-to-the-Sun Road

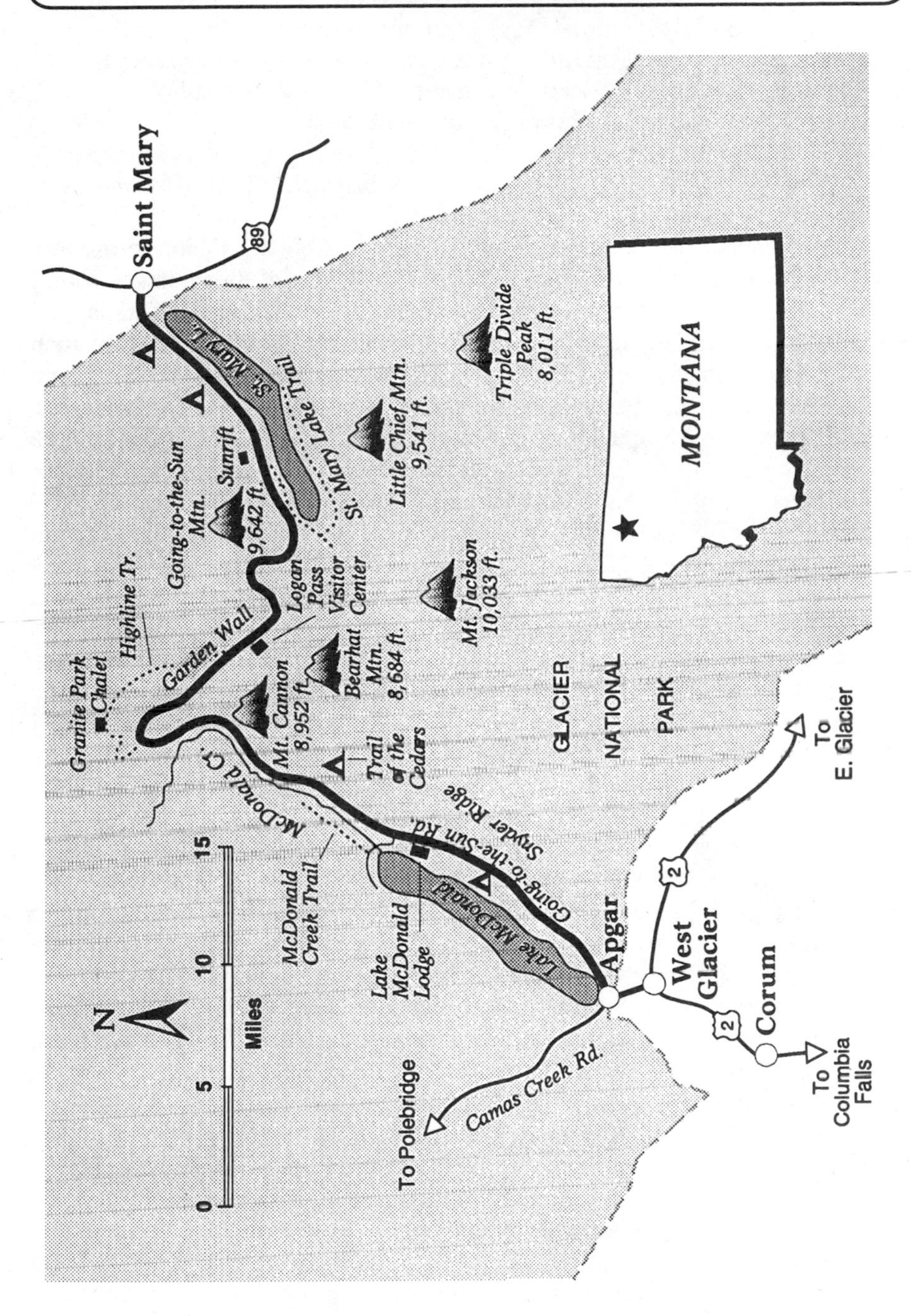

The drive:

> Mountains are as close as the surface of our planet reaches toward the heavens. The purest air, the purest water, and the purest light on earth are found amidst these great uplifted forms. They are the source of awesome natural power, shaping winds and weather and the rivers that flow across the land. And they are the home of very special communities of living creatures.
>
> — Douglas Chadwick,
> *A Beast the Color of Winter*

Not only are there not enough words to describe the Going-to-the-Sun Road, but mere description is not enough. This is one of those drives where you must get out of the car at every opportunity, to take in the smells, feel the weeping rock walls, listen to wind and water, and scan for wildlife, such as mountain goats, harlequin ducks, pine martens, grizzly bears, and raptors.

The road is considered an engineering masterpiece, even by today's standards. Twelve years of construction were finally completed in July 1933 at a cost of $3 million. Crews risked their lives to dynamite the road from sheer cliffs, in some places thousands of feet high. No wonder the employee turnover rate was 300 percent! The road was listed on the National Register of Historic Places in 1983 and was designated a National Historic Civil Engineering Landmark in 1985.

During 1995 and 1996, the road will again be under construction in certain places. A parking lot will be added at Oberlin Bend, just north of Logan Pass, to ease congestion where tourists often stop to look for mountain goats. Going-to-the-Sun Road will be closed at night to accommodate this construction. In addition, the Logan Pass Visitor Center will be closed after August 15 so crews can expand the parking lot there. Beginning after Labor Day 1996, the road near Triple Arches will be reconstructed. These closures and construction projects are only temporary, but they may last longer than anticipated. Weather conditions and other factors can slow such work.

The drive begins in West Glacier, a town at the west entrance to Glacier National Park. From US 2 in the center of town, turn north to Apgar, named for a family who homesteaded here in 1895, and follow signs for Going-to-the-Sun Road. The route will take you along the shore of Lake McDonald. On a clear day you can see Stanton Mountain, Mount Vaught, McPartland Mountain, Mount Cannon, and Mount Brown across the lake. You can trace your route from here: The drive will take you along the farthest point visible, a long arête called the Garden Wall. This sharp ridge forms the Continental Divide as it goes through Glacier National Park.

If visibility is low, or if it is raining, your chances of seeing the deeply gouged canyon of McDonald Creek, the full effect of cataracts on the Garden Wall, Bird Woman Falls, or other magnificent views along this scenic drive are slim. You may want to put off the drive for a day when skies are relatively clear. However, if you are dressed for it, hiking in the cool mist of the park is wonderful. Glacier in fog has its own charm.

Backpackers in Glacier National Park with Mount Clements looming in the background. Photo by Darrin Schreder.

Lake McDonald Lodge in Glacier Park draws guests from around the world.

As you drive the first 8 miles past Lake McDonald, you will see a snarl of spruce-fir and hemlock forest on your right side, while the lake shimmers between scattered trees on your left. There are dozens of pullouts along the lake if you want to get out and walk its shore. On still days, Lake McDonald is glasslike. You can rent boats and explore the lake yourself. It is cold and clear, and its rocky shores are fun places to skip rocks or sit while reflecting or writing in a journal.

The water clarity tempts swimmers, but unless you are tough you might want to wear a dry suit. It's cold! Lake McDonald was formed when a large chunk of ice settled in the depression during the last ice age, preventing glacial sediment from filling up the basin that is now the lake. On windy days the lake can seem like an inland sea, with whitecaps breaking on its gray, cobbled shore. The lake is 9.5 miles long and 1.5 miles wide, the largest lake in the park. It is more than 400 feet deep and has little or no plant life to speak of. For this reason, you can see many feet below its surface. Despite nutrient-poor conditions, it supports some fish, including cutthroat trout and mountain whitefish.

Not long ago the south end of Lake McDonald was a popular stop along the flyway for migrating bald eagles. They came to feed on kokanee salmon that choked McDonald Creek while spawning. Bald eagles, numerous as sparrows in the spruce trees, attracted late autumn visitors, steam from excited whispers swirling around people's heads. But due to changes in the complex food web of the Flathead River Basin, salmon populations began to decline in 1987, and the eagles moved on to other food sources. Today some bald eagles still make the stopover, and others are year-round residents. In late October and November you may still see eagles near Apgar.

Several trails into the forest on the east side of the lake allow visitors to experience a forest ecosystem. At the north end of the lake is Lake McDonald Lodge, built in 1913 and originally called the Lewis Hotel. The National Park Service bought the lodge in 1932. Inside the lodge, mounted animal heads of all the species found in the park hang in the lobby. Made of logs, with balconies overlooking the lobby, it has a rustic, western atmosphere. Boat tours of Lake McDonald leave the dock at the lodge several times a day.

In winter, Going-to-the-Sun Road is plowed only about 2 miles north of the lodge. Here you can park and cross-country ski farther up the road or into the woods on a trail. The snow is usually in good condition, and Glacier has a totally different atmosphere in winter. If you have the opportunity to come here then, I would strongly recommend a midnight cross-country ski during a full moon. A ski up Camas Creek Road can make up for the lack of eagles these days. If you listen carefully, you may hear the ghostly cries of wolves guiding members of their pack to a rendezvous. There are other skiing and hiking opportunities nearby. A short road heading west from the northern tip of Lake McDonald leads to private holdings and a ranger station. Several trailheads take off from this road; consult a park map for further details. Just under a mile up the main road from the ranger station junction, a bridge crosses McDonald Creek. You may want to park here and get out to take a closer look at the creek. The water has carved holes in the bedrock and smoothed the rock surface, giving the creek bed an almost soft appearance. On the other side of the creek, a trail leads through the woods and back to the ranger station road. It is a 2-mile, soothing walk through hemlock and grand fir forest, relatively flat, with only one steep incline.

The road winds around curves and narrows north of Lake McDonald. It follows McDonald Creek, where harlequin ducks dabble from spring to fall. Get out at any one or more of the several turnouts along the creek and search with binoculars for these steel gray, white, and rust-colored ducks quietly bobbing in the ice-blue riffles. During winter these miniature ducks are tossed in the surf along the West Coast.

Farther up the road take your chances and stop at the turnout marked "Moose Country." I've only seen a moose here once in the dozens of times I have traveled this route, but you may get lucky, especially in early morning or evening. If nothing else, you can read the interpretive signs. Remember, moose get aggressive when people approach too close. Always observe wildlife from a distance.

About 4 miles north of Lake McDonald, near Avalanche Campground, the Trail of the Cedars is a popular and worthwhile walk. This short boardwalk tour leads you through a western red-cedar and hemlock forest. A few interpretive signs explain the ecology of this magnificent ecosystem. The ground is carpeted with ferns and devil's club, and a moss-covered rock wall weeps spring water year-round. The 200-foot-high trees filter light so well you need a flash for pictures. The boardwalk crosses Avalanche Creek. Here

Trail of the Cedars near Avalanche Campground in Glacier Park.

you can take pictures of probably one of the most photographed sights in the park: the creek as it tumbles over moss-covered boulders into a narrow gorge. After crossing the bridge, the boardwalk turns into a trail. From here, you can go through the Avalanche Campground on the asphalt road back to your car, or take a left to walk the 4-mile Avalanche Lake Trail.

The Avalanche Lake Trail is not very steep and takes you through the tangled forest to the lake, where you might see mountain goats on rock ledges overlooking the water. It is frequented by grizzly bears, but there will be warnings posted at the trailhead if grizzlies have been spotted recently in the area. In Glacier National Park, it is probably wise to hike with one other person, at the very least. Make plenty of noise (talking is usually noise enough to give bears warning of your approach) and carry bear repellent (a pressurized can of red pepper spray that has proved effective for warding off bears).

Across the main road from the Trail of the Cedars is the Avalanche Picnic Area. If you decide not to head up to the lake, you can sometimes see mountain goats from this vantage point as well. With binoculars scan the ridge to the east. Mountain goats have sharp hooves and spongy foot pads, much like a dog's, allowing them to skip along precipitous ledges with ease. At times they appear to taunt you with their penetrating gazes and the flippant way they bounce along the bluffs.

Shortly after you leave the Avalanche area the road begins its ascent. Vehicles longer than 21 feet and wider than 8 feet are prohibited beyond the Avalanche parking lot. From here the travel will be slow going—especially during summer, when traffic is heaviest. You will pass through a fire-scarred area, burned by a lightning fire in 1967. Notice how the alder thickets provide shade and hold soil moisture for the conifer seedlings that will eventually become giants again here.

The first big hairpin turn you come to is called "The Loop." You can park here and look south across the valley below to the 8,987-foot Heaven's Peak. A trail from here leads up to Granite Park Chalet. Closed in 1993 after a waste-treatment problem that attracted grizzlies, the chalet expects to open again soon for park visitors interested in spending a night or two in a glacier-carved setting. Day visitors to the chalet can enjoy a juicy slice of homemade pie in its small dining room. Granite Park and Sperry chalets are the only remaining chalets of seven built in Glacier backcountry between 1910 and 1917. For overnight stays you must make reservations in advance by mail, starting in January.

The Granite Park area is heavily used by grizzlies, especially in autumn. Again, warnings will be posted if bears have been seen in the area for extended periods, but take extra precautions in any case. People have been mauled and/or killed on this trail by bears. These unfortunate events affect the bears as well: When a bear kills or seriously injures someone, it is caught and usually killed.

You can take the Loop trail beyond the chalet all the way along the Garden Wall to Logan Pass. This is a spectacular hike, mostly level past the chalet, and you are just about guaranteed mountain goats, bighorn sheep, mule deer, hoary marmots, and pikas—little furballs related to rabbits only without the long ears and cotton tails. You can also see stromatolites, formations of fossilized sea creatures, along the trail. If you take the whole trail, give yourself an early morning start and expect to finish by late afternoon.

Continuing on Going-to-the-Sun Road, you gain quite a bit of altitude on your approach to Logan Pass. To one side is a sheer rock wall; to the other, several hundred feet of vertical drop. DRIVE SLOWLY. Several cars have taken unplanned plunges over the edge. Because you must keep your eyes on the road the whole time, you will benefit by getting out of the car at designated pullouts to take in the valley as it unfolds below.

A couple of miles before you reach Logan Pass, you can look for mountain goats at Haystack Bend, which has the only big parking lot between the Loop and the pass. In all but the driest of years water pours seemingly out of the grassy mountainside over Haystack Falls and seeps out of the moss down the Weeping Wall.

Logan Pass, at the Continental Divide, was the meeting point for two glaciers scouring rock in opposite directions. The result was the low, saddlelike cut of the 6,680-foot-high pass. You can see scrape marks in the cliffs above the road. From the Logan Pass Visitor Center, you can take the boardwalk up and over another low pass to the Hidden Lake overlook. You will probably encounter mountain goats somewhere along the trail. They sometimes will graze on grasses only 10 feet away from people. Goats are inquisitive and sometimes follow people; they have been known to lick hikers' urine for its mineral content. Although mountain goats look cute and fuzzy and appear tame, they are wild animals. Do not approach or feed them.

Frequent contact with people can make wild animals aggressive; if this happens, they may have to be killed. Do not be responsible for the destruction of your nation's wildlife.

In wet years, Logan Pass is often covered with snow year-round. The weather here can change every hour, so if you venture out on the boardwalk, dress appropriately. When or if the snow does recede, about July or August, the grassy valley at the top of the pass is blanketed with fragile alpine plants, some only blooming one day a year. Monkey flowers and all shades of Indian paintbrush also color the grassy meadow like a Monet painting. Gnarled pines here are deformed by the intense winter weather at such high elevation. This type of plant community is called *krummholz*, meaning "crooked tree." Step inside the visitor center to read more about the flora and fauna of Glacier.

As you head down from Logan Pass toward Saint Mary, 18 miles away, the terrain and plant communities change dramatically. The west side of Glacier Park is wet and often rainy throughout spring and into midsummer. East of the Continental Divide, moisture is more scarce. Notice the different kinds of vegetation. About 2 miles beyond Siyeh Bend is Jackson Glacier Overlook. This is a good place to see remnants of the massive glaciers, some four thousand years old, still carving the park's terrain. Just below the turnout are trailheads to Gunsight Lake and Pass and Twin lakes. There are a few more pullouts and trailheads along the way, some leading to mountain lakes others to glaciers and ridgelines.

The drop down to Saint Mary Lake is beautiful. At the north end of the lake you will find a trailhead for Saint Mary and Virginia falls. From this trailhead you can also walk along both shores of the south and west portion of Saint Mary Lake. Just below these trailheads on Going-to-the-Sun Road is Sunrift Gorge. You can park on either side of the bridge to go have a look at this unique feature, just a short walk from the road. The gorge is referred to as a geologic curiosity because it was not formed by erosion. Interpretive signs describe the likely processes of its formation.

Saint Mary Lake is 9.5 miles long by just under 1 mile wide at its widest point. At only 300 feet, Saint Mary Lake is not quite as deep as Lake McDonald, and has a much greener hue. Wild Goose Island, another one of the most photographed features in the park, was named for a pair of geese that for years built their nest there.

When you reach the area around Rising Sun, you will have dropped to arid bunchgrass prairie, vastly different from the cedar-hemlock forests of Glacier's west side. At the Triple Divide turnout you can see the only place in the country (and one of two on the continent) where water flows to three different drainage systems: the Gulf of Mexico, Pacific Ocean, and Hudson Bay. Head down to the visitor center at Saint Mary. The Park Service has restored an old ranger station nearby. Inquire at Saint Mary for tour hours. At this point you can either turn around and go back over Logan Pass to West Glacier or drive southeast on US 89 to Kiowa, then take Montana Highway 49 south to US 2, which follows the south and east borders of the park.

As you travel through Glacier you may want to keep in mind t. sacredness of this place to the Blackfeet people, both past and present. Th U.S. government purchased the lands from the Blackfeet for a mere $1.5 million in the late nineteenth century, during a time when Indian peoples were starving and completely dependent on the federal government for support. Until 1910, when these lands became a national park, the Blackfeet were allowed to use the area for hunting and fishing as well as for spiritual rituals. Today some Blackfeet Indians believe their ancestors' sacred lands ought to be off-limits to those who do not belong to the tribe.

3 SEELEY LAKE AND THE SWAN VALLEY

Montana Highway 83

General description: This 91-mile trek through the Swan Valley is flanked by the Swan and Mission mountains. It follows the Clearwater and Swan rivers and a chain of glistening lakes through larch, spruce, and pine forests with great hiking opportunities.
Special attractions: Blackfoot-Clearwater Game Range, Seeley Lake, Bob Marshall Wilderness, Mission Mountain Wilderness, Swan Lake, Swan Lake National Wildlife Refuge, Bigfork, Flathead Lake; boating, fishing, camping, wildlife viewing, hiking, backpacking, skiing, snowmobiling, ice skating.
Location: Northwest Montana. The drive begins at Clearwater Junction, 33 miles east of Missoula on Montana Highway 200, and ends near Bigfork at the north end of Flathead Lake.
Drive route number: Montana Highway 83.
Travel season: Year-round. Snow and ice make winter travel hazardous, and summertime storm squalls can whip around the mountain peaks with all the ferocity of winter in them.
Camping: Forest Service and private campgrounds are numerous for the most of the route. There is also unlimited camping off many Forest Service roads.
Services: Full services at Seeley Lake, Condon, Swan Lake, and Bigfork. Limited services at Clearwater Junction and various places along the way.
For more information: Lolo National Forest, Seeley Lake Ranger District; Flathead National Forest, Swan Lake Ranger District; Confederated Salish and Kootenai Tribes; Seeley Lake Chamber of Commerce; Swan Lake Chamber of Commerce; Bigfork Chamber of Commerce (see Appendix).

3 SEELEY LAKE AND THE SWAN VALLEY

Montana Highway 83

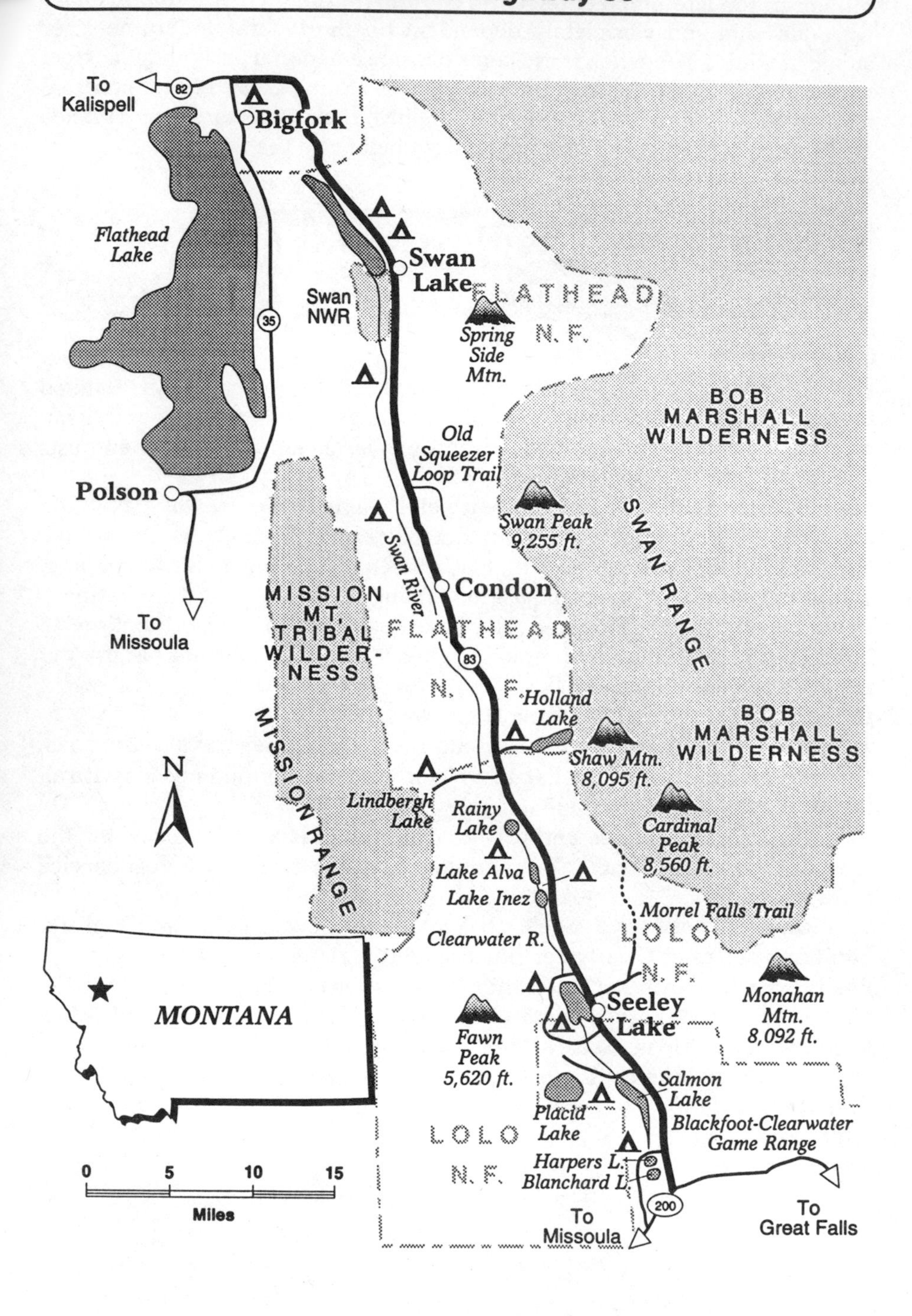

The drive:

> The common loon is our link to the environment. The calls of the common loon are truly reminiscent of a wilderness concerto. This one avian species stands out in bold relief against nature's complex orchestra of sounds.
>
> — Terry McEneaney,
> *The Uncommon Loon*

This drive begins at Clearwater Junction, 33 miles east of Missoula on MT 200. Turn north at the junction by the giant statue of a Hereford bull at the combination gift shop, grocery store, cafe, and gas station.

Just after you begin the drive look for a pullout on the west side of the road. Here, an exhibit offers interpretive information about the Blackfoot-Clearwater Game Range, a 50,000-acre refuge for elk and other wildlife, including deer, grouse, ducks, Canada geese, eagles, and bears. You can drive, walk, or mountain bike through the refuge from late May to the end of November. The dirt road is passable for most vehicles. It heads east just beyond the interpretive sign and viewing area. Beginning in December, about 1,400 elk migrate from the high mountains of the Bob Marshall Wilderness to winter on these sage-covered hills. The elk then head back to high country sometime in April. With binoculars, you can view them from the road in early winter and in late March, before they trek back to summer range.

Just beyond the game range pullout is a turnoff leading to tiny Harpers and Blanchard lakes, which offer opportunities for fishing, boating, and swimming. Because of its small size, Harpers Lake warms up quickly in the summer and is one of the few lakes in Montana where you can swim comfortably without turning blue. It is an ideal lake for paddling around in a small raft or canoe, especially for kids. No motorboats are allowed, and the lake is always calm.

Farther north, MT 83 begins to wind and narrow as it approaches Salmon Lake, the southernmost in the series of lakes along the Clearwater River. The lakes were created as flood depressions in a glacial moraine, filled when giant chunks of ice melted in each depression. At Salmon Lake, motorboats are permitted and summer weekend warriors ski until nightfall. There is a state park along its southeast shore with a boat launch and fishing access. Just north of that is a campground. The lake is set in a basin surrounded by conifer forest, as are all of the lakes in the Clearwater chain. These lakes get a lot of weekend use during summer, but on weekdays you might find some quiet time. Watch for deer all along this route, especially in early mornings, late afternoons, and evenings. Also found here are bald eagles, red-necked grebes, great blue herons, and yellow warblers that migrate in spring and fall.

Common loons nest on the shores of Salmon and Seeley lakes and Lake Alva. This region supports the largest nesting population of loons in the

Winter view of the Swan Mountains.

western states, with an estimated summer population of more than two hundred. A wildlife viewing area on the west side of the road has an interpretive sign about loons in the area. Loons use at least four basic sounds, classified by biologists as wails, tremolos, hoots, and yodels. One of the loon's most identifying characteristics is its wailing call, which can pierce the most dense spruce-fir forests. The birds' haunting wails shatter tranquillity and evoke images of the truly wild. The tremolo is what people call the loon's laugh. It is a warning cry that intruders are near. Loons are also tremendous divers. Adult birds can dive deeper than 200 feet, but typically dive from 6 to 120 feet. Chicks less than one week old have been filmed diving as deep as 15 feet. Loons are also able to swim submerged for a few hundred yards and have been known to streak beneath boats.

If you want to view loons you can do so on the northeast shore of Salmon Lake, the western shore of Seeley Lake at Seeley Lake Campground, the northeast shore of the lake near the ranger station, and the northeast shore of Lake Alva. From May through mid-June, nesting time, please keep your distance from these wonderful birds. Loons will readily abandon their nests if disturbed by people coming within 200 to 300 yards, whether by boat or on foot. Even anglers can unknowingly fish too close to nesting loons, forcing the birds to abandon their usual two eggs.

Northwest of Salmon Lake is the turnoff to Placid Lake and its state park, often used for boating, fishing, and camping. As the name suggests, it is usually quieter than Salmon Lake. Anglers may want to try for trout and kokanee salmon. The lake is surrounded by forested, rolling hills with many

private cabins along its shores. Follow the signs to the park. There i
range here, so be mindful of cattle along the gravel road.

Back on MT 83, north of Placid Lake and south of the town of Seeley L
(named for the first white man to live there), the road passes through m
open rangeland. Here you get a great view of the Swan Mountains to the ea
and the Mission Mountains to the west. The Swan Mountains are heavily
roaded from logging. This does not bode well for wildlife, especially grizzly bears, since it allows access for people who explore the forested mountains. The best way to explore this country is by foot, skis, or mountain bike. Please respect road closure signs for wildlife's sake.

The town of Seeley Lake thrives on both winter and summer recreation, serving boaters, anglers, hunters, snowmobilers, and cross-country skiers. Just north of town is the road to Morrel Falls National Recreation Trail. This relatively flat trail, about 2.5 miles long, will guide you through the forest to a set of tiered waterfalls that tumble over high rock bluffs. Two small lakes (or ponds, really) catch the water streaming in from the falls. It is a great hike for those who do not like steep trails, and the falls at the end are worth the walk. If you are feeling adventurous when you get to the falls, take a steep hike up the trail along the falls and you will see another tier. Keep going and you will find smaller and smaller tiers as you head up the mountainside.

To get to the trailhead, take Forest Road 477 heading east just north of the town of Seeley Lake. (Follow the signs to the medical center.) The road becomes gravel shortly after you turn. Follow the road for about a mile until you get to a left-hand turnoff. This is still FR 477. The route is well marked with wooden Forest Service signs, and the gravel road is in good condition. Watch for other traffic, though, as the road narrows. The trailhead is 8 miles in from the main road.

Back on MT 83 at the north end of Seeley Lake is a ranger station where you can get information and directions for boating the Clearwater Canoe Trail. This is a gentle, 3.5-mile float along the Clearwater River that connects the southern chain of lakes in the Swan Valley. Watch for muskrats, beavers, turtles, warblers, common loons, wood ducks, kingfishers, snipes, and other shorebirds and waterfowl. This float is especially nice if you have only one vehicle because you can park it at the ranger station and take a short walk (1.5 miles) back to the put-in point. During winter, cross-country ski trails south of the ranger station offer both easy and difficult trails for Nordic skiers. You can also ice skate on this and many of the other lakes in the chain. Ask at the ranger station for directions to the wildlife viewing blind nearby.

North of the ranger station, the road is heavily forested on both sides, mostly with larches, Douglas-firs, and lodgepole pines. In autumn, the larches, our only deciduous conifer, turn gold before dropping their needles. Watch for deer on the road here and throughout the drive. The Swan Valley is full of whitetails, many of which are hit by cars.

If you want to take a drive through the forest off the main road, there are many Forest Service roads on which to do so. Some of these turnoffs are loop drives, clearly marked with signs. I recommend getting a Lolo National Forest map for more details about forest road driving. These roads will give

Canoe lessons on Harpers Lake in the Swan Valley.

you a better vantage point for viewing the Swan and Mission ranges, and can provide access for hiking.

North of Seeley Lake is another short chain of lakes—Inez, Alva, and Rainy lakes—all with access to boating, fishing, and camping. These are the larger of the northernmost lakes in the Clearwater chain. Several smaller lakes to the north and west also trickle into the Clearwater River. Dense forest along both sides of the road allows you to catch only glimpses here and there of the Swan and Mission mountains, which are most stunning when snow-capped.

North of Lake Inez, the West Fork of the Clearwater Road leads to several other small lakes in the foothills of the Mission Mountains. In order to hike in the Mission Mountain Tribal Wilderness, you need to buy a tribal permit. For information contact the Confederated Salish and Kootenai Tribes.

At about mile marker 29, the trees clear from the road for a moment for a staggering view of the Swan Mountains. Pull over and have a look. Just over a mile up the road at Summit Lake is a turnout on the west side where the sharp peaks of the Mission Mountains come into view. A mile north of that, Beaver Creek Road turns off, leading to Lindbergh Lake and the Mission Mountains Wilderness. From this road the lake is accessible only by trail. A few miles farther up the road is another turnoff to Lindbergh Lake and a campground.

Lindbergh and Holland lakes are the southernmost lakes in what is the Swan River chain. About 2 miles north of Lindbergh Lake Road is the turnoff to Holland Lake on the east side of MT 83. You can boat, camp, fish, and swim here, as well as enjoy many hiking trails, including the Holland Falls National Recreation Trail. Holland Lake has a guest lodge for those who would rather not camp, and campers can use showers there for a small fee. This is a great place to enter the 1-million-acre Bob Marshall Wilderness comple… locally as "The Bob," just east of Holland Lake.

Bob Marshall was an avid outdoorsman with a keen interest in pres… remote national lands of scenic significance. He was founder of the W… ness Society, which helped pass the 1964 National Wilderness Preserva… Act that today protects millions of acres of wildlands from development. 1930, Bob Marshall wrote an article for *Scientific Monthly* in which he state… that there was only "one hope of repulsing the tyrannical ambition of civilization to conquer every niche on the whole earth. That hope is the organization of spirited people who will fight for the freedom of the wilderness." If you have a chance, experience Bob's wilderness.

North of Holland Lake, MT 83 flows past meadows, some separated from the road by copses. In early morning or evening you may want to pull over where it is safe to do so and look for wildlife. You will likely see small groups of white-tailed deer and possibly hear coyotes getting ready for their evening hunt. Grizzly and black bears also use these meadows to forage for food. Remember to keep your distance from these and all wildlife.

North of Condon you enter the Swan River State Forest. At the forest headquarters building, you can take the Old Squeezer Loop Road to a couple of short loop trails through the conifer forest and add birds to your "life list." You may see hairy woodpeckers, warblers, Swainson's thrushes, and hummingbirds. Take Forest Road 554 (Goat Creek Road) for 1.5 miles, then turn right onto Squeezer Creek Road. The trails are about 2 miles farther up the road. You can also follow FR 554 to the north and back out onto the main highway. Consult a Flathead National Forest map.

About a mile south of Swan Lake is the Swan River National Wildlife Refuge, containing marshland and meadow. This 1,568-acre refuge supports at least 170 bird species as well as deer, moose, elk, bears, and river otters. Turn west off the highway and go down a narrow dirt track to watch for black terns, bald eagles, great blue herons, tundra swans, wood ducks, and yellowlegs. You can paddle a canoe through the water and get a better view of these birds and more. Put in at the bridge on Porcupine Road (Forest Road 10229) south of the lake and float the 3.5 miles to a boat ramp on the southeast shore of Swan Lake.

The small town of Swan Lake lies at the southern end of the lake that bears the same name. There are a few campgrounds here, and fishing and boating access. There are also full services and many trails and Forest Service roads in the foothills on both sides of the lake. The road skirts the entire east shore of Swan Lake before making its way toward Bigfork. Look for signs for the turnoff to the west.

Bigfork was once described as a "huddle of little gray houses in a hollow" but has now become a trendy tourist town with coffeehouses, art galleries, and gift shops. During summer, Bigfork hosts art fairs as well as theater performances. It is on the northeast shore of Flathead Lake, which, as the largest natural freshwater lake west of the Mississippi, is also one of Montana's most gorgeous.

From Bigfork you can explore the shores of Flathead Lake, or head northwest to Scenic Drive 1 or northeast to Scenic Drive 22. Missoula, where Scenic Drive 4 begins, is about 2 hours south.

THE BITTERROOT VALLEY
U.S. Highway 93

General description: This 95-mile drive up the Bitterroot Valley to the Idaho border goes from the urban setting of Missoula and south along the beautiful Bitterroot Mountains, with a view of the rolling Sapphire Mountains across the valley.
Special attractions: Fort Missoula, the University of Montana, USDAFS Aerial Fire Depot and Smokejumper Visitor Center, International Wildlife Film Festival, Ravalli County Museum, Saint Mary's Mission, Daly Mansion; wildlife refuges, urban and mountain trails, hot springs, theater, concerts, museums, art fairs, county fairs, lectures; skiing, bicycling, floating, fishing, shopping.
Location: West-central Montana. The drive begins in Missoula and goes to the Idaho border. Drivers may elect to loop back to Missoula via the East Side Highway.
Drive route number: U.S. Highway 93.
Travel season: Year-round.
Camping: There are several Forest Service campgrounds in the Bitterroot Mountains, and unlimited camping (undeveloped) in the national forest surrounding the valley. Missoula has a commercial KOA Campground.
Services: Full services in Missoula, Lolo, Hamilton, Darby, and Sula. Most services, and limited lodging, in other towns along the route. There are numerous private guest ranches and lodges.
For more information: Lolo National Forest; Bitterroot National Forest; Missoula Chamber of Commerce, Bitterroot Valley Chamber of Commerce in Hamilton (see Appendix).

The drive:

> The road through this hilley Countrey is verry bad passing over hills & thro' Steep hollows, over falling timber... continued on & passed Some most intolerable road on the Sides of the Steep Stoney mountains, which might be avoided by keeping up the Creek which is thickly covered with under groth & falling timber...
>
> — Captain William Clark,
> September 12, 1805

This drive begins in Missoula, one of Montana's largest cities. There is some discrepancy about where the name Missoula comes from, but the most commonly accepted story says it comes from the Salish word for "river of awe" or "by the chilling waters." Whatever the origin, there is no doubt that the river passing through Missoula, the Clark Fork, is both awesome and chilly.

4 THE BITTERROOT VALLEY

U.S. Highway 93

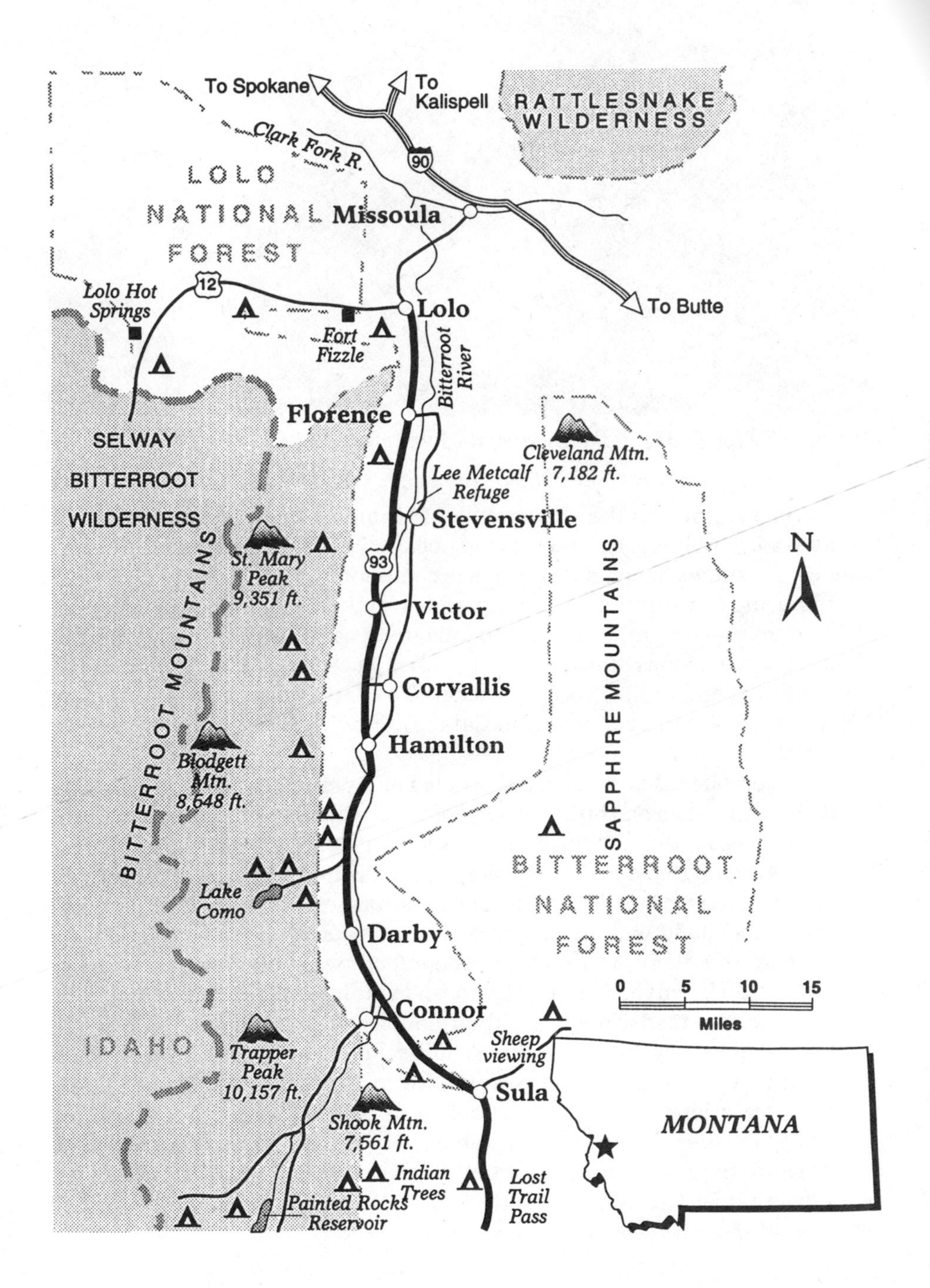

Heavenly Twins Peaks in the Bitterroot Mountains. Photo by Paul Dumond.

Missoula is home to the University of Montana, which hosts a variety of events and activities for visitors and locals, year-round. Theater performances, art shows, concerts, and sports competitions will keep you busy in town. During summers, many special music and entertainment events take place in downtown parks and on the university campus. A farmers' market in Circle Square runs Saturday mornings and Tuesday evenings from about June until the end of the growing season. On Wednesdays during summer, Out to Lunch features a food fair in Caras Park, with entertainment starting at noon.

The historical museum at Fort Missoula has a permanent exhibit detailing Missoula's more than one hundred-year-old past. Changing exhibits document various trades in which Missoulians have thrived. Visit the USDA Forest Service's Aerial Fire Depot and Smokejumper Visitor Center near the airport and learn about the history of jumping out of airplanes into forest fires. It might help you understand why these brave men and women do what they do.

Hundreds of miles of trails both in and out of town will keep you busy on foot or bike. Fishermen, floaters, skiers, and wildlife watchers find plenty of water, snow, and landscape to ply their hobbies. If you are visiting in early April, the week-long International Wildlife Film Festival shows the best wildlife films of the year from all over the world and features film workshops and demonstrations. If you enjoy walking or biking, Missoula has several unique urban trails where you can watch for birds, watch people, or picnic. For those wanting more solitude, three major mountain national recreation areas just minutes from town—Rattlesnake, Pattee Canyon, and Blue Mountain—might have what you are looking for.

Begin the scenic drive by heading south from town on US 93. As yc
the road toward Lolo, you will pass Blue Mountain Recreation Area
Bitterroot Mountains. To access its hiking, biking, and motorbiking
turn right at the Montana Athletic Club, a bluish building that looks l
round spacecraft. The road turns to gravel shortly after the turn. There
three different places along Blue Mountain Road to park your car and enj
the outdoors; all are adequately marked. You can sled at Blue Mountain i
winter or visit a fire lookout in summer. A small observatory near the lookout opens its telescope to the public for star- and planet-gazing on certain Fridays during summer.

South of Missoula, the road skirts the flanks of the Bitterroot Mountains, affording nice views of the Sapphire Mountains to the east. The low, grassy hills of the Sapphires provide a stark contrast to the higher, forested arêtes of the Bitterroots. Composed of sedimentary rocks that in places oozed granite, the Sapphires were never molded by glaciers like their valley neighbors, which were heavily glaciated. The route between Missoula and Lolo is the windiest section of road until you get to Darby. A word of caution: Even though much of this route is straight, US 93 has a lot of traffic, and many deer cross the road. These factors make driving hazardous at night and during winter.

The town of Lolo is about 8 miles south of Missoula on US 93. The origin of the name Lolo is disputed. Some think it was an Indian corruption of the word for Lewis, as in Lewis and Clark, or for Lawrence, a French trapper. Others say there is a Nez Perce word *lolo* meaning "muddy water." At the south end of town, U.S. Highway 12 heads west into Idaho. Traveler's Rest, near here, is where Lewis and Clark camped September 9-10, 1805, and again on their return from the West Coast June 30-July 3, 1806. This spot was so named because it was an ideal spot for the explorers to rest up before continuing on their journey. It was here, too, that the Lewis and Clark party split on their return trip, Clark going southeast to explore Yellowstone country and Lewis heading northeast to the Sun and Marias rivers.

The expedition's passage through Lolo Creek proved to be the most difficult portion of their entire journey. Today US 12 seems like an easy route for the team to have negotiated, but much of the canyon had to be blasted to build the highway, and the route was much narrower then. Instead, the expeditionary group took the high road, crossing ridge after ridge after ridge. The weather was cold, the mountain travel strenuous, and the food scarce. To get an idea of the approximate trail Lewis and Clark took through the Lolo Creek drainage, look for the red dotted line on a Lolo National Forest map.

About 5 miles west of Lolo on US 12 is another historic site. Fort Fizzle, as it was later dubbed, was a blockade built by Captain Charles Rawn of the U.S. Army infantry from Fort Shaw. It was built in 1877, and was intended to stop advancing non-treaty Nez Perce Indians from entering the Bitterroot Valley as they fled toward Canada. But the blockade did not work. The Nez Perce were camped near the hot springs 20 miles upstream and got wind of

A beaver slide in the East Fork of the Bitterroot.

plans to stop them. They sent a small delegation to negotiate with the soldiers, and while they parleyed, Nez Perce scouts led the main band of eight hundred people up and over a hill past the army. A fire burned what remained of the "fort" in the 1930s. Lolo Hot Springs is a small resort now, with a hot pool for soaking, a warm pool for swimming, a restaurant, a bar, and lodging. It makes a nice stop for cross-country skiers coming back from a day at Lolo Pass.

South of Lolo, the Bitterroot Valley opens wide. As the chain of Sapphire Mountains continues south, the mountaintops become more fully dressed in Douglas-firs and ponderosa pines. The Bitterroot's fertile farmlands are quickly being subdivided, but the valley still comprises large private ranches. At the turn of the century, apple orchards blossomed across the valley; at one time Montana become a leading producer of this fruit. Apples were shipped to the East by rail, and some of the orchards were so productive they filled more than five hundred rail cars a season. But the apple boom was short-lived. Better fruits could easily be produced in other parts of the country, sending many of the Bitterroot orchards out of business. Remnants of these orchards can still be found on the benches above the valley floor, and some orchards still produce commercially.

Florence is the next town you'll pass through, one of several tiny burgs in the valley. The town was named for Florence Hammond, the wife of prominent Missoula businessman A. B. Hammond. He also named a hotel for her in Missoula, now used as an office building. At one time the town of Florence sported a cheese factory, a creamery, and a greenhouse. From here you can take the East Side Highway, clearly marked by signs and directly across from the town's northernmost gas stations on US 93; if you are driving from Missoula and heading back there, the East Side Highway makes a nice return route.

The Bitterroot River flows east of the highway, carving a winding path to Missoula where it joins the Clark Fork. Floaters enjoy the gentle Bitterroot, although spring thaw often brings down large cottonwoods along its bank, making some spots a bit hard to maneuver around. There are many fishing access sites along the Bitterroot, most marked clearly with signs on US 93. One interesting spot 2.5 miles south of Florence is called the "car pool," because for a short stretch of river the banks are lined with rusted car bodies. Several other rivers in Montana also have "car pools," which started as a plan promoted by Lady Bird Johnson to prevent stream bank erosion. Fortunately, the plan is no longer practiced, but its legacy remains in steel. Today the cars provide pools and hiding cover for fish. Pull off the highway where you see a Forest Service sign indicating the Charles Waters Campground, just 0.25 mile farther. The "car pool" is a short walk down the dirt road beyond the closed gate.

For hikers there are trails up just about every drainage in the Bitterroots, and all are easily accessible. Most lead directly to mountain lakes, and many feature waterfalls in the creeks along the trails. I recommend using a Bitterroot National Forest map, or reading about trails here in *Hiking Montana*, also published by Falcon. The 9,351-foot Saint Mary's Peak, often covered in snow, is a popular spot. You can hike to the fire lookout on top of the peak via a 4-mile, at times steep, trail. From the top of Saint Mary's, or any other peak in the Bitterroots, you can appreciate the vast mountain wilderness to the west into Idaho. There are no settlements for hundreds of square miles, so if you want to get lost, this is the place to do it.

Stevensville is the next town along this route, but you'll have to drive east off the highway to see it. Stevensville is said to be the oldest community in Montana, having been established in 1841 with the founding of Saint Mary's Mission. (It was actually authorized as a town in 1864 and called Stevensville after its founding father, Isaac Stevens.) Father Pierre Jean de Smet was a Jesuit priest who was sent to the valley to bring Christianity to the Flathead Indians. Saint Mary's Mission is believed to be Montana's first church, and it may be where the first oats and wheat were harvested in Montana. You can tour the tiny mission and some of the outbuildings. To get there from Stevensville, turn west on Fourth Street and go to the end of the block. At the south end of town you will find the newly reopened Stevensville Museum, which houses artifacts and displays of the valley's history.

In 1850 Saint Mary's Mission was sold to John Owen, who eventually opened a trading post just north of the mission grounds. Fort Owen is said to be the first territorial capital of Montana, although Bannack is recognized as such. Flathead Indians, miners, settlers, and fur traders all did business here. Some remains of the original fort lie northwest of Stevensville and are well marked with signs. They are on part of a private ranch, so it may seem as if you are driving up a private road to get to the fort.

Lee Metcalf National Wildlife Refuge is just northeast of town. From Stevensville, turn east on the East Side Highway. The turnoff for the refuge

An autumn celebration at the Daly Mansion in Hamilton.

is just past the ranger station on the left. Large signs clearly point the way to the refuge. There are several wonderful walking trails through the cottonwood forest and along the Bitterroot River. You can expect to see white-tailed deer, muskrats, and many species of waterfowl most of the year. Other species common on the refuge include pileated, hairy, and downy woodpeckers, common flickers, great horned owls, bald eagles, ospreys, wood ducks, ruddy ducks, and teal, in addition to many other ducks and geese during spring and fall migration. In summer you may see a tireless beaver, a turtle basking on a fallen log in the water, or a porcupine napping on a ponderosa pine limb.

South of the turnoff to Stevensville, US 93 continues to make a straight course through ranchland and growing subdivisions. The view of the Bitterroots becomes more spectacular. The peaks farther south seem to be more sharply carved and defined, with chiseled ridgelines covered in snow at least nine months of the year. The north end of the Bitterroots is largely composed of metamorphic rocks, while the end south of Stevensville is granite. The granite makes for some nice rock climbing in some of the drainages. If you are interested in watching climbers, a good spot is just a short way up the North Kootenai Creek trail. Watch for climbers on the low bluffs just off the trail to the right.

Next along the drive route is the little town of Victor, which has a small museum and a few antique shops. If you're hungry at this point, you might try the Mexican restaurant right on the highway.

A few miles north of Hamilton, and east of US 93, lies the tiny town of Corvallis. This community was named for the town with the same name in

Oregon, from which people had come to settle in Montana. The word originated from two French words, *coeur*, meaning "heart," and *valle*, meaning "valley."

Hamilton is the biggest town in the Bitterroot Valley, fast becoming a popular retirement place because of its small-town atmosphere, low crime, and scenery. The town was named for J. W. Hamilton, from whom the Northern Pacific Railroad got its right-of-way here. Marcus Daly, one of the "copper kings," built a summer mansion here among his thousands of acres of ranchland for cattle and horses. Daly's wealth came from his copper mines and smelter in Anaconda. The Daly Mansion has twenty-four bedrooms, fifteen bathrooms, and a sprawling lawn shaded with maples and cottonwoods. You can tour the mansion for a fee; you might find it entertaining to do so during special events that take place throughout the summer on the mansion grounds. Daly's horses had it posh too. Their barn (across the East Side Highway from the mansion) resembled a large, fancy house more than a stable and was called Tammany Castle, for one of Daly's prized racing horses.

Hamilton is home to the Ravalli County Museum, run by the Bitter Root Valley Historical Society. It is housed in the old county courthouse and has interesting exhibits in many rooms. On Sundays during winter, the museum hosts special programs, ranging from musical performances to slide shows. In October its grounds are the site of the annual Apple Festival, with music, arts, crafts, baked goods, and, of course, apple stuff for sale. To get to the museum, turn west off of US 93 onto Bedford Street. The museum is on the second block on the left, just behind the new county government building.

South of Hamilton the road begins to wind more on its way to Darby, and the valley narrows. To the southwest lie the tallest and most pointed peaks of Montana's Bitterroots: El Capitan, Como, North Trapper, and Trapper peaks. Only Trapper Peak breaks the 10,000-foot level, by just over 150 feet. The rest fall from 7 to a few hundred feet short. Hiking to the tops of these peaks is usually reserved for the hardy.

About 9 miles south of Hamilton is the turnoff for Como Lake Recreation Area. Just before the turnoff, the road curves along the Bitterroot River, becoming narrow and hazardous under less-than-ideal conditions. From this point south it is much the same in many spots, so use caution as you drive. Como Lake is a popular spot for locals because of its scenery and proximity. It has a boat ramp and three campgrounds. You can fish and swim in this manmade lake also. There is a hiking trail around the lake and two additional trails that lead to higher mountain lakes after several miles.

Just south of Como Lake, the town of Darby springs up in a narrow passage between the mountains. Darby grew up out of the mining and fur trade, then saw a minor boom from the timber industry. Today it relies more and more on agriculture and cattle ranching, but timber is still a viable industry here. Tourism has recently come into its own in Darby, as evidenced by the many hunting outfitters, fishing guides, and numerous guest ranches. Its new one-block stretch with gift shops, a cafe, and a coffeehouse seems strangely out of place, but attests to the town's willingness to cash in on Montana's tourism boom. A small museum next to the Darby Ranger District has exhibits about the lives of early foresters here. A couple other tiny museums in Darby exhibit wildlife mounts and tell local history.

You may have noticed that west of Darby the mountain vegetation appears more moist, and that there are more trees and shrubs. East of the Bitterroot River the scrubby hillsides are covered with sagebrush and scattered with dryland ponderosa pine. You can travel up both the East and West forks of the Bitterroot River, and the difference in vegetation is much the same. This is because storms moving from west to east usually dump their wet loads on the Bitterroots, leaving little for the drier, and lower, Sapphires.

Three miles south of Darby is the turnoff to the West Fork of the Bitterroot River. About 20 miles southwest on this road, you will enjoy Painted Rocks Reservoir, a flooded, narrow canyon where you can boat, and in places where it is warm enough, swim. About 10 miles south of Darby you may notice a ponderosa pine on the east side of the highway with colorful ribbons hanging from its branches. Called the Medicine Tree, it is estimated to be more than four hundred years old. The tree is sacred to the Salish Indians and was recently spared the axe in plans to widen US 93. Supposedly it has a bighorn ram's horn imbedded in its trunk. Others say the horn has been removed. Today, people leave offerings of cloth and beads, as well as other objects at the tree for "good medicine," good luck.

South of Darby lies Sula, named for Ursula Thompson, the first white child born there. This area, also called Ross Hole, is depicted in the Charles M. Russell painting in the state capitol in Helena, depicting Lewis and Clark meeting with Flathead Indians. From here you can take the East Fork Road to view bighorn sheep near the Broad Axe Lodge and Restaurant. The road takes off east just before you cross the bridge. Follow the wildlife viewing signs (depicting binoculars) 5.5 miles to the viewing site. A few interpretive signs along the road discuss sheep and where to look for them. The best time to see sheep is during winter. You may even see them grazing along US 93—another good reason to take blind curves slowly.

South of Sula, Indian Tree Campground is laid out among large ponderosa pines. The area was used for camping by Native Americans as recently as this century and as long ago as several hundred years. Turn west and follow the gravel road to the campground near the Lost Trail Hot Springs Resort. Look for the giant ponderosa pines with long, wide scars in their bark. Indians would peel the bark and eat the inner portion, called the cambium. The sweet sap and soft cambium of ponderosa were delicacies. Although quite large and visible, the scars do not appear to have harmed the trees.

Just south of the campground, a stop at Lost Trail Hot Springs is a great, cozy way to finish off a day of downhill skiing at Lost Trail Pass, on the Montana-Idaho border, or a day of cross-country skiing on trails at Chief Joseph Pass. From this point you can go back up the valley by way of the East Side Highway, or take Montana Highway 43 (Chief Joseph Pass) at Lost Trail Pass to the Big Hole Valley and Scenic Drive 6.

If you are heading back to Missoula, the East Side Highway makes a nice alternate route. It is much narrower than US 93 in places, with several elbow curves, and it makes you feel like you are really in the country as you pass cow pastures, Victorian-styled farm houses, and rundown barns and homesteads. If you take the East Side Highway north from Hamilton, you will go through the towns of Stevensville and Corvallis, coming out at Florence. To find this route from Hamilton, follow the signs east on County Road 269 by the Safeway grocery store from US 93. You will pass the Daly Mansion, if you have not already seen it. From Missoula you can pick up Scenic Drives 3 or 5 by heading east.

5 THE ANACONDA–PINTLER SCENIC ROUTE

Montana Highway 1

General description: This 63-mile drive goes from Anaconda, one of Montana's most historic towns, to Georgetown Lake and Philipsburg. The road penetrates both conifer-clad mountains and sage-covered hills and is a wonderful alternative to Interstate 90 when traveling between Butte and Missoula.
Special attractions: Historic Anaconda, Georgetown Lake, Philipsburg, Granite ghost town; gem mining, fishing, skiing, camping, hiking, boating, biking, wildlife viewing.
Location: Southwestern Montana. The drive begins in Anaconda and ends at Drummond on I-90 east of Missoula.
Drive route number: Montana Highway 1.
Travel season: Year-round.
Camping: Several public campgrounds are found on nearby national forest land, especially around Georgetown Lake. There are some camping sites near Anaconda at Lost Creek State Park.
Services: Full services at Anaconda, Georgetown Lake, Philipsburg, and Drummond.
For more information: Deerlodge National Forest, Philipsburg Ranger District; Montana Department of Fish, Wildlife, & Parks; Anaconda Chamber of Commerce; Philipsburg Chamber of Commerce (see Appendix).

The drive:

> Thou shalt tell no false tales about good diggins in the mountains, to benefit a friend who may have mule, blankets or provisions and tools that he wishes to sell lest thy neighbor deceived by thee into making the trip shall one day return through the snow with naught left but his rifle, contents of which he shall present to you in a manner that shall cause thee to fall down and die like a dog.
>
> — Miner's Ninth Commandment,
> from *Ghost Towns of Montana*

5 THE ANACONDA–PINTLER SCENIC ROUTE

Montana Highway 1

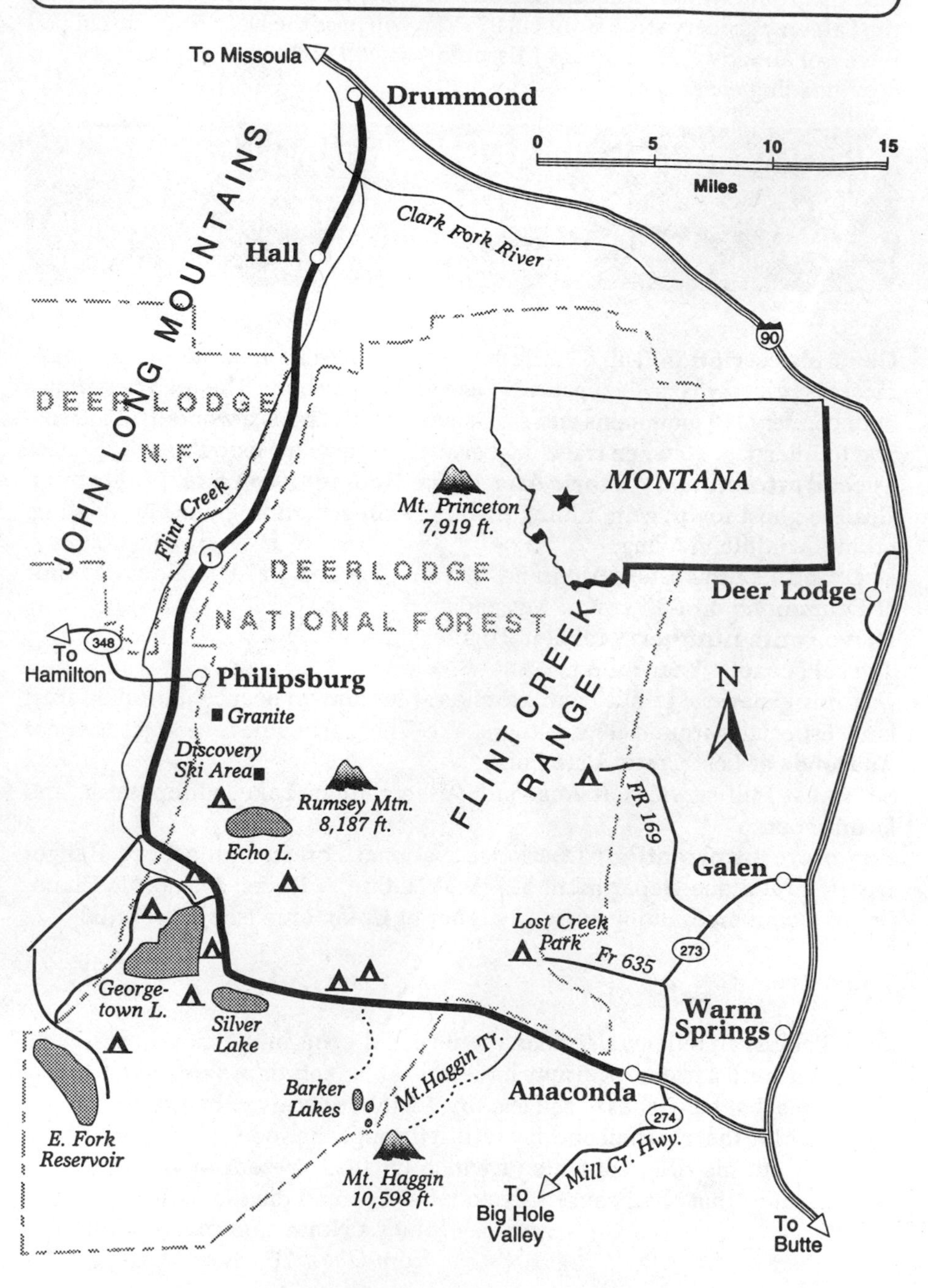

This drive begins off I-90 just east of Anaconda. Take the exit to Anaconda and follow the signs marked "Pintler Scenic Route." You will go through downtown Anaconda, a town with history as rich as the precious metals mined from its hills.

Anaconda, named for a giant, South American snake, was originally called Copperopolis for the rich veins of copper mined here. But because the name Copperopolis was already claimed by another Montana town, Anaconda's first postmaster was asked to choose another. Anaconda was the dream town of mining giant Marcus Daly, who made it the site of the Anaconda Copper Mining Company's Washoe Smelter. Daly chose this site to process ore from his mines in Butte, 25 miles east, because of its plentiful water supply. The smelter closed in 1980, but its 585-foot smokestack, the largest in North America, still stands. The stack's diameter is 86 feet at its base, making it large enough to fit the Washington Monument inside its core. You can see ruins of Anaconda's first smelters, built in the 1880s, along the hillsides north and east of town. Golfer Jack Nicklaus has designed a golf course that will reclaim the site of the smelter ruins, scheduled to open in 1996.

During February, Anaconda hosts a chocolate festival that includes a bake-off and window decorating contest. "Fines" are issued to businesses that fail to hand out chocolates to clients. Anaconda also has several winter sports events. When summer arrives, add art fairs, historic bus tours, and drag races to the list of activities here. I highly recommend the bus tour, during which your guide relates colorful tidbits of Anaconda's early days. You can also take a historic walking tour of downtown; inquire at the chamber of commerce for details. Peek your head inside what the Smithsonian Institution has called the fifth most beautiful theater in the country, the Washoe Theatre, built in 1937. Silver, copper, and gold leaf accentuate its WPA-era wall murals, and hand-carved rams' heads stand guard on the ceiling.

About 2 miles east of Anaconda you can see live bighorn sheep and mountain goats at Lost Trail State Park as they perform death-defying leaps across the steep limestone cliffs. The best times to see both animals are winter and spring; during summer you may be able to see sheep in Olsen Gulch, 4 miles west. You can usually see mountain goats from a pullout by the entrance to the park. The road beyond the lower picnic grounds is too narrow and windy to accommodate large trailers, however. Be sure to visit Lost Creek Falls, via a short walk along a trail. You can also ride your bike along a closed portion of road here and look for moose in the creek bottom.

To continue the scenic drive, take MT 1 from downtown Anaconda. The highway is in good condition. It passes through forested foothills and past Mount Haggin on the way to Georgetown Lake. The valleys here were once home to giant glaciers that left their calling card of debris in the moraines and granite boulders that give this area its bumpy appearance. There is a trail to several lakes below Mount Haggin, south of the highway. To get to Mount Haggin Wildlife Management Area, take the Mill Creek Highway (County Road 274) off of MT 1, heading south. There is evidence that people used the Mount Haggin area as long as 10,500 years ago. These early residents mined

A relic of Anaconda's rich past.

chert for spearheads and hunted game in the hills. If you hike in this area, remember that arrowheads and other artifacts are protected under the Antiquities Act, so resist the temptation to bring any home. Mountain bikers will find this area to be a pleasant place to ride. Farther up MT 1 and to the south is another set of trails, in Barker Creek, leading to Barker Lakes.

As the highway winds through the canyon heading west, it breaks out onto a small body of water called Silver Lake. From here a few Forest Service roads head up into the mountains above the lake, where you will find several smaller mountain lakes and a few nice meadows. This is the Anaconda Range; the Anaconda–Pintler Wilderness is just beyond. Check wilderness and Forest Service maps for details on hiking trails. Part of the Continental Divide National Scenic Trail passes through here as well.

Just past Silver Lake, manmade Georgetown Lake is a year-round mecca for Anaconda residents. The lake has all the standard recreational opportunities—boating, fishing, swimming, water skiing, camping, and hiking. During winter, many people find pleasure ice-fishing here. A road borders the entire shoreline and provides access to ten campgrounds. The outlet of Flint Creek was dammed in 1885 to create what is now the lake, which used to be a cattle ranch. The dam provided power for the Bi-Metallic Mining Company in Philipsburg and Granite.

Overlooking Georgetown Lake is Discovery Basin, a downhill ski area with beautiful, long, open runs for both beginners and experts. From the top of Discovery, you can view the Anaconda–Pintler Mountains to the south, spectacular when covered by snow. This area prides itself on having plenty of sunshine, so even during the winter you have a good chance of having sunny ski days.

From Georgetown Lake, MT 1 turns north toward the mining town Philipsburg. The road goes over a short pass then descends through a narro canyon into the Philipsburg area. As you head up to the pass, look up at th rock walls to see ruins of an aqueduct running along the side of the bluffs. These flumes once carried the water from Georgetown Lake to generate power for the Bi-Metallic Mining Company. In winter water that has collected in the remains of the wooden structure dribbles and freezes on the rock, making beautiful aqua blue ice sculptures on the rock faces.

During summer you can take an alternate route through the mountains to your west on what is called the Skalkaho Pass Road. *Skalkaho* is Salish for "beaver." The turnoff is 6 miles south of Philipsburg. It is not paved for most of the way and is quite curvy, with sheer drops down a canyon in places. The road comes out just south of the town of Hamilton in the Bitterroot Valley, where you can pick up Scenic Drive 4. There are several hiking trails along the way and a beautiful set of waterfalls right along the road. If you like off-road driving and exploring, this might be a fun route for you. Otherwise continue on the Anaconda–Pintler Scenic Route to Philipsburg.

Philipsburg started out as a mining camp in the 1860s and soon reached a population of 1,500. With other camps and settlements in surrounding areas, Philipsburg served as many as 8,000 people in the late nineteenth century, following a population crash in the 1870s. The town has survived; its schoolhouse, built in 1895, is still in use. In Philipsburg, visit the Ghost Town Hall of Fame at the Granite County Museum and Cultural Center. This photographic display features ghost towns from around the state. The

Young anglers at Georgetown Lake.

Built in 1896, the Granite County Jail in Philipsburg was made from locally-fired bricks and is still in use today. Photo by Randall Green.

museum has plans to open a new exhibit that is a recreated underground mine operation with authentic equipment. "Mine" your own gems by buying a bucket of rocks at the Sapphire Gallery on Broadway, washing the gravel to find sapphires from local sources. It is fun, and probably about as close as you will ever get to experiencing the livelihood of early miners—and it is a much easier way to dig for stones. During winter save your lift ticket from Discovery Basin and turn it in for a free beer at the Sunshine Station here. Your beer will taste good with a homemade bowl of chili. The proprietors say that if the sun fails to shine at all one day, drinks are on the house.

About 5 miles southeast of Philipsburg, in the Flint Creek Range, is the ghost town of Granite. In the mid-1880s, Granite boasted the largest silver-producing mines in the world, with $20 million worth of silver coming from its bowels in just a few short years. As quickly as it boomed, it died; the silver panic of 1893 drastically reduced the price of silver and emptied the town of its 3,000 residents in less than two days. Today you can explore what little is left of the town; most of it burned in the 1950s. Unfortunately, some of the few remaining buildings were burned and vandalized in recent years, including the Miner's Union Hall, once a magnificent structure and no doubt witness to many a good time. The buildings that remain standing are rickety and dangerous, so use caution when exploring.

To get to Granite from Philipsburg, head up Broadway and turn right on South Montgomery Street. Turn left immediately after the pile of wooden freight decks and follow the signs. The road to Granite can be rough and is steep in places, so do not drive it unless you have a vehicle with good clearance—no trailers. It is sometimes well marked, sometimes not. Help from a Deerlodge National Forest map might be necessary. Many other ghost towns, some with only a few buildings, litter the hillsides around Philipsburg and Georgetown Lake. Many are on private property, are relatively inaccessible, and are not worth exploring unless you happen upon them while hiking.

From Philipsburg, MT 1 heads north toward I-90 again, cutting between the Flint Creek Range and the John Long Mountains. The road passes through a somewhat narrow canyon north of Philipsburg for about 9 miles before entering open sagebrush cattle range south of Hall. When you come out of this low canyon you will see large granite boulders littering the fields. The boulders arrived via mudflow from Boulder Creek sometime after the last ice age.

About 70 million years ago, the Sapphire Mountains, just west of the John Long Mountains, moved east out of Idaho, shoving the Flint Creek Range out of their way. As a result, the western portion of the Flint Creeks are crumpled and folded. Magma oozed into the crevices of the folds to eventually form granite. It was in these granite intrusions that ore deposits were found.

The drive ends as it intersects I-90 near Drummond.

Along Flint Creek north of Philipsburg. Photo by Randall Green.

6 THE BIG HOLE

Montana Highway 43, County Road 278

General description: This 113-mile drive meanders through the Big Hole Valley to the ghost town of Bannack. You can end the route there or go an additional 40 miles through the Pioneer Mountains to loop back to where you started. Ghost towns, hot springs, and great hiking opportunities make this drive one on which you will want to spend some time.
Special attractions: Big Hole Battlefield, Bannack and Coolidge ghost towns, Crystal Park, Elkhorn and Jackson hot springs; hiking, camping, boating, fishing, backpacking, mountain biking.
Location: Southwestern Montana. The drive begins at Divide, off Interstate 15, south of Butte. It circles the Pioneer Mountains and ends back on I-15, a few miles south of Dillon; an alternate return route cuts through the Pioneers and ends at Wise River.
Drive route numbers: Montana Highway 43, County Road 278; optional return route via Pioneer Mountains National Scenic Byway.
Travel season: Year-round from Divide to Bannack. Upper portions of the road through the Pioneer Mountains are closed during winter.
Camping: There are several Forest Service campgrounds along Montana Highway 43, and many along the optional return route through the Pioneers. There is also camping at Bannack State Park.
Services: Full services in Wisdom, Wise River, Jackson, and nearby Dillon. Limited services in most other towns along the way.
For more information: Big Hole National Battlefield; Beaverhead National Forest, Wise River and Wisdom ranger districts; Bannack State Park; Dillon Chamber of Commerce (see Appendix).

The drive:

> Few of us will soon forget the wail of mingled grief, rage, and horror which came from the camp four or five hundred yards from us when the Indians returned to it and recognized their slaughtered warriors, women, and children.
>
> — Colonel John Gibbon, 1879

To begin this drive, exit I-15 at Divide, where the landscape is open with scattered buttes. Look for the slender pillar of Maiden Rock on the ridge north of town. From Divide, follow MT 43 toward the town of Wisdom. The highway winds around the Big Hole River, passing through a narrow canyon at the start. Just a few miles west is Divide Ridge Recreation Area, offering camping facilities and fishing access on the Big Hole River. The road continues to wind along the river to the one-block-long town of Dewey, which has a café and lodging as well as fishing access and fishing guide service.

6 THE BIG HOLE

Montana Highway 43, County Road 278

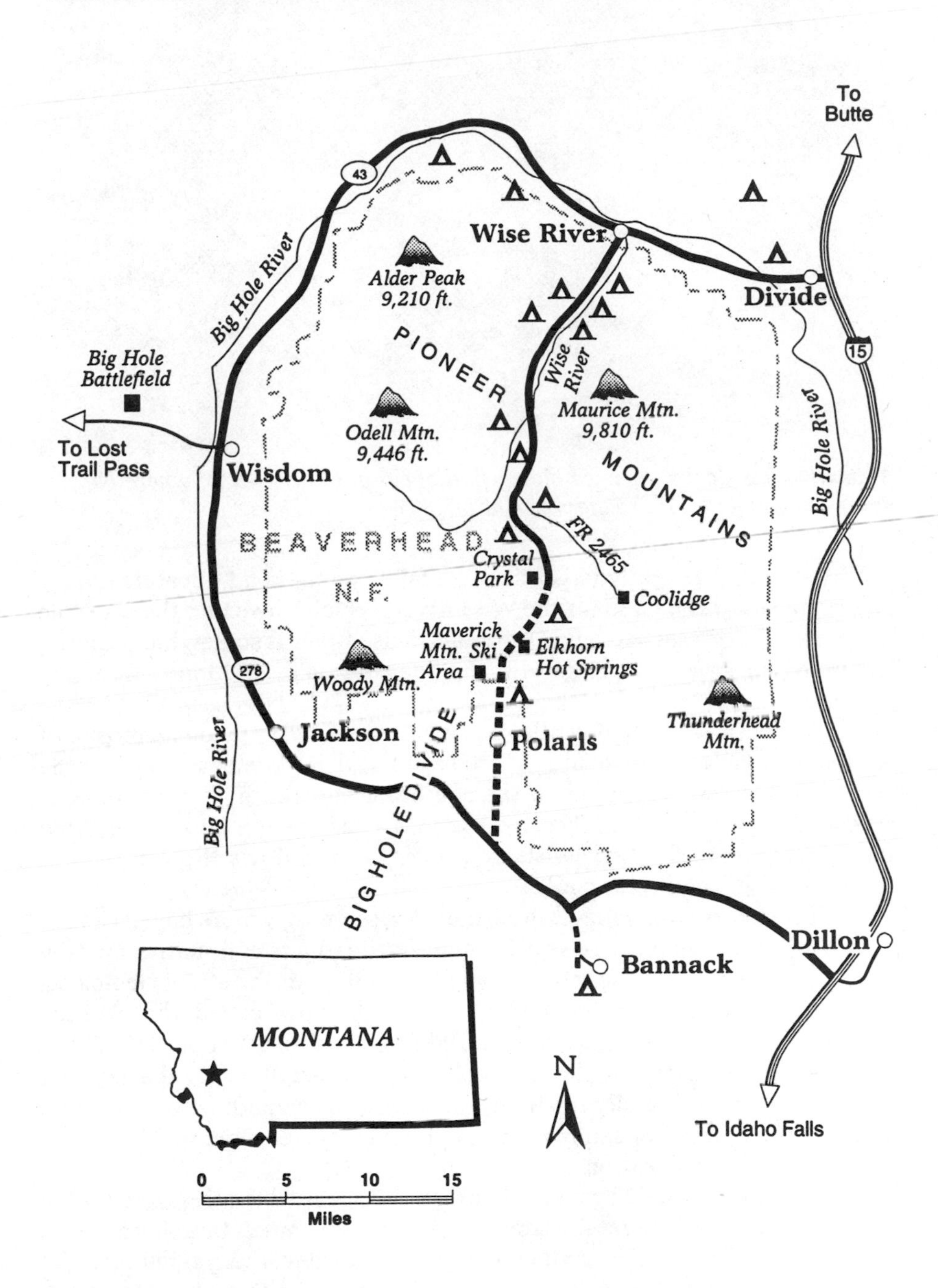

A howitzer overlooks the once bloody battlefield in the Big Hole, where Nez Perce Indians and U.S. soldiers fought in 1877.

Wise River is a slightly larger town 23 miles up the road. It caters mostly to anglers and was named for the Wise River, which flows into the Big Hole River here. The route between Dewey and Wise River is somewhat pastoral, traversing sagebrush rangeland with the Anaconda-Pintler Mountains rising to the north.

Continuing on MT 43 to Wisdom, you will see country made up mostly of wide open hills and rangeland covered with sage. In the backdrop are the pine-clad Pioneer Mountains to the southeast and the higher Anaconda-Pintlers to the northwest. The road is in average shape and has narrow shoulders. It makes a few twists and turns, as it follows the contours of creeks, sloughs, and rolling hills.

The openness of this valley, where there are seemingly more haystacks per square mile than anywhere else in the state, is the source of its name: the "Big Hole." It is considered the largest "hole," or valley, in the state. Geologists estimate it was created by a block of rocks, now called the Pioneer Mountains, that slid off the top of another block of rocks about 70 million years ago. Moving from Idaho, the rocks pushed east, creating the gap that is the Big Hole. To literally top it off, the valley has something on the order of 14,000 feet worth of sediment and fill covering bedrock, making it the deepest valley in the region.

A character in Ivan Doig's novel *English Creek* called the Big Hole Valley the "front parlor of heaven." Many who have spent much time here agree.

Because the Big Hole has not really been discovered yet, unlike the Bozeman and Missoula areas, traffic is usually sparse—although anglers from all over the country descend on the river during fly hatches, adding a noticeable increase at various times of the year. There are one or two pullouts along the route, with roadside picnic tables by the river, offering the only few places to stop and look around.

Near Fishtrap Creek, the Big Hole starts to look even larger as it turns into a gigantic valley. The forested folds of the Pioneer Mountains close in, while the higher peaks that separate Atlantic from Pacific waters at the Continental Divide can be seen in the distant northwest.

As the road turns south toward Wisdom (14 miles north of town) and crosses the river, a gravel road to the west follows the west side of the Big Hole River. The river branches quite a bit here, and other creeks flow into it from the mountains. Take this gravel road, passing through private ranchland, to enjoy the valley views. You will miss the town of Wisdom, but hit MT 43 again in 20 miles, a few miles west of town, so you can backtrack to it easily.

Wisdom has one main road with an art gallery and few bars and cafes—one of which serves buffalo burgers. South of the main drag on County Road 278 a woman hand-shapes custom cowboy hats for sale. Despite the trendy art gallery, this mostly ranching town still appears well worn. That is part of Wisdom's charm and helps make the Big Hole what it is: a ranching haven held together with cowboys whose weather-chiseled faces speak volumes about Montana ranch life in this 6,000-foot-high valley. A cowboy from Wisdom once told me, "Yeah, we get summer in the Big Hole, and on that day everybody gets together for a picnic."

Wisdom was originally called Crossings, and later derived its name from the river that passes by. The river was originally named by Lewis and Clark. The explorers named the three rivers in this area after the three virtues of their president, Thomas Jefferson: Wisdom, Philosophy, and Philanthropy. Somewhere along the way the rivers' names were changed to the Big Hole, Beaverhead, and Ruby.

A 15-mile side trip from Wisdom on MT 43 west toward Chief Joseph Pass takes you to the Big Hole Battlefield National Monument. Here, 163 soldiers of the U.S. Seventh Infantry, along with 33 civilian volunteers, attacked about 800 men, women, and children of the Nez Perce tribe, on August 9, 1877. The Nez Perce had already journeyed several hundred miles from their homeland in Idaho in search of a new home where they could live in peace. The soldiers mounted a surprise attack that lasted for 36 hours and ended when Colonel John Gibbon's troops were forced to retreat. In all, between 70 and 90 Nez Perce were killed, most of them women, children, and elderly men. Dead U.S. soldiers numbered about twenty.

Today, the battlefield is silent and sorrowful. Tepee poles stand like skeletons scattered about the meadow where the Nez Perce camped more than a century ago. In the forest overlooking the campsite, shallow pits in the ground have slowly become filled with duff and debris. Soldiers dug these pits for shelter from flying bullets. The howitzer on the mountain above looks out over the battlefield like a vicious guard dog, a cold reminder of what

Some of Bannack's more well preserved buildings in Grasshopper Creek.

happened here. Take a self-guided tour of the battlefield's three walking trails, with a pamphlet relating the events that took place. The visitor center shows a short film explaining more details of the Nez Perce flight.

To reconnect with the main scenic drive, head south from Wisdom on CR 278 toward Jackson. The road is fairly straight with a few turns. The Bitterroot Mountains, now to the west, contrast sharply with the softer Pioneers in the distant east. The Big Hole River continues to meander as if someone took a giant wad of string and dropped it from the clouds. Tangled willows bind the water's edge. Ranches and hayfields cover the valley floor. In late summer and autumn, large loaves of hay pimple the mown fields. The hay is stacked with a large wooden contraption called a beaver slide. The device was invented and built in the Big Hole Valley around 1907 and patented in 1910. The slides can stack about 20 tons of hay as high as 30 feet.

The town of Jackson has a small hot springs and motel. A gravel road southwest of town will take you to several lakes and hiking trails with fishing and camping access in the Bitterroot Mountains. You can hike up to the Continental Divide, which draws the line between Montana and Idaho in this region.

South of Jackson the road heads due east and climbs up Big Hole Pass into the grassy and pine-dotted foothills. The 7,000-foot pass is not a difficult climb, since the valley floor is already more than 6,000 feet above sea level. Over the pass the peaks of the Pioneer Mountains come into view. To the south, thick conifer forests blanket the hills. Aspen groves on both sides of the road set off the green forest in autumn when the leaves turn gold. The bald mountain to the east in front of you, appropriately named Baldy Mountain, is 10,568 feet high.

About 7 miles from the top of the pass is the northbound turnoff to Polaris, Maverick Mountain, and Elkhorn Hot Springs. This is your optional return route, but don't take it now. First head south to Bannack State Park, another 7 or 8 miles along CR 278.

From the Bannack turnoff, follow the signs and gravel road to this well-preserved ghost town. The road is fairly wide and smooth. It heads into some dry, scrubby hills that probably look much the same today as they did a century ago when Bannack was a bustling, rough-and-tumble gold town and Montana's first territorial capital. The town's name was derived from the Bannocks, Native Americans who lived in the area. Like most Montana towns, Bannack began with a gold strike, in Grasshopper Creek in 1862. By 1863 it drew more than three thousand people. At the time, Montana was just a territory, and the strike was the first major claim within its boundaries.

Bannack was as rough as any frontier gold town, despite the efforts of wives and "civilized folk" to bring decency to it. As was true of all booming towns in Montana, Bannack had more saloons than churches. As noted in the Montana Department of Fish, Wildlife & Parks publication, the *Bannack Free Press*, one resident wrote:

> There was nothing visible to remind a person in the slightest degree that it was Sunday. Every store, saloon, and dancing hall was in full blast. Hacks running, auctioneering, mining and indeed every business, is carried on with more zeal than on week days.

Even the sheriff had better things to do than protect law-abiding citizens. Sheriff Henry Plummer was the leader of a gang of thieves and road agents who, during their gold-plundering careers, murdered more than one hundred people. But like the rich gold strikes in Bannack, Plummer's days came to an end. A citizen's group, the Vigilantes, formed with the intent to end the robbery and murder. Their first action was the hanging of road agent George Ives in Nevada City (see Scenic Drive 9). Eventually they caught up with Plummer and the rest of his gang. All but three were hanged or banished. The Vigilantes left a mysterious mark on cabin doors and tent flaps of known road agents. The mark, 3-7-77, struck fear in those who received it, knowing they were marked for certain hanging. Although its meaning is still a mystery (many theories abound), the numbers adorn the badges of Montana sheriffs to this day.

Plan on spending several hours at Bannack. With remnants of more than sixty preserved buildings, a cemetery, and mine works, you will have plenty to keep you busy. Bannack Days, the third weekend in July, is a two-day event, providing visitors with music, food cooked the pioneer way, wagon rides, old-time crafts, black powder shooting events, and live drama in the dusty streets. Some years, local Masons perform a play about the Vigilantes. During these festival days, church services are held in Bannack's only remaining church. For a limited time during winter, park officials flood a dredge pond for ice skaters. (Skates are available free of charge.) A warming hut is an added attraction for both skaters and skiers.

Some of the treasures found at Crystal Park in the Pioneer Mountains.

From Bannack you can either end your scenic drive by heading north again to CR 278 and Polaris or I-15, or head south on the gravel road from Bannack to County Road 324 and pick up Scenic Drive 7, Big Sheep Creek Road, through the Tendoy Mountains. Drivers who continue on CR 278 toward I-15 will go through more open sagebrush. From atop another small pass, called Badger Pass, at 6,700 feet, the Ruby Range is visible to the east. The paved road is in good shape and comes out just south of the town of Dillon.

Drivers who choose to extend this scenic drive by taking the alternate route through Polaris back to their starting point should go north from Bannack to CR 278 and retrace their route to the intersection with the road leading to Polaris, and turn north. The one-time mining camp of Polaris was originally about 2 miles north of where the town by the same name is now. With a single-digit population, Polaris consists of a post office, a few buildings, and the Polar Bar, supposedly moved here from Bannack and the place where Sheriff Plummer had his last drink. Not much is left of the original silver-mining camp in the hills.

The fair gravel road traverses sagebrush country with the rolling hills of the Pioneer Mountains on either side. The road is in fairly decent shape. It will be gravel until you reach the top of the pass north of Elkhorn Hot Springs, which has hot springs, a cafe, and lodging. The Pioneers are encompassed by the Beaverhead National Forest, and a few hiking trails lead to high mountain lakes between Polaris and Elkhorn Hot Springs to the east. Developed campgrounds are found here and there, but the adventurous can camp just about anywhere in national forest.

Maverick Mountain Ski Area is in the western Pioneers near Elkhorn Hot

Springs. Near Maverick Mountain, the road passes through thick spruce-fir forest and a small community of vacation cabins. Along the road, Grasshopper Creek, with its boulders and cool water, is the same creek that bled gold for the nineteenth-century residents of Bannack.

From Elkhorn Hot Springs north, the road is part of the Pioneer Mountains National Scenic Byway. It climbs to a pass through the forest to a place called Crystal Park, about 6 miles from the hot springs, where the pavement begins. At Crystal Park you can dig for crystals and keep whatever you find. Be mindful of the posted rules, though. The forest here is pockmarked with small craters from people digging for the clear stones, formed from molten rock intruding through limestone. Some of the lodgepole pines have fallen over and others look unsteady from people digging under the roots. (This is NOT allowed.) The dig sites and parking lot, built to accommodate RVs and trailers, are to the west.

The elevation at the top of the pass near Crystal Park is around 7,000 feet. The air is cool and the scenery wonderful. It is somewhat flat on top with grassy meadows on either side of the road. The high peaks of the Pioneers form the backdrop. Several trails take off from the road and many lead to high mountain lakes. The road surface is fairly new, and it winds down from the top of the pass for 25 miles to Wise River. The trees close in again as you head down, so drive carefully.

Just below Crystal Park a gravel road to the east will take you to the ghost town of Coolidge (named for the former president). Heed the warning signs if there is logging going on. Sometimes log truck drivers like to go as fast as negotiable on these narrow, winding Forest Service roads. The route to Coolidge is rough and rocky in spots and not suited for RVs and cars pulling trailers. If you want to make the trip, go slowly and carefully. Better yet, take a not-too-grueling mountain bike ride to the town. A campground up this road is nicely situated in the woods.

From a small parking area below Coolidge, it is about a 0.75-mile walk to the town. Coolidge sits in a narrow, high mountain valley sliced down the middle by Elkhorn Creek, which drains the steep ridges that face it. The town is mostly in shambles, but there are a few standing buildings you can explore. The schoolhouse now rests in the middle of Elkhorn Creek. The main mine site is still intact, but very dangerous to explore. I do not recommend it. Due to a lack of funding, the Forest Service cannot adequately preserve Coolidge. Buildings are crumbling and vandals destroy property. Use extreme caution when exploring Coolidge and PLEASE resist the temptation to take a piece of its history home with you.

Continuing on the main road, you will find plenty more hiking opportunities and a few more campgrounds. The road follows the Wise River and has virtually no shoulder since it is closed in by forest. About 5 or 6 miles before you get to the town of Wise River, the scenery opens up to sage land. The Anaconda–Pintler Mountains rise sharply to the north. From here you can head back to I-15 where you started and pick up Scenic Drive 5 north or Scenic Drive 7 south.

7 BIG SHEEP CREEK
Forest Road 302

General description: This 55-mile gravel road—in some places a dirt track—traverses arid country cut by veinlike creeks and dry washes. Although rough in spots, the road glides through the grassy meadows of the valley between the Tendoy and Bitterroot mountains.
Special attractions: Clark Canyon Reservoir; wildlife viewing, fishing, hiking, mountain biking.
Location: Southwest Montana. The drive begins near Dell off Interstate 15, 24 miles north of the Idaho border. It ends at Clark Canyon Reservoir, 19 miles south of Dillon on I-15.
Drive route number: Big Sheep Creek Road (Forest Road 302).
Travel season: Spring through autumn.
Camping: Clark Canyon Reservoir has a few campgrounds. Camping at undeveloped sites is available on Forest Service and Bureau of Land Management lands. Camping on private land with owner permission only. There is one primitive campground (outhouse only) near the beginning of the drive.
Services: Full services at Dillon. Limited services in Dell and at Clark Canyon Reservoir.
For more information: Beaverhead National Forest, Dillon Ranger District; Bureau of Land Management, Dillon Office (see Appendix).

The drive:

> . . . at the distance of 4 miles further the road took us to the most distant fountain of the waters of the Mighty Missouri in surch of which we have spent so many toilsome days and wristless nights. thus far I had accomplished one of those great objects on which my mind has been unalterably fixed for many years, judge then of the pleasure I felt in all[a]ying my thirst with this pure and ice-cold water which issues from the base of a low mountain . . . below McNeal had exultingly stood with a foot on each side of this little rivulet and thanked his god that he had lived to bestride the mighty & heretofore deemed endless Missouri.
>
> — Meriwether Lewis,
> August 12, 1805

The Big Sheep Creek scenic drive starts south of the town of Dell, turning off the frontage road along I-15. About 1.5 miles south of town, turn west onto a gravel road. The route is clearly marked with small, brown signs. Pay

7 BIG SHEEP CREEK
Forest Road 302

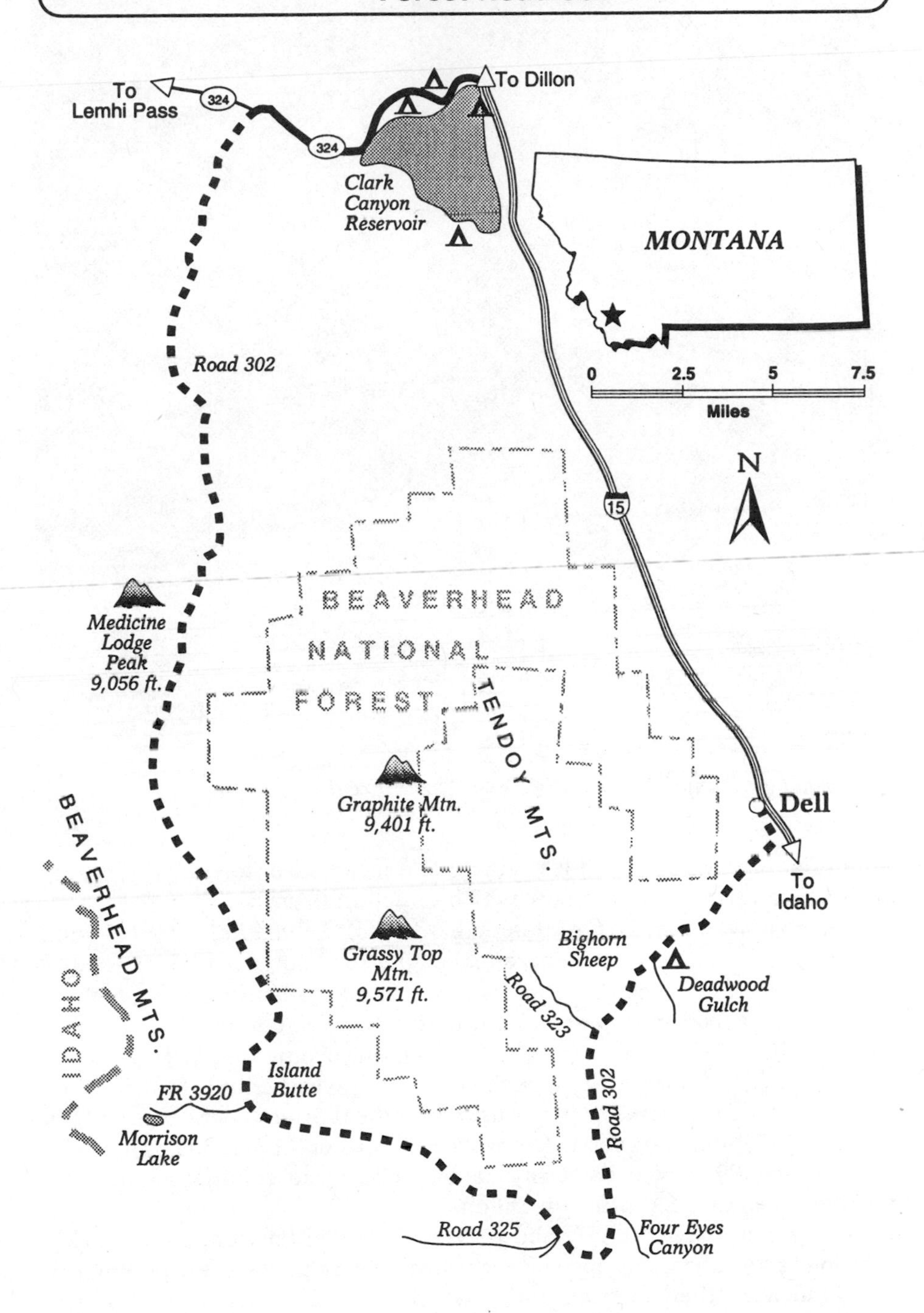

The Tendoy Mountains along Big Sheep Creek Road.

attention to these: The road forks in quite a few places, so you will have to read the signs carefully to know which direction to go.

A word of warning: Do not attempt this drive if the weather looks like rain. The slightest wetting of soils here makes the road surface slick as ice and impassable. In case you do get stuck in a surprise rainstorm, I recommend bringing extra food and water and waiting out the weather. DO NOT attempt to drive out. The Bureau of Land Management claims that large RVs and vehicles towing trailers can make the trip in dry weather only, and in some places the road can develop deep ruts. Four-wheel-drive is not necessary but could be helpful if you get stuck in wet conditions or if the road has not been graded recently. If you have any doubts about road conditions and local weather, call the BLM office in Dillon.

In general, the gravel Big Sheep Creek Rd. is in fair shape but quickly develops a washboard surface after grading. The road has a few potholes. It starts out wide, then narrows, and it winds quite a bit at the beginning. You may not run into anyone else on this route; if you do, it may be ranchers checking on their cattle. On the drive, you must pass through three or four gates, so please remember to leave each one as you found it. If the gate is closed and latched, close and latch it again behind you.

As you begin the drive, the Tendoy Mountains rise ahead. Tendoy was a chief of the Lemhi, a band of Shoshoni Indians who lived in Idaho and this part of Montana. Dixon Mountain, at 9,674 feet, stands guard to the west while rangeland dominates the foreground.

The road follows Big Sheep Creek. Alder and willow thickets seem to hold the creek in place. There is a spot or two to camp along the creek, or you can stop to drop a line in or swim. Keep your eyes on the rocky hillsides along the road for bighorn sheep, which were prolific in the area until disease nearly wiped them out in the early 1990s. The population is slowly recovering, so if you watch carefully you may see a few ewes or rams. The best place to look is about 4.5 miles up the road, where the canyon narrows and becomes quite rocky. You might also try a hike up Hidden Pasture Trail near Deadwood Gulch or along Muddy Creek for both scenery and sheep.

Many trails along the route provide hikers with a chance to explore this arid country. If you venture out, take plenty of water, since there is not much cover; you may want to hike in the cooler hours of morning or evening. Also remember that much of this passes through leased rangeland and a few private ranches, so stick to established trails if you leave your car to explore.

About 10 miles up the road you will pass the mouth of a gulch called Four Eyes Canyon. Three miles past this, you will come to a major fork in the road. Bear to the right. Shortly after you turn, there should be a sign confirming that this is Forest Road 302, the Sheep Creek route. If you take a left onto Forest Road 326 at this junction instead, you can hike part of the Continental Divide Scenic Trail, which takes you into the hills to the southwest. Continuing on FR 302 after the right turn, the country opens up quite a bit to wide, flat land with buttes and the Beaverhead Mountains in the background to the west. The Beaverheads are actually a continuation of the Bitterroot Mountains. Eighteenmile Peak, rising to 11,141 feet to your south, is the highest point on the Continental Divide between Banff, Alberta, and central Wyoming.

The Beaverhead Mountains and national forest got their name from a rock formation near Dillon which supposedly resembles a beaver's head. (It was recognized by the Shoshoni as such, although you might have to use your imagination.) Sacagawea, the Lemhi Shoshoni woman who served as guide for the Lewis and Clark expedition, recognized the rock as she and the explorers approached it. At the sight of the familiar outcropping, she knew she had returned to the land of her ancestors. Sacagawea's affiliation with her homeland proved to be just what the expedition needed. At this point in their journey, Lewis and Clark needed horses desperately. When Sacagawea recognized the landscape, she knew that her people were near, and that the expedition could count on the Shoshoni to supply them with the animals. For this reason, Beaverhead Rock is now a state monument, 19 miles north of Dillon on Montana Highway 41.

The arid, monolith-studded range of Big Sheep Creek.

As FR 302 begins to stretch across the open plain, it heads toward a power line, crosses under it, then makes a few twists and turns, swinging back to the power line near Island Butte. Island Butte is a large, grassy, round bump seemingly plopped down and forgotten in the plains. If you want to hike on it, the best place to access the butte is across BLM land on the south end. A sign near the south end of the butte will point you west to Morrison Lake. The road is a bumpy dirt track 2.5 to 3 miles long. It is a small lake with good fishing, and you can camp there on undeveloped sites. From the Morrison Lake turnoff, FR 302 swings around Island Butte and travels under the power line again.

Near Sawlog Creek the road cuts through a long-abandoned homestead, testament to days of hard living in this arid country. After passing the homestead, the road begins to go through rolling country. If you have not gotten out of the car yet, you will have to now in order to open a series of gates.

When you get around Island Butte, take the road that follows the power line north. You pass a sign that marks the old Bannack Road. Once connecting the gold-mining town of Bannack with Corrine, Utah, this 1862 road was used to move freight and possibly gold. Its two-wheeled tracks are still clearly visible.

Just below the Bannack Rd. crossing, you will go over a small pass. Parts of it can be steep for short pitches, so go slowly. As the road draws closer to Hildreth Creek, it smoothes out and widens a bit. Ranch homes are scattered about these ranges. The mountains are closer to the road, and the landscape is not as open. Some of the foothills are scattered with pine, but the country is still arid.

The road now follows Medicine Lodge Creek, which provides water here; the rangeland is noticeably more lush than the country through which you just passed. During drought years, however, the creek can disappear as quickly as it can pour from the volcano-like Medicine Lodge Peak to the west. Look for the bright blue mountain bluebirds here, flitting low to the ground on a feeding frenzy of insects. American kestrels hover over the grasslands here, too, in their hunt for small rodents and insects. As you near the end of the drive, look for pronghorn in the hayfields along the road.

You will soon come to an intersection with the obviously main road, paved County Road 324, where a right turn takes you to Clark Canyon Reservoir and back to I-15. Clark Canyon has plenty of camping, boating, and fishing opportunities. Cattail Marsh Nature Trail, along its edge, is a good place to see yellow-headed and red-wing blackbirds, snipes, and many waterfowl species. Interpretive signs describe the various birds and other wildlife.

A left turn at the paved road will take you to Lemhi Pass, the Sacagawea Historical Area, where Lewis and Clark crossed the Continental Divide on August 12, 1805. The road is paved until the turnoff to the pass to the west. After you turn, follow Forest Road 300 and the signs for 18 miles on the gravel road to the top of the 7,300-foot pass. The last mile up to the pass can get rugged. Large RVs and trailers are not recommended, but it is a nice walk if you need a leg-stretcher. You can camp at Sacagawea Memorial Camp, just below the pass.

From Clark Canyon Reservoir you can head north and pick up Scenic Drive 6, just south of Dillon. Or you can head south on I-15 and pick up Scenic Drive 8 in Monida.

8 THE CENTENNIAL VALLEY
Red Rock Pass, Centennial Valley Road

General description: This 51-mile gravel road skirts the Centennial Mountains, offering views across marshland and a valley bounded by the Gravelly and Snowcrest ranges. In autumn the foothills display groves of golden quaking aspen, in brilliant contrast to deep green conifers. Wildlife is abundant.
Special attractions: Red Rock Lakes National Wildlife Refuge; backpacking, camping, fishing, floating, hiking, mountain biking, wildlife viewing.
Location: The extreme southwest of the state, just north of Idaho. The drive begins off Montana/Idaho Highway 87, just south of the Montana border on Raynolds Pass. It ends at Interstate 15 in Monida.
Drive route numbers: Centennial Valley Road, Red Rock Pass Road.
Travel season: The main road (Red Rock Pass), Elk Lake Road, and the North Side Road are open year-round, weather permitting. Other roads have seasonal restrictions. Snow conditions often close the main road in winter, leaving it open to local traffic only.
Camping: Henrys Lake (Idaho) has a few campgrounds. Two more are located at Red Rock Lakes National Wildlife Refuge, one at Upper Red Rock Lake and one at River Marsh on Lower Red Rock Lake. There is a commercial campground at Elk Lake.
Services: Lodging and food are available at a few resorts near the wildlife refuge. There are also limited services at Henrys Lake in Idaho. There are no services at Monida along I-15. You can get gas in Lima.
For more information: Red Rock Lakes National Wildlife Refuge; Bureau of Land Management, Dillon (see Appendix).

The drive:

> High horns, low horns, silence, and finally a pandemonium of trumpets, rattles, croaks, and cries that almost shakes the bog with its nearness, but without yet disclosing whence it comes. At last a glint of sun reveals the approach of a great echelon of birds. On motionless wing they emerge from the lifting mists, sweep a final arc of sky, and settle in clangorous descending spirals to their feeding grounds. A new day has begun on the crane marsh.
>
> — Aldo Leopold,
> *Sketches Here and There*

You can approach this scenic drive from Raynolds Pass on Montana Highway 87, or from West Yellowstone on MT 20. From either direction, head to Henrys Lake, Idaho, a popular fishing and boating site—check Idaho regulations if you intend to do either of these activities. Follow the paved road

8 THE CENTENNIAL VALLEY

Red Rock Pass, Centennial Valley Road

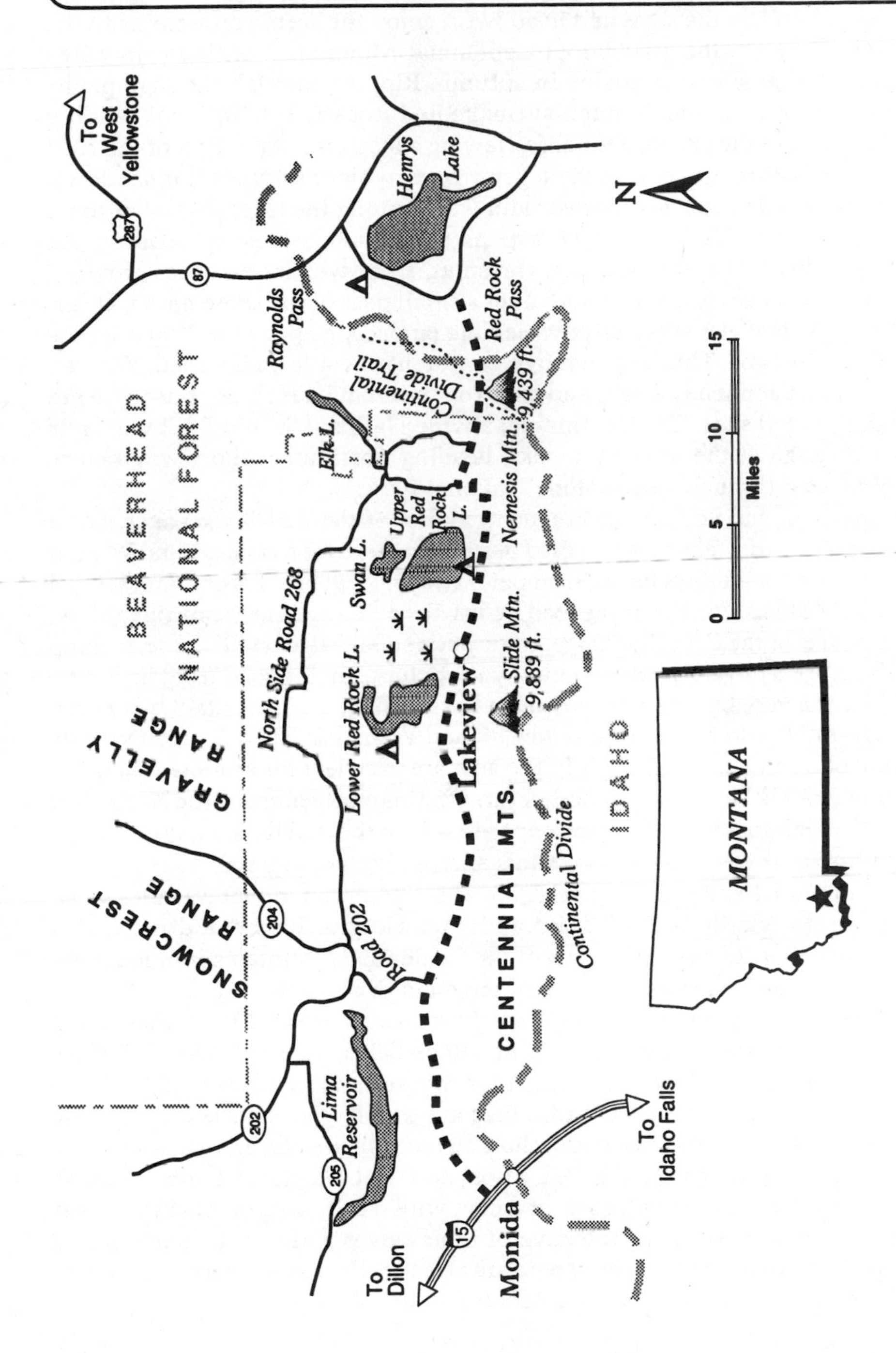

along the lakeshore, then turn west where signs indicate the route to Red Rock Lakes. From the north, the first 3 miles of this road are paved. It soon turns to gravel. The road is in good shape but narrow in spots, especially when there is traffic in both directions.

As you follow the signs and head west, enjoy the scenic mountains to the south. They are the 10,000-foot Centennial Mountains, with aspen grove hemlines that shimmer golden in autumn. Ripping through the high plains from east to west, the Centennials make Red Rock Lakes National Wildlife Refuge one of the prettiest wildlife viewing sites in the state. Part of the road passes right through some of the aspen groves, which cast sparkling shadows. Look for a safe place to pull over and walk among the trees. Many of them are genetically identical, since aspens clone themselves by sending out tremendous root systems, called rhizomes, from which new trees grow.

Red Rock Pass Road then goes over a small pass of the same name, at just over 7,000 feet elevation, after which the landscape opens up. You are now back in Montana. This is open range, so watch for cattle on the road. You can pull off just about anywhere and camp on national forest land, but there are no designated sites. The Continental Divide National Scenic Trail winds its way through at the top of the pass, heading north for a short way before trailing east through Yellowstone National Park.

Drive on, and you will soon reach the first of the Red Rock Lakes. For a pleasant side trip, take a right at Elk Lake Road and go for a walk around Wigeon Pond. Look for white pelicans, trumpeter swans, great blue herons, and several species of ducks. Farther up the road is Elk Lake, where you can camp in the low, grassy hills of the Gravelly Range, or stay at a small lodge on Elk Lake or camp at the lodge's private campground. If you continue up the road from here, you will have a very bumpy ride to Hidden Lake. Hikers and mountain bikers can take a trail beyond Hidden Lake to Cliff and Wade lakes (see Scenic Drive 9). Many other unimproved roads in the area are excellent for mountain biking.

South of Elk Lake there is another turnoff, this one heading to the North Side Road, which goes west along the opposite side of the Red Rock Lakes from the main route. If you choose to take this alternate route, you will meet up with the Centennial Valley Road just east of Lima Reservoir, about 30 miles west. You can also take the North Side Rd. and make a loop of this scenic drive, taking the North Side Rd. west (the view of the Centennial Mountains is much more panoramic) and returning by way of the main drive route.

After taking one or the other of these short side trips, return to the main road, where the marshy land and lakes of Red Rock Lakes National Wildlife Refuge come into view to the north. Watch for moose in the willow thickets here, especially during autumn. Because they are so tall, you can see these gangly creatures of the family Cervidae for long distances across the marsh. Moose are mostly solitary animals, unlike elk, bison, and deer, but it is not uncommon to see two bulls, a bull with a cow, or a cow with a calf. Like others in the deer family, females are very protective of their calves and can seriously injure people who venture too close. Moose are also excellent swimmers and are said to be able to swim as fast as two people can paddle a canoe.

The Centennial Mountains loom over Red Rock Lakes National Wildlife Refuge and the surrounding rangeland.

The 32,350-acre Red Rock Lakes refuge was established in 1935 to protect trumpeter swans, the largest of all North American waterfowl, which were nearing extinction at that time from unregulated hunting. In 1939 only sixty-nine swans existed in the Greater Yellowstone Ecosystem, of which Red Rock Lakes are a part. A year-round resident population of trumpeters in this region now numbers about three hundred; during winter another two thousand swans arrive from Canada. Many of them settle at the refuge. Unfortunately, Greater Yellowstone can only support about half of the swans that winter here. A severe winter or disease outbreak could kill hundreds of trumpeters. Biologists have tried to capture and relocate many of the birds so they are not so vulnerable. But because swans tend to return to their same wintering habitat every year, getting them to winter elsewhere has proved difficult.

Other refuge residents and visitors include a number of raptor species: ferruginous hawks, red-tailed hawks, Swainson's hawks, and peregrine falcons. Shorebirds such as willets, avocets, long-billed curlews, in addition to terns, gulls, and sandhill cranes, wade in the shallows, probing for insects and small shellfish in the mud. Look for cranes west of Upper Red Rock Lake and south of Lower Red Rock Lake. You can canoe from the upper to the lower lake and see wildlife that you may otherwise miss. Mink usually cavort along the water's edge and, if you are lucky, you may see a river otter. Red fox have also been seen skulking around the marsh edges, especially at nesting time. Check at refuge headquarters for boating regulations and restrictions.

One of two campgrounds on the refuge lies just below the road at Upper Red Rock Lake, situated in a small grove of quaking aspen. This campground offers one of the best places to view trumpeter swans. You have a good chance of seeing swans at both Shambow and Culver ponds as well, or from the Lower Red Rock Lake turnout. There is a visitor center at the refuge headquarters in Lakeview, open Monday through Friday, 7:30 a.m. to 4 p.m.

After spending as much time as you can at the lakes, drive west. Keep your eyes peeled for pronghorn on the sagebrush north of the lakes in the Centennial Valley. Hundreds of mountain bluebirds use the fence posts on the refuge and national forest for perches; these beautifully colored birds hunt for flying insects close to the ground, sometimes hovering in midair before they swoop down on their insect prey. Just east of Mud Lake, you can take County Road 202 north to Lima Reservoir. This is the same road you would come out on if you had taken the North Side Road from Elk Lake. It will also take you to the Gravelly Range Road and into the town of Ennis, more than 70 miles north.

Just west of this turnoff, the road begins to climb to a plateau before dropping into the town of Monida. Here the landscape is much drier than it was around the refuge. There is not a tree in sight—except at the horizon, where the Bitterroot, Beaverhead, and Lemhi ranges mingle along Montana's southern border. For the most part, Monida is a ghost town, with a row of boarded-up storefronts facing I-15. One or two families live here, but travelers will find no services. Because it rests on the border of Montana and

The road near Red Rock Lakes National Wildlife Refuge.
Photo by Paul Dumond.

Idaho, Monida's name was derived by combining the first three letters of both states.

From here you can head north on I-15 and go 23 miles to Dell, where Scenic Drive 7 starts. Scenic Drive 6 begins about 13 miles beyond Dell and north of Dillon.

9 MADISON RIVER COUNTRY

Montana Highway 2, U.S. Highway 287

General description: This 90-mile drive skirts the folds, crinkles, and arêtes of the high Madison Range and the sparkling waters of the Madison River and nearby lakes. Enjoy this fly-fisher's paradise, or take a 28-mile side trip and relive Montana's gold rush in Virginia City, a restored ghost town.
Special attractions: Missouri Headwaters State Park, Lewis and Clark Caverns, Virginia City, Nevada City, Madison River, Quake Lake, Hebgen Lake; camping, boating, fishing, hiking, mountain biking, wildlife viewing.
Location: Southwestern Montana. The drive begins at Three Forks, on Interstate 90. It ends at West Yellowstone or at Cliff and Wade lakes.
Drive route numbers: Montana Highway 2, U.S. Highway 287, Montana Highway 287.
Travel season: Year-round, but narrow roads can make winter travel hazardous.
Camping: Campers can find places at Headwaters State Park and Lewis and Clark Caverns State Park, along the Jefferson River. There are several Bureau of Land Management and commercial campgrounds along the Madison River, especially south of Ennis. There are also campgrounds at Virginia City (commercial) and Cliff and Wade lakes (on national forest land).
Services: Full services at Three Forks, Ennis, Virginia City, and West Yellowstone; limited services at Cardwell, Harrison, Norris, and Cameron.
For more information: Beaverhead National Forest, Madison Ranger District; Ennis Chamber of Commerce; Lewis and Clark Caverns State Park; West Yellowstone Chamber of Commerce; Virginia City Chamber of Commerce (see Appendix).

The drive:

> *Sah-cah-gar-we-ah* (our) Indian woman was one of the female prisoners taken at that time; tho' I cannot discover that she shews any immotion of sorrow in recollecting this event, or of joy in being restored to her native country; if she has enough to eat and a few trinkets to wear I believe she would be perfectly content anywhere.
> — Meriwether Lewis, July 28, 1805

Begin this scenic trip up the Madison River at Missouri Headwaters State Park, where the Madison, Jefferson and Gallatin rivers join to form the

9 MADISON RIVER COUNTRY

Montana Highway 2, U.S. Highway 287

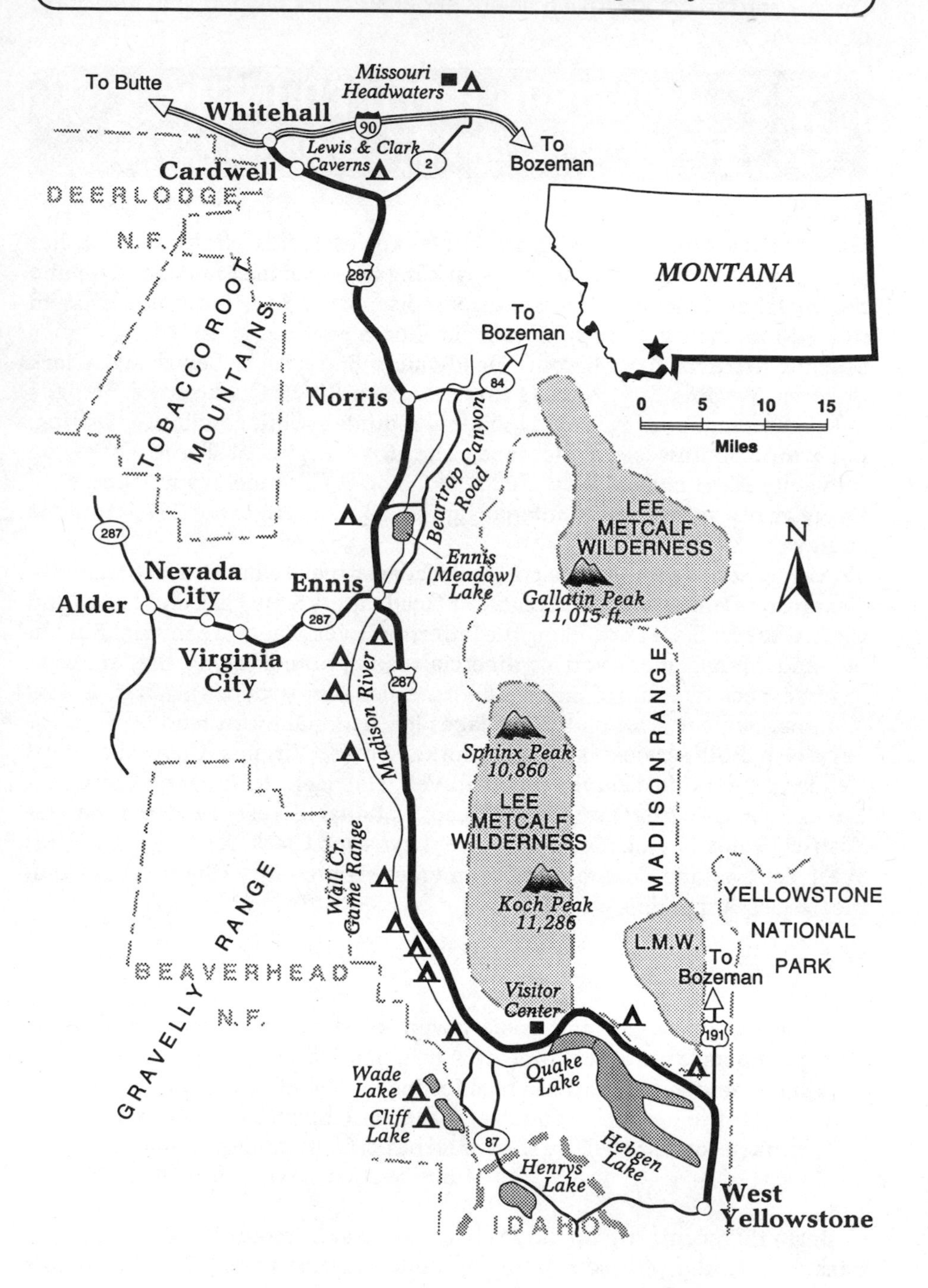

mighty Missouri. The three rivers were named by explorers Meriwether Lewis and William Clark for their president Thomas Jefferson ("that illustrious personage," according to Lewis), James Madison (then secretary of state), and Albert Gallatin (secretary of the treasury, who, incidentally, had refused financing for the expedition, believing it was a waste of money.) The site where the "three forks" of the Missouri come together was also the place where the Shoshoni Indian woman Sacagawea was kidnapped before being sold to Hidatsa Indians in North Dakota, where she met her husband, a French trapper named Charbonneau, and, later, Lewis and Clark.

The state park also marks the history of later years. In 1863, Gallatin City was laid out near the Missouri headwaters. Its founders envisioned the area as the perfect spot for a regional commercial center, given the dependence on water travel at the time. The town founders' dreams never materialized, however. Gallatin City experienced brief prosperity in the 1870s when supplies were ferried up the Missouri and then taken overland to the mining boomtowns of Bannack and Virginia City, then several days' travel south. But the town breathed its last when the railroad bypassed it in 1883.

The headwaters area today is a fine place to camp or enjoy riverine habitat. Rocky buttes and knobs punctuate the low cliffs along the river within Missouri Headwaters State Park. The campsites have few trees and are mainly arid, but the picnic area is very pleasant—a big, grassy, shady place along the Jefferson River. Barrier-free trails with interpretive displays about the landscape are an added feature. Boaters can launch their crafts on the Missouri by means of an access ramp here.

The drive heads south of the Missouri Headwaters park, going through the town of Three Forks. Take MT 2 south and west of town about 16 miles to Montana's oldest state park, Lewis and Clark Caverns. If you are coming from the west on I-90, you may want to skip the Missouri Headwaters and begin the drive at Cardwell instead, taking MT 2 east to the caverns. The road to the caverns is quite narrow with sharp curves as it snakes along the Jefferson River. Look for raptors sailing above the narrow, rocky canyon.

Lewis and Clark Caverns, the largest caves in Montana, were once tilted layers of limestone filled with acidic water. As the water dissolved the limestone over thousands of years, the ceiling of the newly formed openings collapsed numerous times. Today the caves' glistening limestone insides are still growing stalactites and stalagmites. These underground rooms also are home to a rare Montana mammal, the western big-eared bat. You are bound to see one or two streak by you on the 2-hour tour through the caverns. Tour guides discuss various limestone formations and cave history. The state park also has camping, rental cabins, nature trails, concessions, and picnicking from May through September. It is open for tours on weekends in April and October. Reservations are required for candlelight tours during December.

After you visit the caverns, head back toward Three Forks on MT 2 until you reach US 287. Turn right (south) on US 287, following signs to Yellowstone National Park. The road crosses the Jefferson River, then rolls over cattle and sheep pastures and grain fields dissected by shallow coulees.

Down time on the Madison River, one of Montana's premiere fishing spots.

Surrounding hillsides sport scrubby lodgepole pines and junipers and are hemmed in with willow- and cottonwood-choked stream bottoms. The Tobacco Root Mountains, bored by hundreds of old mine shafts and a few mining towns, rise to the west.

At Norris, a wide spot in the road, you will find a small campground and hot springs, a cafe, and a few tattered houses. After Norris, US 287 takes on more hills and curves through the still scrubby foothills of the northern Madison Range. The road climbs a pass known as Norris Hill. Look closely at the grass on top, since remnants of the Bozeman Trail still scar the hillside. A shortcut to Bannack and Virginia City, the trail was used to transport supplies to the gold rush towns. Stop at the historical marker atop the pass and look just beyond it, imagining what it was like to draw wagons over such jarring terrain.

At the bottom of Norris Hill, Ennis Lake sits in a small basin below the impressive Madison Range. The lake has access for camping, boating, and fishing. White pelicans glide above its surface and bob along its marshy shoreline. You can also access several trails into the Madisons to the east of the lake or follow roads into the Tobacco Root Mountains, to the west.

Farther south, the town of Ennis bustles in summer. A road sign near the community limits attests to Ennis's bread and butter: "Ennis, 660 people and 11 million trout." Several fishing guides are available for trips on the blue-ribbon trout stream, the Madison River. Among the angler's quarry are cutthroat trout, brown trout, brook trout, rainbow trout (although a recent outbreak of "whirling" disease has killed most of these), mountain whitefish, and Arctic grayling. Check local closure areas before fishing, since the river is still recovering from the disease outbreak.

Ennis is an odd mix of museums—a wildlife museum, an antler museum, and a rockhound museum among them—cafes, fly shops, art galleries, and real estate brokers. The children of Irishman William Ennis, for whom the town was named, were supposedly the first white children to see Yellowstone National Park in 1873.

From Ennis, take a side trip west on MT 287, which snakes its way to the still lively ghost towns of Virginia City and Nevada City. On the way there, from the top of the pass between Ennis and the other two towns, an overlook provides a stunning 180-degree view of the Madison River valley below. As you descend the steep pass and enter Virginia City, you will see remains of broken dreams in the form of tattered cabins dotting sagebrush hills. Newer homes scattered among the century-old ruins are strangely conspicuous, as if some treasure hunters have not yet given up.

Virginia City sprung up when gold was discovered in Alder Gulch (named for the bushes that line it) in 1863, another rich deposit like that found in Bannack a year earlier. The Alder and Grasshopper creeks strikes were two of the richest ever discovered in Montana. Many prospectors left Bannack for the newer strikes in Virginia City, and the latter town managed to wrest from the former designation as territorial capital by 1865. The two boomtowns shared the notorious Road Agents, however, the gang of thieves and murderers who reportedly killed more than one hundred people and robbed countless others before their glory days were over (see Scenic Drive 6).

At Virginia City, take a historical bus tour through town and into the hills, where men dizzy with gold fever sweated to find the mother lode. This crash course in history is a delightful look into Montana's beginnings. You can also relive the drama by watching the Virginia City Players perform melodramas and variety shows nightly. In its heyday, Virginia City had the largest mercantile shop in all of Montana Territory. Many of its original buildings now house modern-day shops, while others have been left more or less in their original condition. The modern shops peddle everything from candy to trinkets to cappuccino. The old buildings are not open, but you can look through windows at displays of nineteenth-century goods and services. Many of the buildings bulge with artifacts from clothing to foodstuffs, tools, and dry goods.

Nevada City, down the road a mile or two, is not so alive as its counterpart. A small fee grants you access to this little town beyond the storefronts on the main road. The original Nevada City, a mining camp and trading post that thrived in the 1860s, is not really intact. Many of the buildings here now did not make up the original town, but were brought in from other sites. Many of them are open, so you can wander inside on your tour. Most buildings have been restored or rebuilt to give visitors an idea of what a real western mining town might have been like. Another tour train ride through the gold-robbed hills relates historical accounts of mining life.

Oddly enough, one hundred years after the death of these two boomtowns, the futures of both Virginia and Nevada cities are uncertain. Virginia City is vying for an unlikely designation as a national park, while the operators of Nevada City are hard-pressed to upkeep the historic landmark, and have

Lone Mountain, the centerpiece of Big Sky Ski Area.

begun to sell off assets. Both towns lack finances to preserve the deteriorating buildings. For information on possible limited access to Nevada and Virginia cities, call or write the Virginia City Chamber of Commerce, listed in the appendix.

After taking the side trip to two of Montana's historical ghost towns, head back the fourteen miles to Ennis. From here, take US 287 south. The road narrows and straightens with only a few dips in the pavement. To the east, the Madison Range crowns the sprawling ranchland. Sphinx Peak, which can be seen best from the overlook on the way to Virginia City, stands sentinel over the valley. Its 10,000-foot red-rock cliffs cast a striking glow in the setting sun. The gravel conglomerate forming the Sphinx is unique to that mountain in all of the range.

There are many campgrounds along the Madison River. Most of them are open and flat with wonderful views of the Madison Range and its river. The campgrounds tend to fill up quickly during the summer when fishing is good. During winter you can view a thousand or so elk on the sagebrush flats of Wall Creek Wildlife Management Area, near the McAtee Bridge campground.

The road is in good shape for 20 miles south of Ennis with a wide shoulder. It begins to curve a bit when it turns into the mountains again near Quake Lake. Where US 287 meets Montana Highway 87, the vista narrows as the road passes through a narrow canyon. As you drive on, you will see much rubble and rock bars providing a rapid course for the Madison River. You will notice the river runs much more quickly through here than it did farther downstream.

Pull over into the interpretive center describing the origins of Quake Lake when you reach it. Look across the lake to the south, where a mountainside is visible. On August 17, 1959, an earthquake measuring 7.5 on the Richter scale shook loose 80 million tons of rock and sent it sliding 100 mph downhill toward the Madison River. The road you just drove came over the top of this 300-foot-deep rubble pile, which now forms a bench and dam across the river. The visitor center here overlooks the 37,800-acre slide area where twenty-eight people were killed. Although the earthquake formed Quake Lake more than thirty years ago, the mountain that dropped a load on the area is still sparsely vegetated.

Continuing on US 287, you will wind around Quake Lake where you can see the tops of dead trees (called snags) sticking out of the water. When the earthquake struck, the Madison River dammed to form this body of water. Many summer cabins now lie beneath its waves. If you get out and walk around parts of the lake you can see a rooftop or two protruding from the water. As you drive east toward Hebgen Lake, several pullouts along the road tell stories about events that took place the night of the huge quake. At point number seven, you can take a short walk and see where cabins were submerged in the lake when the shoreline dropped 19 feet.

At Hebgen Lake, farther east, there is plenty of access to boating and fishing, as well as to campgrounds around the lake. The mountains on the other side of Hebgen form the Continental Divide. Lionhead Mountain thrusts its rocky nose southeast into Idaho. On the left (north) side of the road, sage-covered hills are punctuated by groves of quaking aspen. As you near the east end of Hebgen Lake, deeper waters give way to shallow marshes choked with willow. US 287 bumps into the southern end of US Highway 191 shortly after passing the lake. At the junction, head south to the tourist town of West Yellowstone and Yellowstone National Park. (For a description of West Yellowstone, see Scenic Drive 10.)

You can end your drive in West Yellowstone or take another side trip back to Cliff and Wade lakes. To do the latter, head west from West Yellowstone on US Highway 20, which dips into Idaho for about 12 miles, going over Targhee Pass (7,072 feet high), then pick up MT 87 heading north toward Henrys Lake. This short loop passes through sagebrush range rimmed by rolling hills. Henrys Lake sits below the road to the southwest. You then go over another pass, 6,800-foot Raynolds Pass, and go north back into Montana.

Two miles beyond the top of the pass, a gravel road to the west leads to Cliff and Wade lakes. The road is in good condition and probably smooth enough for bikes. The blue-green lakes sit in deep basins surrounded by high pine ridges. Both have nice, lightly forested campgrounds. Drop a boat in the water and spend an hour or two fishing. If you are brave enough, or a little crazy, you can even go for a swim. Bald eagles and ospreys nest along the shores. In winter you stand a good chance of seeing moose, elk, and trumpeter swans; look for river otters in Wade Lake. You can cross-country ski at Wade Lake Resort or above Cliff Lake at the Cliff Lake Natural Area. You can also hike the trails here.

From these jewel-like lakes, you can pick up Scenic Drive 8 to the south or Scenic Drive 10 from West Yellowstone.

10 GALLATIN CANYON
U.S. Highway 191

General description: This 83-mile trip takes you from West Yellowstone to Bozeman through a narrow, mountain canyon cut by the sometimes green, sometimes whitewater Gallatin River. The drive passes through a little-used but attractive portion of Yellowstone National Park.
Special attractions: Yellowstone National Park, Lee Metcalf Wilderness, Big Sky Resort, Museum of the Rockies, Montana State University; petrified forest, hot springs, concerts, festivals, art shows, county fairs; hiking, camping, fishing, whitewater rafting, floating, backpacking, skiing, snowmobiling, wildlife viewing, swimming, shopping.
Location: Southwestern Montana, beginning in West Yellowstone and ending in Bozeman.
Drive route number: U.S. Highway 191.
Travel season: Year-round. Extreme snowfall and slick ice conditions can make winter travel extremely treacherous along portions of US 191.
Camping: Campgrounds in Yellowstone National Park fill up quickly during summer and even after Labor Day. There are numerous Forest Service campgrounds along the Gallatin River and many undeveloped places to camp in Beaverhead and Gallatin national forests. There are KOAs and other commercial campgrounds in and around West Yellowstone and Bozeman.
Services: Full services in West Yellowstone, Big Sky, Gallatin Gateway, and Bozeman. There are a few gas stations, restaurants, and food stores along the way.
For more information: Yellowstone National Park; Beaverhead National Forest, Madison Ranger District; Gallatin National Forest, Bozeman and Hebgen Lake ranger districts; West Yellowstone Chamber of Commerce; Bozeman Chamber of Commerce; Big Sky Resort; Museum of the Rockies (see Appendix).

The drive:

> Regardless of the fact that they had been harassed and hard pressed and expected battle any moment . . . the majority of the Nez Perces were light-hearted and seemed not to worry over the outcome of their campaign.
>
> — Emma Carpenter Cowan,
> "A Trip to the National Park in 1877"

West Yellowstone, as the name suggests, is the western gateway to Yellowstone National Park. It is also the starting point for this scenic drive. West Yellowstone is quite the tourist town year-round. In summer it takes

10 GALLATIN CANYON
U.S. Highway 191

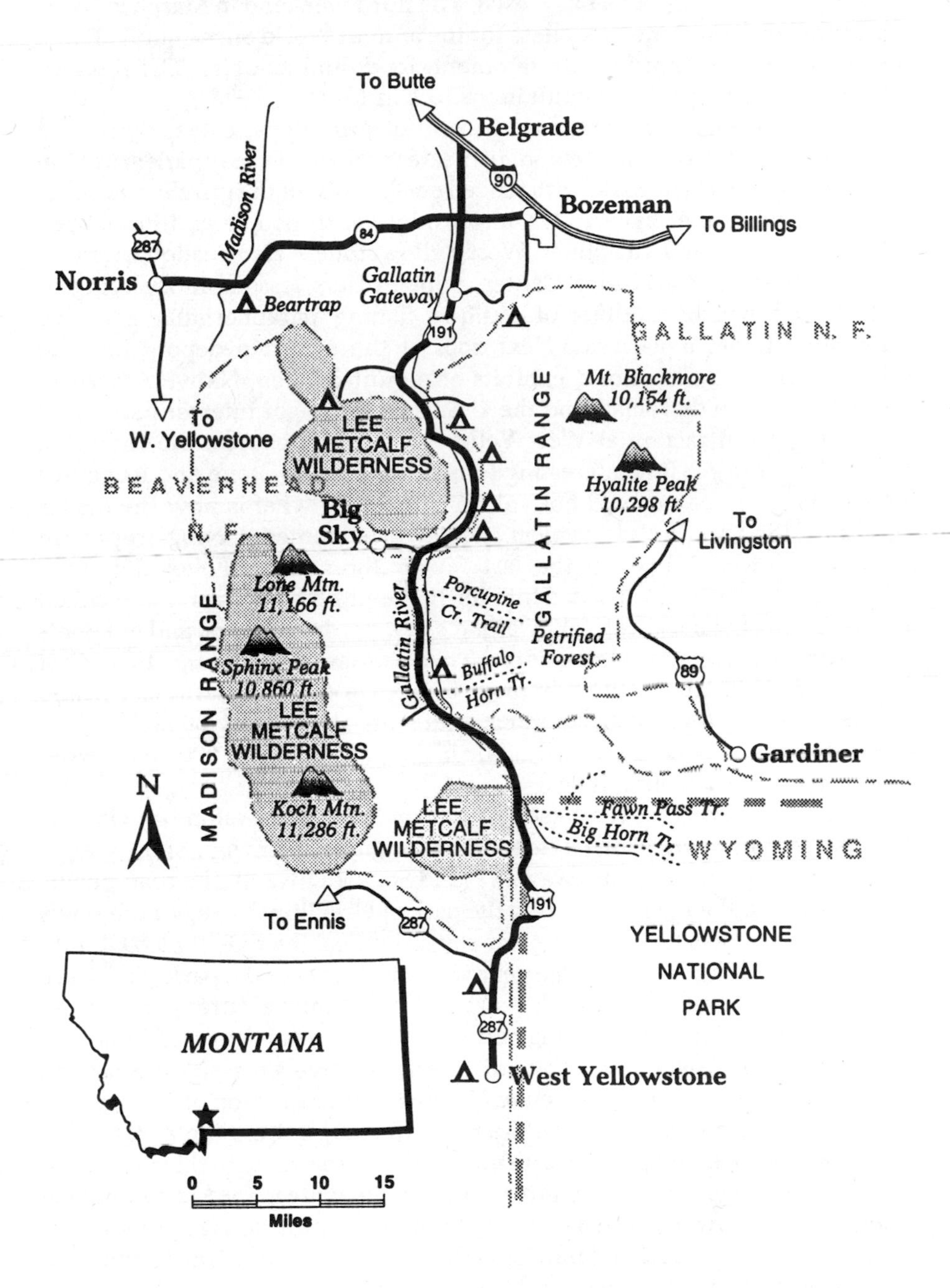

in the traffic from visitors to the park; in winter it is a haven for snowmobilers and cross-country skiers. Be warned that the first few weeks after Labor Day are not yet off-season for Yellowstone. Although there are significantly less tourists, West Yellowstone still has full motels well into September. Other times of the year also find a busy town. The third weekend in March is abuzz with a few thousand snowmobilers for the annual World Snowmobile Expo, which holds races, music, entertainment, food, and exhibits. The Rendezvous cross-country ski races pull in visitors in March.

West Yellowstone is composed mostly of gift shops, cafes, fly-fishing shops, and motels. A brand new Imax theater and grizzly bear park are at the south end of town. The park, with fenced enclosures for the grizzlies, is home to captive bears that have gotten into trouble with people and have been banished from their own habitat. West Yellowstone is also headquarters for the International Fly Fishing Center, which offers lessons in fly tying or casting and houses exhibits of antique fishing paraphernalia and live coldwater stream aquariums. Next door at the old train depot, now the Museum of the Yellowstone, exhibits of mountain men, Native American artifacts, wildlife dioramas, and the U.S. Cavalry might interest you.

The largest attraction at West Yellowstone is, of course, the first U.S. national park itself. It is interesting to note that Yellowstone and its geyser activity takes place in a still-hot volcanic basin. In what is now the center portion of the park, a classic volcanic cone once loomed, having erupted in a big way several times in the last few million years. Following these eruptions, the volcano collapsed into itself, leaving a giant depression called a caldera. Most, if not all, of Yellowstone's geysers, hot springs, and hot pools lie within the perimeter of this caldera. There is some evidence that these "hot spots" may be getting hotter. Geologists believe the Yellowstone volcano erupted with the force of a giant nuclear arsenal about every 600,000 years. Interestingly, the last time Yellowstone blew was about 600,000 years ago—give or take a few thousand years.

To begin this scenic drive, head north from West Yellowstone on US 191. The road out of town is long, wide, and straight as a runway. Shortly after passing a turnoff to U.S. Highway 287 (and Scenic Drive 9), the road begins to climb hills and wind a bit, tracing the path of Grayling Creek, which flows from Yellowstone's high peaks. After several miles, the road dips back into Yellowstone, going just inside the very western border of the park. There are places to pull over and fish the streams here (make sure you have a Yellowstone National Park fishing permit) or hike the sage-covered hills. The dead forest you see was created by a double whammy—a massive disease kill and part of the infamous, spectacular Yellowstone fire season of 1988, when seven major fires roared through the park, burning 1.4 million acres.

Notice the green understory returning to the burned area in this fire-prone and fire-dependent ecosystem. Fires can bring new life to forests by burning older trees, dead wood, and shrubs that are not as nutritious for wildlife as younger plants. Fires release nutrients stored in forest litter (dead branches, leaves, cones, conifer needles, and grasses) back to the soil, which are then used to grow new plants. Some trees, such as older lodgepole pines, need fire to rid the trees of diseases and provide a seedbed for more pines to grow. Lodgepole pine has serotinous cones, and needs intense heat, either from hot sun or fire, to open the cones and release the seeds.

Cottonwoods and willows along the creek bottoms here are brilliant gold in autumn. The Madison Range and Taylor Peaks lie to the west of the highway. Due to moving faults along the edges of the mountains, the Madisons continue to rise. The same is true of the Gallatin Range, on the east side of the highway.

Fawn Pass and Bighorn Pass trails offer pleasant hiking in a mostly open landscape on the east, Yellowstone Park side of the road. Keep your eyes open for hot springs along these trails if you feel like a soak. North of here are Tepee Creek and Buffalo Horn Creek trailheads. These trails will lead you into part of the Gallatin's petrified forest. About 50 million years ago lava coated these mountains. Ash, lava, and mudflows overcame trees and other vegetation. Some of the trees were so well preserved that paleobotanists can identify tropical and temperate species. The cooler-weather species were carried down from higher elevations as the mudflows destroyed everything in their paths. If you hike in the area, please don't remove petrified wood; leave it for others to enjoy. For trail information, refer to a Gallatin National Forest map.

The road begins to follow a windy route along the Gallatin River just before you leave this little piece of Yellowstone Park. Winter travel on this highway can be extremely hazardous, so please use caution. Even when the

Birding along the Gallatin River north of West Yellowstone.

Mountain goats in the Bridger Range near Bozeman.

roads are dry, negotiating through the tight curves is easily underestimated. Truck traffic can frighten the best of drivers here. Also, watch for wildlife (as on any road in Montana), especially bison which occasionally wander to this part of the park during winter months.

As you leave park boundaries and enter the Gallatin Canyon, many wonderful hiking trails take off from US 191. Look for turnoffs to Taylor Fork and Porcupine Wildlife Management Area. If you are in search of a wildlife experience, watch for the elk, deer, moose, and grizzly bears that frequent these areas. Please be mindful of wildlife by keeping your distance and minimizing any disturbance. You can fish just about anywhere along the Gallatin River, and numerous pullouts offer places to park. There are several designated camping sites as well. This is bear country, however, so be sure to store all food in your vehicle overnight. If you fancy a tumble in the river rapids, watch for signs directing you to rafting outfitters along the way.

Between Buffalo Horn Creek and Buck Creek the canyon closes in to steep rocky cliffs on both sides of the road before opening up again north of Buck Creek all the way to Big Sky. Big Sky is a destination ski resort. It offers plenty of hiking, mountain bike riding, fishing, and rafting during summer months. There is also a golf course. An outdoor recreation shop at Big Sky rents mountain bikes and other outdoor toys if you don't have your own. At the ski hill you can buy a ticket to ride the gondola up Lone Mountain for a head start on hikes along the ridge and scenic views of the Gallatin and Madison mountain ranges. Some of the several guest ranches at and around Big Sky allow drop in visitors for trail rides and have restaurants open to the public.

Check with local chambers of commerce for reservation details.

North of Big Sky, the narrow US 191 bends and turns recklessly until you get to Spanish Creek. Several more hiking trails cut up the steep ridges on both sides of the highway. Most of the trails on the east side in the Gallatin Range go up over the divide and into the Paradise Valley (see Scenic Drive 11). From Spanish Creek the drive into Bozeman is mostly straight, and the road widens out to much safer dimensions. You will pass through flat, open range not far from urban sprawl. At Gallatin Gateway, stop at the Gallatin Gateway Inn, along the highway. Once a destination on the Milwaukee Road train route, the inn has been refurbished. Its Spanish-style architecture and painted cathedral ceilings impress. The food is also worth stopping for.

About 5 miles north of Gallatin Gateway, just before you get to Four Corners (a four-way stop with a traffic light), Bozeman Hot Springs offer a pleasant soak—especially after a day of skiing at Big Sky or floating the Gallatin River. From Four Corners, head east into Bozeman or, alternately, take Montana Highway 84 west, which is a cutoff to Norris (and Scenic Drive 9). This cutoff is a nice little drive that winds over hills and along part of the Madison River. The Madison is a popular place on weekends during summer for floaters, swimmers, and fly-fishers. You will reach the river at Black's Ford, about 18 miles west of Four Corners. The Madison River here is gentle and somewhat warm.

If you continue along the Madison, you will find another recreation area. At Bear Trap Road, head south along a dirt track on the east side of the river. The large campground at the Bear Trap turnoff is on flat, arid ground, and no longer maintains services. Past Bear Trap, MT 84 crosses the Madison and snakes along the river's course for a few more miles before following a small creek cutting through low red bluffs. At Norris you can pick up Scenic Drive 9 or turn around and head back to Bozeman.

If you turn east at Four Corners instead, you will follow a straight road right into Bozeman. Bozeman is a college town with plenty to see and do. You can enjoy concerts, lectures, film festivals, art galleries, gift shops, and good food. Visit the Montana State University campus, which houses the Museum of the Rockies. This world-class museum is the home of dinosaur eggs and a nest; these were part of the first North American discovery of dinosaur eggs, found near Choteau, Montana (see Scenic Drive 22). The museum has a wonderful and limited display of dinosaur bones and eggs, complete with fossilized embryos. The museum staff is now in the process of constructing a nearly intact skeleton of *Tyrannosaurus rex*, scheduled for display before the end of the decade. Other museum exhibits include pioneer and Native American artifacts, western art, and photographs. The planetarium at the museum runs several different sky and laser shows throughout the year. Ask at the museum for directions and a guide to Kirk Hill, a wildlife area managed by the museum, about 5 miles south of town.

Be sure to visit Bozeman's computer museum, a unique and impressive collection of those machines that make you wonder how you ever lived without them. During summer catch an outdoor performance of Shakespeare in the Park, or attend the Sweet Pea Festival, which features music, dance, food, sports events, and artisans selling their beautiful craft work.

The mountains surrounding Bozeman offer great hiking to panoramic vistas, canyons, scenic lakes, and waterfalls. You might want to drive up to either Hyalite Reservoir, south of town, or Bridger Canyon, north of town. Both offer hiking and recreation around high mountain lakes. You can get to Hyalite Canyon (named for a translucent mineral) via South 19th Street, going about seven miles out of town to Hyalite Canyon Road. Take the winding Hyalite Canyon Rd. for 10 miles to the reservoir. Check with the Gallatin National Forest for details about recreational activities here. Beyond Hyalite Reservoir the East Fork of Hyalite road will take you to the Palisade Falls trail. This unique area is specially designed for people with disabilities. Scan the cliff walls and rocky slopes for nesting golden eagles, pikas, and marmots.

To get to Bridger Canyon, head northeast of town on Bridger Drive. There are several hiking trails along this road, and downhill skiing at Bridger Bowl Ski Area. Check a Gallatin National Forest map for directions to Fairy Lake and accompanying trailheads. Hardy hikers will enjoy climbing to the top of Sacagawea Peak. You may even run into some inquisitive mountain goats.

From Bozeman you can head west to pick up Scenic Drive 9 or go east toward Livingston to pick up Scenic Drives 11 and 23.

11 PARADISE VALLEY
U.S. Highway 89

General description: Following the Yellowstone River from Livingston to Gardiner, this 53-mile drive through the well-named Paradise Valley features some of Montana's highest peaks. Take in Livingston's annual rodeo or art galleries, soak in hot springs, or watch for herds of elk, deer, and pronghorn that migrate out of Yellowstone National Park in winter.
Special attractions: Park County Rodeo, Chico Hot Springs resort, Jardine ghost town, Yellowstone National Park; galleries, shopping, museums, county fairs, concerts, fishing, floating, hiking, backpacking, wildlife viewing.
Location: Southwest Montana. The drive begins in Livingston, 26 miles east of Bozeman, and heads south to Gardiner, at the North Entrance to Yellowstone National Park, just north of the Wyoming border.
Drive route number: U.S. Highway 89.
Travel season: Year-round. Snow, ice, and strong local winds can make winter driving hazardous.
Camping: Campgrounds in Yellowstone fill up quickly during summer and after Labor Day. There are Forest Service campgrounds at Pine and Mill creeks, and undeveloped camping places elsewhere in Gallatin National Forest. There are also several RV parks and private guest ranches in the valley.
Services: Full services in Livingston and Gardiner. Emigrant has a store and gas station, and nearby Chico Hot Springs has camping, lodging, and food.
For more information: Gallatin National Forest, Livingston and Gardiner ranger districts; Livingston Chamber of Commerce; Chico Hot Springs resort; Gardiner Chamber of Commerce; Yellowstone National Park (see Appendix).

The drive:

> Yankee Jim was a picturesque old man with a talent for yarns. . . . It seemed to me . . . that I might hold my own with the old-timer if I judiciously painted up a few lies gathered in the course of my wandering. Yankee Jim saw every one of my tales and went fifty better on the spot. He dealt in bears and Indians—never less than twenty of each.
>
> — Rudyard Kipling,
> *From Sea to Sea*

Begin this drive in Livingston, an attractive Old West town gone trendy, with many gift shops, art galleries, cafes, and bookstores. The town more or less grew out of the rails in 1882 and was named for Crawford Livingston, once director of the Northern Pacific Railroad. In this neo-pioneer age, people are streaming into Livingston; its residents recently have had to grapple with growth issues affecting environmental quality.

11 PARADISE VALLEY

U.S. Highway 89

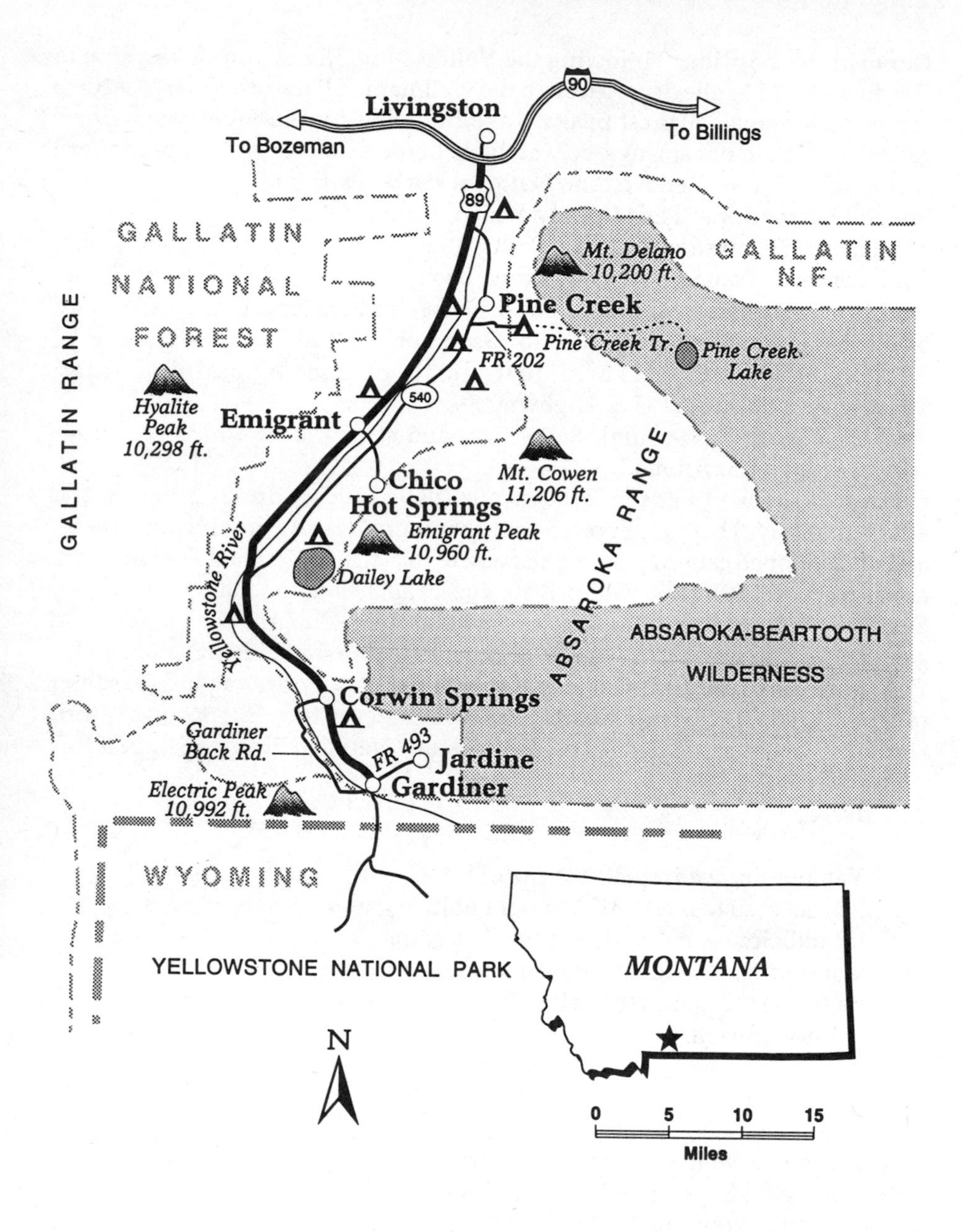

Nevertheless, Livingston is a fun place with many year-round activities. Events include theater, art shows, and music festivals. The county's annual rodeo, held in Livingston July 2-4, draws top cowboys and cowgirls from all over the country. The Park County Museum, open summers only, houses rocks and minerals, pioneer artifacts, archaeological finds, and displays of Yellowstone National Park's early explorers. The museum has an original Yellowstone stagecoach, a caboose from the 1890s, and a railroad room. Museum staff have also recreated a Shoshoni bison kill site from an actual one near here, used from 700 to 300 years ago. The Depot Center, a former passenger depot for the Northern Pacific Railroad, has also been turned into a museum with changing exhibits. The building is on the National Register of Historic Places, as are 436 other structures in Livingston, including private homes and downtown businesses.

Calamity Jane first strolled into Livingston in the 1880s, and from then on made Livingston her occasional watering hole. Her exploits were detailed in early newspaper accounts, and reporters must have had fun tracing her path through various saloons. In June 1901 the *Livingston Post* noted the following of the famous Western woman:

> She reports having had great success in "hot airing" the tourists who are making park trips [Yellowstone], and says that if she could only hold onto the money she is making she would be a bloomin' millionaire in a short time. Unfortunately, however, she is unable to keep the proceeds of her work in this wet weather, when keeping the outside dry does no good unless the inside is kept in exactly a reverse condition.

Take US 89 south of Livingston, where it follows the Yellowstone River toward its source. The river is visible from the highway for most of the drive. Just south of town, you enter the wide Paradise Valley, hemmed by the Absaroka Range to the east and the Gallatin Range to the west. The Absaroka Mountains (pronounced Ab-SOR-kee) are high, steep, and sharply defined. Several trails head into the mountains and the Absaroka–Beartooth Wilderness Area, where hikers must be prepared for all kinds of weather conditions. The most popular trail, probably because it is easy and leads to a set of waterfalls, is along Pine Creek. To get to the trailhead, turn east on Pine Creek Road about 11 miles south of Livingston. When you get to the little community of Pine Creek, turn south (right) on East River Road and then make a left on Forest Road 202, following signs to the Pine Creek campground. Mill Creek, 7.5 miles south of Pine Creek, has many additional trails that lead to lakes within the Absaroka–Beartooth. I recommend the Gallatin National Forest map for details on the various trails.

Once you've finished hiking, go back to US 89. The highway is in good shape and fairly straight, with few turns. It cuts through terrain that is arid and scrubby on the west side of the road, with a long stretch of ground between the pavement and the Gallatin Mountains. On the east side of the

The streets of Livingston were once a hang-out for Calamity Jane.

valley, the Absarokas spring seemingly from the river's edge. These mountains are ancient volcanoes, the site of many eruptions and mudflows. Such cataclysmic events left tons of petrified logs in the southern portion of the range.

The Paradise Valley is mostly ranchland, although there are a few settlements here, and newcomers are quickly snatching up lots on recently subdivided ranches. The Yellowstone River meanders through the valley, and several access points for fishing and floating on the river are well marked. At Point of Rocks fishing access, look for rounded hills west of the highway. These were vents for volcanoes that erupted some 50 million years ago.

The valley was also paradise for miners. Gold was discovered in Emigrant Gulch, east of the modern "town" of Emigrant, near Chico Hot Springs. Miners used the natural hot springs for bathing, and a community developed around them. The young town of Chico had a store, meat market, hotel, schoolhouse, five dozen cabins, and a blacksmith shop. Crow Indians made frequent attacks on settlers here, stealing horses and supplies. Today Chico Hot Springs serves a slightly different clientele, with clean, developed pools and quaint, moderately priced hotel rooms. Two small restaurants and a saloon serve the inn, and a few log cabins, cottages, and houses are for rent as well. The resort offers horseback riding in summer and dog-sledding and cross-country skiing in winter. You can rent mountain bikes and skis here, too.

South of Emigrant, past Big Creek, US 89 makes a left-hand curve into Yankee Jim Canyon, named for James George, a gold prospector in the mid-

1800s who built a toll road through here. Yankee Jim was renowned for his cantankerous nature and for his tall tales, as Rudyard Kipling noted. The canyon is narrow for just a few miles before the landscape opens up again to reveal high plateaus to the west on the other side of the river. A stretch of challenging rapids through Yankee Jim Canyon makes a good run for experienced rafters.

The road winds a little more on its way into Gardiner, spruces and Douglas-firs scattered on the hillsides. As you drive this section of US 89, watch for wildlife crossing the road. The Corwin Springs area is winter range for the largest group of hoofed animals in the country. Antelope (October), bighorn sheep and mule deer (November–December), and elk move here (January) from the highlands of Yellowstone National Park. About 20,000 elk of the northern herd winter in the area. From December to May, you may see some of these animals along the base of Cinnabar Mountain. To view wildlife, cross the river on the bridge at Corwin Springs. Turn left once you are past the bridge and head south on the gravel Gardiner Back Road. During winter, watch for bald eagles along the river. It is about 8 miles to Gardiner.

You may also view some of the wintering animals from the main highway, at a turnout near Devil's Slide. The "slide" is made of sedimentary deposits that are about 200 million years old. Some geologists speculate from its red color that Earth's atmosphere may have had more oxygen during the Triassic period (from which these deposits hail). The oxygen would have reacted with iron to create the red pigment and devilish color.

The Absaroka Range in Paradise Valley contains some of Montana's highest peaks.

Teddy Roosevelt's gateway to Yellowstone National Park in Gardiner.

When you get to Gardiner by way of the main highway or the back road, take a side trip on the gravel road that leads northeast to Jardine. More winter range is scattered throughout the hills near the Jardine mine and ghost town, where arsenic was mined for use by the U.S. government during World War II. Evidence of a 1994 wildfire in the area can still be seen.

Gardiner itself was named for an early day trapper, Johnston Gardiner, who spent much of his time along the upper tributaries of the Yellowstone River. Crow Indians hunted here, and conflicts with Gardiner's first settlers were frequent. The new town had no sawmill, and its pioneers were forced to live in tents or hand-hewn log shacks. By 1883 Gardiner bustled with a half-dozen restaurants, five stores, a couple of fruit stands and barber shops, twenty-one saloons, and four brothels to serve its two hundred residents.

Today Gardiner is surprisingly busy year-round, the attraction, of course, being the northern entrance to Yellowstone National Park through Teddy Roosevelt Arch. The town's somewhat drab character makes it unique among the so-called gateway towns of national parks. Art galleries and espresso bars don't haunt every block, and Gardiner still very much caters to snowmobilers, cross-country skiers, and late season elk hunters. Its gift shops still sell cheap "genuine" Indian trinkets and Yellowstone paraphernalia—the plastic kind made in Taiwan. Floaters and fly-fishers have begun to find an outpost in Gardiner as well. It is the nearest town to Cooke City on the eastern border of the park, and kids endure long bus rides to go to school in Gardiner during winter.

A few miles inside the park boundary is the town of Mammoth Hot Springs, Yellowstone National Park headquarters. The Horace Albright

Top: *St. Mary's Lake, Glacier National Park.*
JOHN REDDY

At right: *Pasque flowers.*
DARRIN A. SCHREDER

Top: *Giant cedars, Bull River valley, Cabinet Mountains.* JOHN REDDY

At left: *Wild rose.* JOHN REDDY

Top: *Blackfoot River.* MICHAEL S. SAMPLE
Bottom: *Como Peaks, Bitterroot valley.* JOHN REDDY

Top: *Haystacks in the Big Hole valley.* JOHN REDDY

At left: *Pronghorns.* MICHAEL S. SAMPLE

Winter in the Tobacco Root Mountains. DARRIN A. SCHREDER

Top: *Pintler Mountains southwest of Anaconda.*
JOHN REDDY

At right: *Ladybug.*
DARRIN A. SCHREDER

At left: *Lightning storm near Jordan.* DARRIN A. SCHREDER

Below: *Sage grouse.* MICHAEL S. SAMPLE

Missouri River Breaks from Sunshine Ridge. S. A. SNYDER

Above: *Foggy East Front northwest of Dupuyer.*
RANDALL GREEN

At right: *Fancy Dancer at the Big Sky Pow Wow.*
DARRIN A. SCHREDER

Above: *Sunset in Glacier National Park during forest fire season.* JOHN REDDY

At left: *Tamaracks in autumn, Bitterroot Mountains.* JOHN REDDY

Visitor Center has information about park events and exhibits of natural and human history in the park, as well as photographs of Yellowstone taken during the 1850s Hayden Expedition by W. H. Jackson. These pictures are magnificent, and were largely responsible for convincing the government to preserve Yellowstone as parkland. From Mammoth and its giant hot springs terrace, you can take a road through the Lamar Valley to pick up stunning Scenic Drive 13. Or, you can drive through the park to West Yellowstone and pick up Scenic Drive 9 or 10. Check with the National Park Service for months of winter road closure in the park.

12 THE BOULDER RIVER ROAD

County Road 298

General description: This 50-mile drive on both paved and gravel roads takes you from Big Timber toward the heart of the Absaroka-Beartooth Mountains. The route follows the Boulder River, passing hay fields and a gatelike wall of mountains with cliffs and other geologic features before reaching a wilderness area boundary.
Special attractions: Absaroka-Beartooth Wilderness; waterfalls; fishing, hiking, camping, backpacking, wildlife viewing.
Location: South-central Montana. The drive begins in Big Timber, off Interstate 90, and heads south past McLeod to the Absaroka-Beartooth Wilderness.
Drive route number: County Road 298 (Boulder River Road).
Travel season: In winter the road is maintained to the national forest boundary; beyond that, it is open, weather permitting. Weekday traffic can be heavy during hunting season.
Camping: There is one campground without water near McLeod. There are also several Forest Service campgrounds as you get into the mountains.
Services: Full services in Big Timber; food in McLeod.
For more information: Big Timber Chamber of Commerce; Gallatin National Forest, Big Timber Ranger District (see Appendix).

The drive:

> If you travel with a wagon, provide yourself with a jackscrew, extra tongue, and coupling pole; also, axle-grease, a hatchet and nails, auger, rope, twine, and one or two chains for wheel locking, and one or two extra whippletrees. . . . Never take anything not absolutely necessary. This is a rule of all experienced voyageurs.
>
> — Captain John Mullan,
> *Miners and Travelers' Guide to Oregon,*
> *Washington, Idaho, Montana, 1865*

12 THE BOULDER RIVER ROAD

County Road 298

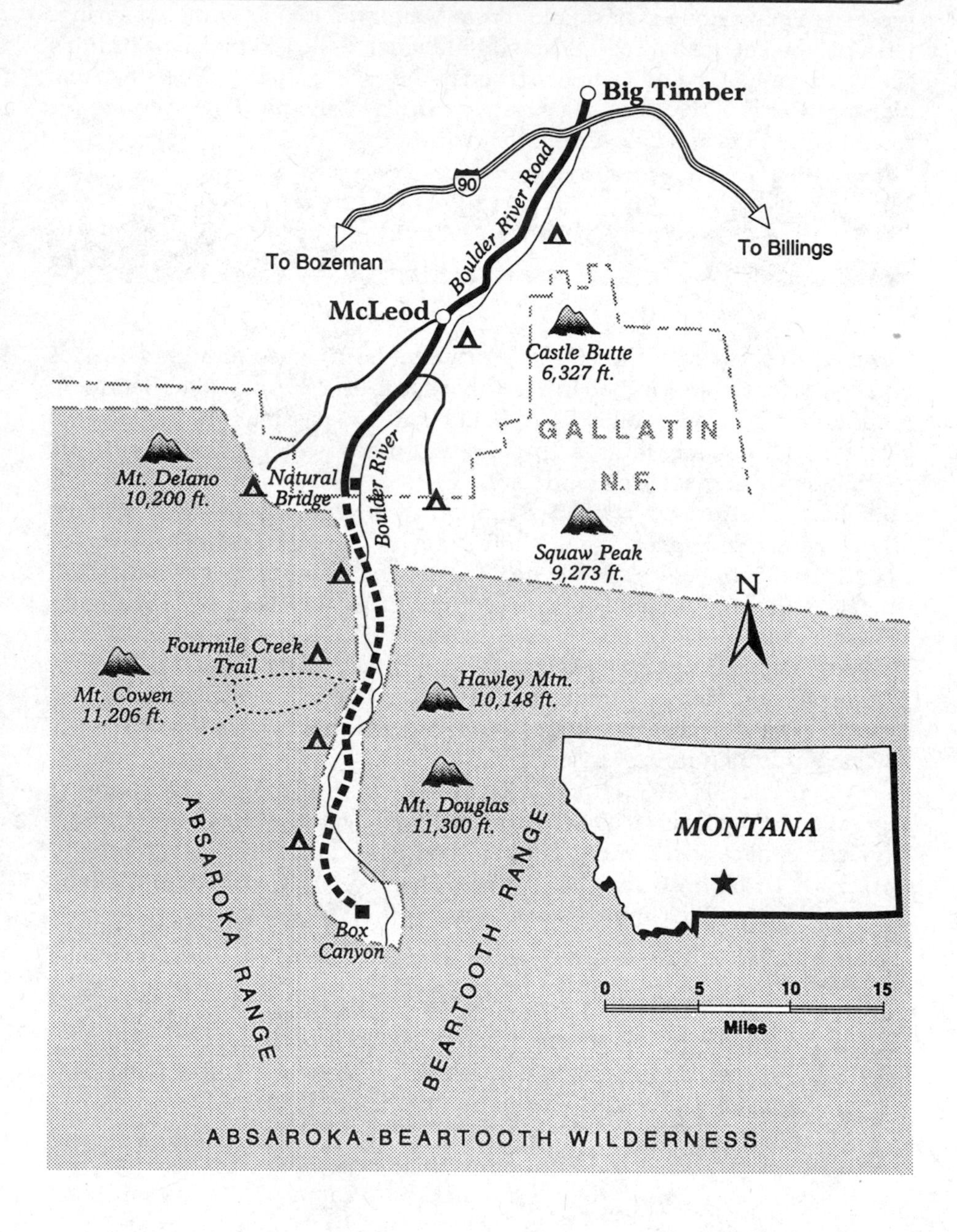

The Boulder River Road is a one-way-in, one-way-out drive on mostly gravel road that is slow going and rough in spots. But this route is worth the trip if your vehicle can handle it, taking you right into the heart of the Absaroka-Beartooth Wilderness. You'll find several wilderness access trails, campgrounds, and plenty of fishing opportunities. The end of the road is a well-used trailhead for horsepackers.

The route begins in the small sheep and cattle town of Big Timber. Follow the signs for CR 298 through downtown Big Timber, heading south. (For a description of things to see and do in Big Timber see Scenic Drive 24.) The first 24 miles of the road are paved and pass through private and state rangeland. There are several fishing access sites and one or two campgrounds between Big Timber and the small community of McLeod.

Near McLeod you can turn off the main road and take side trips up either the East Fork or the West Fork of the Boulder River. Both roads are gravel and cross private land, so heed all "no trespassing" signs. The West Boulder road dead-ends after about 15 miles at a trailhead just outside the Absaroka–Beartooth Wilderness boundary. There is a campground at the end of the road. The East Boulder road takes you upstream for about 4 miles before branching in a "Y." Either of the options will take you into the mountains and to hiking trails.

If you decide to follow the main Boulder River Road instead, pull over at the Natural Bridge interpretive site just before the pavement ends. What was once a natural arch over the Boulder River has fallen in recent years and no longer exists. But the geologic natural formation of limestone under the narrow river canyon here still proves of interest. The roiling Boulder River flows over it during high water (usually in spring) and tumbles over the rock,

The Boulder River flows from the Absaroka Mountains.

The Boulder River's Natural Bridge.

plunging 80 feet to a large pool and riverbed below. During drier periods, the river seems to disappear, since the water goes underneath the limestone and blows out a hole in the cliff as a waterfall. Signs along a short interpretive trail explain how this interesting gorge was formed; another, longer trail leads across the river. When the limestone riverbed is dry, you can look for fossils in the calcite. There is no guardrail where the water falls, so mind small, inquisitive children.

After the Natural Bridge turnout, the Main Boulder River Rd. turns to gravel for the remaining 22 miles. It also turns rough and narrow in places. The road begins to enter a more pinched canyon after leaving the more open ranchland. As you drive south from the Natural Bridge site, look to the west (right) to see a band of rock called Coal Mine Rim, running across the bluff like a jeweled necklace.

There are a half-dozen campgrounds along the route, some of which are in known grizzly habitat. Please follow the food storage instructions posted at each campground and avoid a tragic bear encounter. The road also passes several trailheads, most marked with small signs depicting a hiker. This is steep country, so hiking here is not for those looking to stroll leisurely through the forest. At Fourmile Guard Station you can take a 15-mile loop trail up and around 9,000-foot-high Carbonate Mountain and come out near Hick's Park Campground, about 4 miles farther up the road.

Once the road turns gravel, the scenic drive cuts through lodgepole pine and Douglas-fir forest with a few open meadows scattered throughout. There are several patches of private property, so be sure to do your recreating on

Forest Service land. Just beyond the Fourmile area, the road becomes particularly bumpy and tight. An early hunting season (late September) in the wilderness area brings out outfitters on horseback, making some weekday travel busy. If you plan to hike during the hunting season, be sure to stay on well-used trails, wear hunter orange clothing of some type, and keep unleashed dogs within sight.

Box Canyon, near the end of the road, has a large parking lot. From here, a main trail continues into the wilderness. You can choose from several trails, some of which lead into the northern reaches of Yellowstone National Park. Another bumpy road to the south goes through the forest for a few more miles to an outfitter's camp. If you plan to hike, however, Box Canyon would be a good place to stop.

Retrace your route back to Big Timber, watching for white-tailed deer in the lower meadows. On your way back to town, you may want to stop at the Road Kill Cafe, a bar and restaurant with the motto, "From your grill to ours," just north of McLeod.

A visit to Greycliff Prairie Dog Town, about 7 miles east of Big Timber along I-90, makes an interesting side trip. You can take a short drive or walk through the shortgrass prairie here, where interpretive signs teach you all about black-tailed prairie dogs. You may even witness a hawk or golden eagle swipe one of the furry creatures from its mound. Western bluebirds, meadowlarks, and vesper sparrows also flit about.

From Big Timber you can take Scenic Drive 24 north, or head west to Livingston and pick up Scenic Drives 23 and 11.

Early evening diners along the Boulder River.

13 THE BEARTOOTH HIGHWAY
U.S. Highway 212

General description: This 70-mile drive passes through alpine meadows and glacial lakes at the top of the world, providing access to the highest terrain in Montana. Unless you are an avid backpacker, you will probably never experience such incredible alpine scenery and habitat as that found on the Beartooth Plateau.
Special attractions: Silver Gate, Cooke City, Red Lodge; alpine lakes and tundra; canoeing, fishing, camping, hiking, backpacking, wildlife viewing.
Location: South-central Montana. The drive begins just northeast of Yellowstone National Park in Cooke City. The road dips into a portion of Wyoming and climbs a giant mountain plateau before dropping down to Red Lodge, Montana.
Drive route number: U.S. Highway 212 (Beartooth Highway).
Travel season: Late spring or early summer until snow season. The lower sections of road are well-used by snowmobilers in winter.
Camping: There are three Forest Service campgrounds just east of Cooke City, and five campgrounds in Shoshone National Forest in Wyoming. Seven more campgrounds can be found on the other side of the plateau at Rock Creek, just south of Red Lodge.
Services: Full services at Cooke City and Red Lodge. Limited services at Top of the World store.
For more information: Gallatin National Forest; Custer National Forest, Beartooth Ranger District; Shoshone National Forest, Clarks Fork Ranger District; Red Lodge Chamber of Commerce (see Appendix).

The drive:

> It is a convention of Western thought to believe all cultures are compelled to explore, that human beings seek new land because their economies drive them onward. Lost in the valid but nevertheless impersonal observation is the notion of a simpler longing, of a human desire for a less complicated life, for fresh intimacy and renewal. These, too, draw us into new landscapes.
>
> — Barry Lopez,
> *Arctic Dreams*

Like Scenic Drive 2, Going-to-the-Sun Road in Glacier National Park, this route is probably one of Montana's most stunning. The Beartooth Highway takes travelers to the edge of an alpine wilderness, a rare treat for those who do not travel high mountains on foot. To truly experience the world you are about to enter, however, you must get out of the car as often as possible. Be warned about the weather: It can snow any time of year here, and during bad

13 THE BEARTOOTH HIGHWAY

U.S. Highway 212

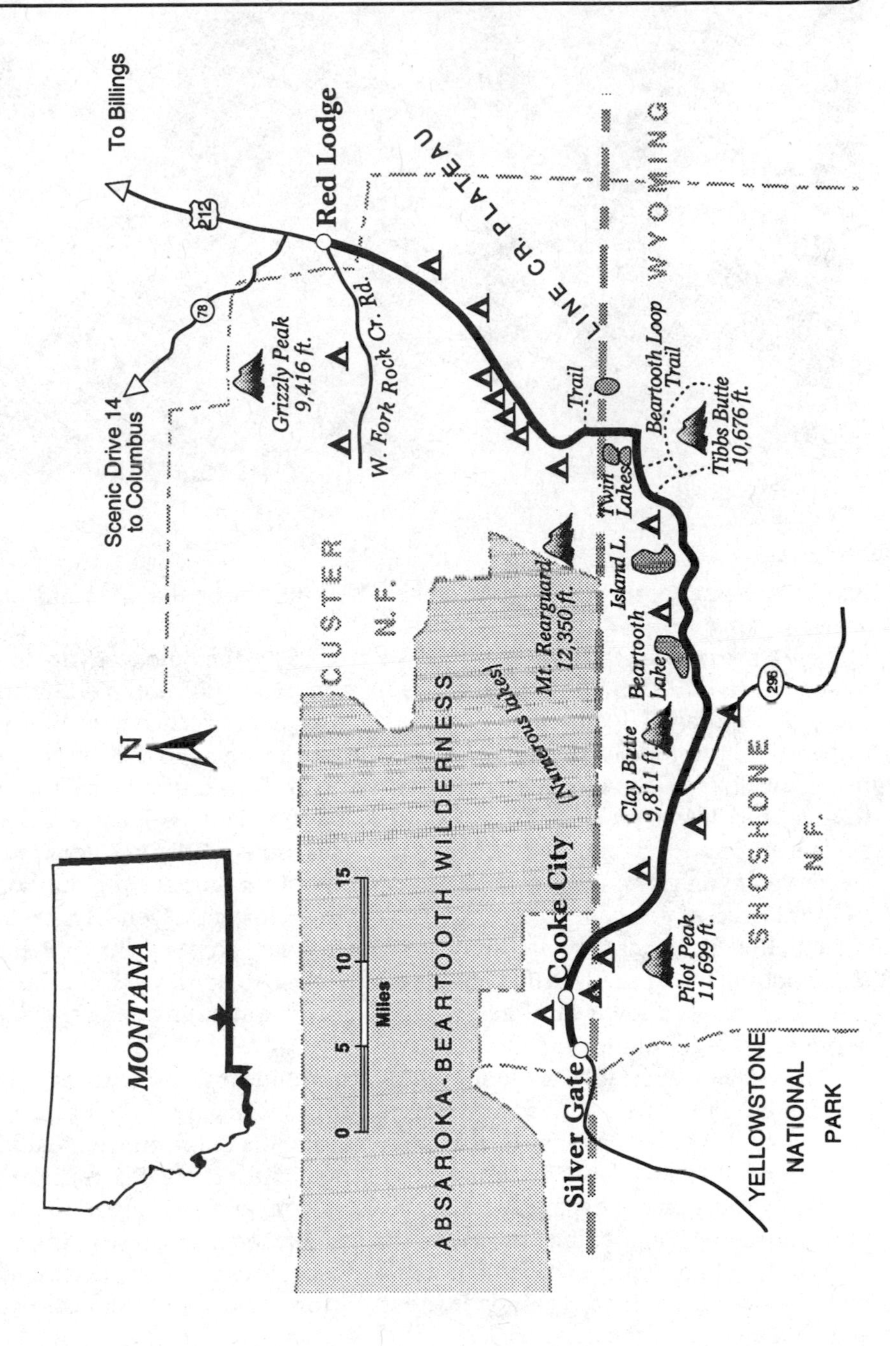

Quaking aspen along the Beartooth Highway.

storms, portions of the road may be closed. Keep an eye on the skies and bring warm clothes.

If you are coming from Scenic Drives 9, 10, or 11, the quickest way to get to the Beartooth Highway is to go through the Lamar Valley of Yellowstone Park, a wonderful scenic drive in itself. This majestic drive begins just outside Yellowstone National Park's Northeast Entrance, in the tiny mining towns of Silver Gate and Cooke City. Silver Gate is the smaller of the two towns, and less developed than Cooke City, but it does have a saloon, restaurant, and lodging. Both Silver Gate and Cooke City are situated in narrow canyons with vertical rock walls, and both towns are the only ones in Montana that you have to go through Wyoming to get to. Densely forested hills below the rocky bluffs slope to the towns' borders. In 1988, the Yellowstone forest fires burned frighteningly close to homes and businesses here. You can see how near the fires raged from the standing dead trees that serve as an eerie reminder.

Cooke City was established in the 1870s as a mining town. It was named for Jay Cooke, a man who had mining claims here. Cooke City is about three or four blocks long and comprises a general store (owners Ralph and Sue Glidden delight in talking to the people who pass through) and a few cafes, motels, gift shops, and bars. In its heyday the town had 13 saloons and 135 log cabins. Short of having a meal or popping into one of the few gift shops in Cooke City, your stay here probably will not be long. If you do decide to camp, you have a choice of three designated campgrounds just east of town. Be sure to have a warm sleeping bag, since the elevation here is close to 8,000 feet.

As soon as you leave Cooke City the road climbs and winds on its way up to the Beartooth Plateau. Much of the drive passes through Wyoming, so remember that fishing regulations differ for both states if you plan to wet a line. NOTE: This entire drive passes through superb grizzly bear habitat. Please mind campground and trail signs regarding proper storage of food and use bear avoidance techniques if you plan to camp or hike anywhere along the way. Do not let your careless behavior lead to the death of an awesome animal.

The Beartooth Highway was conceived in 1919 by J. F. Siegfriedt, a Red Lodge doctor, as a way to save the dying mining towns the route connects. People thought that if a road were built through some of the most amazing landscape of the Beartooth Plateau, the mining towns could survive on tourist dollars. Construction began in 1931, and the road was completed in 1936, costing $2.5 million.

As you wind your way upward through the spruce and fir forest, watch for wildlife on the road. Listen to the rustle of quaking aspen that form shimmering groves along the roadside. In autumn their brilliant gold is the perfect color scheme against a dark green forest and blue sky backdrop. There are a few ranches in the meadows below the road with open livestock range, so be on the lookout for cattle wandering across your path.

The geology of the Beartooth Plateau is mostly Precambrian metamorphic rock, a mere 3.2 billion years old. The rock here is by far the oldest in Montana and among some of the oldest in the world. Hugging the steep crests of Mount Wilse and Iceburg Peak is another ancient part of the terrain, Grasshopper Glacier. Millions of frozen grasshoppers are visible beneath the ice of this snowfield. Only the hardiest hikers should attempt the Grasshopper Glacier trail, which heads up from Goose Lake. Check Gallatin or Custer national forest maps for details.

Wyoming Highway 296, the Chief Joseph Scenic Byway, takes off from US 212 about 14 miles east of Cooke City. You can take this route, heading southeast through an area known as Sunlight Basin, to Cody, Wyoming. Near the WY 296 turnoff, the foreground opens up to sagebrush hills. The bottomlands here are grassy with forested pockets to break up the continuity. A rift of rock to the south of the road juts out from the block of mountain like a bulging vein.

Several scenic turnouts give you the chance to get out and look at the view behind you. The spirelike point of 11,313-foot Index Peak and its neighbor, Pilot Peak, piercing 11,708 feet into the sky, are well-worth the stop. Pilot-Index Overlook, marked with signs, offers almost a 180-degree view of the plateau along its southern border. Just up the road is Clay Butte Lookout, where you can expand the view to 360 degrees. Turn off the main road to the north. The Clay Butte road is gated in autumn, but you can still walk up to the lookout if you need to stretch your legs. It is about 2 miles, if you follow the road. Shortly after the turnoff to Clay Butte the Beartooth Highway narrows, winding past vertical walls to the north and vertical cliffs to the south. Use caution as you drive through this area.

You will soon reach Beartooth Lake, which has a forested campground and a hiking trail leading northward to hundreds of other small lakes on the plateau. Farther up the road is Island Lake, also with a campground and access to the same trail system through the glacial-scoured plateau. The Top of the World store is on the main highway between the two lakes. Here you can buy food, fuel, and camping supplies and get tourist information. A small network of gravel roads on the south side of the highway across from Island Lake will take you to other tiny lakes.

If you choose to walk around up here, tread lightly on the fragile plants. Most alpine plants take decades to develop, growing by the inch and dying underfoot. As you wander, you may wonder why the terrain at the top of the plateau is relatively flat. Only the top several inches of soil here remain unfrozen during summer months. The subsoil is frozen year-round, so water trying to pass through it either freezes or stays on the surface. The surface water flows down even the most trifling of slopes, since it has nowhere else to go. The water brings topsoil with it, filling up basins where it pools and, over years, creating a more level terrain.

East of Long Lake, near the top of Beartooth Pass, look for signs marking the Beartooth Loop Trail. From here you can take the trail a few miles into Losekamp Lake, where you can pick up the Beartooth Loop National Recreation Trail. This loop trail skirts Tibbs Butte through the alpine plateau; the trail is about 10 miles long, so plan on at least a half day if you are a moderately experienced hiker. You can access another trailhead for this loop near Gardiner Lake, farther up the road on the other side of the pass.

After passing Long Lake, the road snakes its way to the top of the pass in loose hairpin loops. Use caution here, since your natural tendency might be to have your eyes wander to the beautiful alpine world around you. The top of the pass comes at 10,947 feet above sea level, and the view, because it is well above tree line, is unobstructed. From here you get a feel for the wide, wild expanse in all directions. Get out and take a stroll through the boulder-strewn meadows. Again, tread lightly. If you happen to be driving this highway on "Snow Bar Day" (one day a year) you will be treated to free drinks at the summit, courtesy of the Red Lodge Chamber of Commerce.

As you descend toward Montana again, the road is steep and twisty in places. Pull out at Twin Lakes Overlook, just south of the Montana border. The view here is worth the short walk, and if you have not already climbed out of your vehicle, it is one of your last opportunities to do so before heading down into Rock Creek. Just north of the Montana state line, one last short trail to the east leads to a small lake that lies on the state borders.

The downside highway has been newly resurfaced, so the road is in good shape. Watch for another big turnout (with restrooms) where you can take a short jaunt down a gravel path to an overlook of the Rock Creek valley, into which the Beartooth Highway descends. The road makes several hairpin curves from this point on as you near Red Lodge.

There are a few hiking trails, Forest Service roads, and several campgrounds along the glacier-gouged Rock Creek drainage. The West Fork of Rock Creek Road, just south of Red Lodge, will take you to Red Lodge Mountain Ski Area and Silver Run Cross-Country Ski Area. You will also find a few campgrounds and hiking trails to cold, tiny lakes. For a detailed description of the town of Red Lodge, refer to Scenic Drive 14, which begins there.

14 RED LODGE AND ROSEBUD COUNTRY

Montana Highway 78

General description: This 48-mile drive takes you from the sharp peaks of the Beartooth Mountains into coulees and grassy foothills that, in summer, smell of sweet, new-mown hay. Side trips to East Rosebud Lake or Mystic Lake will give you a taste for the razorlike mountains here.
Special attractions: Red Lodge Mountain Ski Area, Mountain Man Rendezvous, Festival of Nations, Red Lodge Music Festival, Cooney Reservoir State Park; art shows, museums, alpine lakes; camping, hiking, skiing, backpacking, fishing, mountain biking.
Location: South-central Montana. The drive begins in Red Lodge and ends in Columbus, on Interstate 90.
Drive route number: Montana Highway 78.
Travel season: Year-round. Snow and ice conditions make winter travel hazardous.
Camping: There are several campgrounds south of Red Lodge along Rock Creek. You will also find campgrounds on the way to Mystic and East Rosebud Lakes, and south of Columbus along the Stillwater River.
Services: Red Lodge, Absarokee, and Columbus offer full services. Limited services are available in Fishtail and Dean.
For more information: Custer National Forest, Beartooth Ranger District; Red Lodge Chamber of Commerce; Red Lodge Mountain Ski Area; Columbus Chamber of Commerce (see Appendix).

The drive:

> Walter and Johnny. Good-bye. Wives and daughters. We died an easy death. Love from us both. Be good.
>
> — A note left by two victims of the Smith Mine disaster in 1943

Red Lodge is the quintessential mountain town, with its quaint storefronts, cool climate, and proximity to great hiking, fishing, and skiing. Its immigrant heritage lends it a tiny bit of European flavor, too. The town sits in a small hollow at 4,650 feet above sea level. There are various stories about how Red Lodge got its name. One claims it was because Crow Indians set up camp here frequently and used the abundant local red clay to color their tepees. Another, somewhat derogatory, claim is that the name had more to do with "red men" lodging here than the color of their tepees. A third story points to a red rock outcrop west of town that, when viewed from several miles away, resembles an Indian lodge.

14 RED LODGE AND ROSEBUD COUNTRY

Montana Highway 78

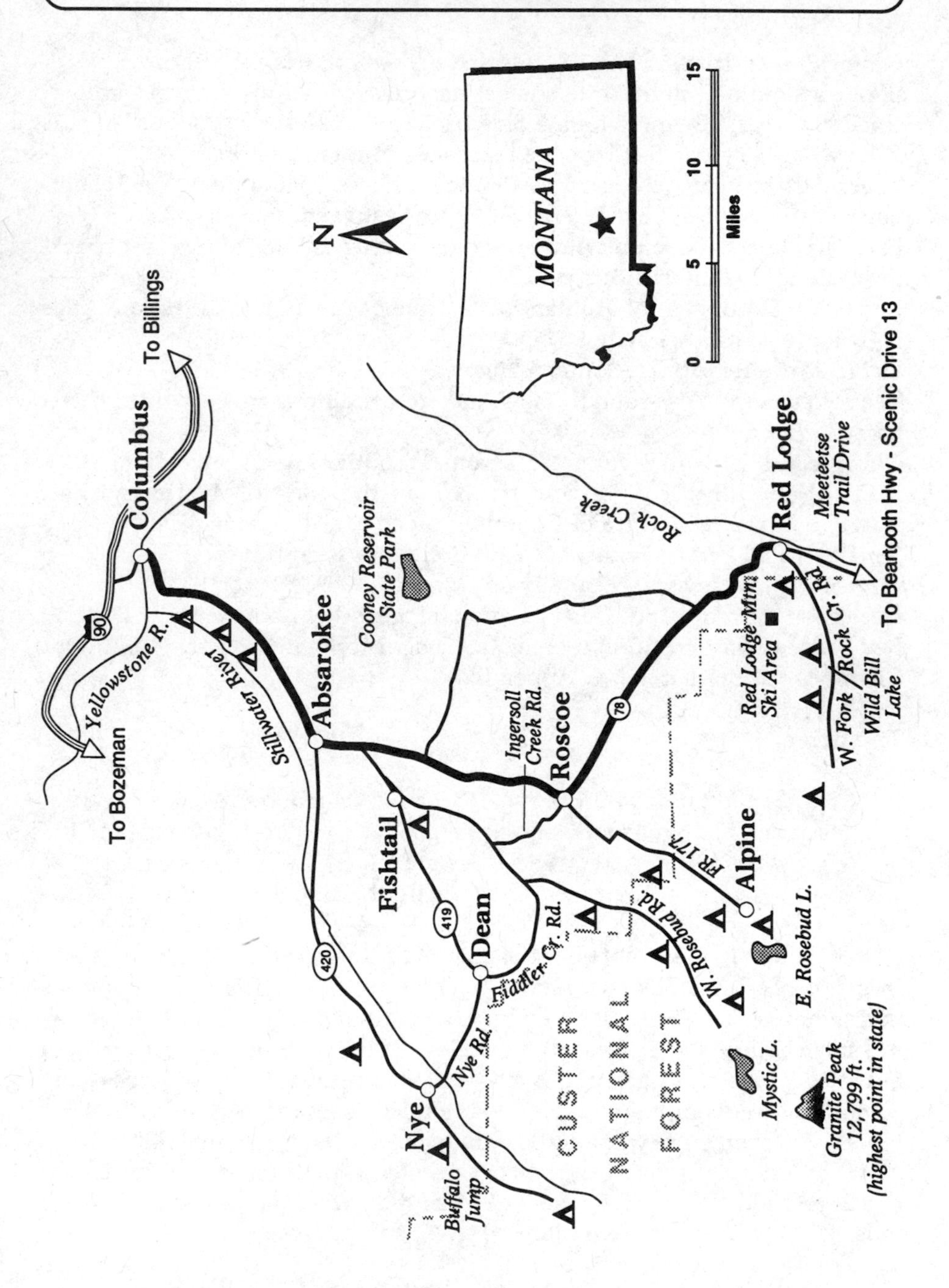

Whatever the origin of the name, coal is what brought European immigrants to the town. By 1911, Red Lodge had a mining town population of five thousand. A tragic mine disaster in 1943 trapped and killed seventy-four miners, however, closing the coal mine permanently. That incident, coupled with the opening of giant coal mines near Colstrip, Montana, farther east, eventually drew many settlers away from Red Lodge. The town's population now hovers around two thousand.

Between Memorial Day and Labor Day, the Carbon County Museum in Red Lodge is open. It houses small displays about mining history and rodeo. For years, the Greenoughs, a local family, have taken top awards at rodeos across the country; the display features this family of riders and ropers. The museum also owns John Johnston's cabin. Johnston is better known as "Liver-eatin' Johnson," a late nineteenth-century mountain man said to have sought vengeance on the men who killed his Native American wife. Once, after killing a man, he supposedly ate his victim's liver. Portrayed by the actor Robert Redford in the film *Jeremiah Johnson*, Johnston was the first constable of Red Lodge.

Children might enjoy the petting zoo at the Beartooth Nature Center in Coal Miners' Memorial Park. Follow the signs on US 212 north of town toward Billings to find it. Visitors to Red Lodge during July will enjoy the Mountain Man Rendezvous, a week-long festival of mountain men, Native Americans, traders, bison hunters, whiskey runners, bullwhackers, horse traders, and other assorted characters. Participants, most dressed in period costume, sell hand-crafted jewelry, beadwork, knives, buckskin-and-fur costumes, and artwork. If you dress in turn-of-the-century costume, you get in free. Games, music, and dance are also part of the rendezvous.

The Festival of Nations, a nine-day event held each August, celebrates the cultures and traditions of the many Europeans who immigrated to Red Lodge. Each day features food, exhibits, a parade, entertainment, crafts, and dancing of some of the countries represented, with the ninth day reserved for one massive European hoopla. If you happen to miss any of these summer events, Red Lodge has a winter carnival in March to help chase away cabin fever and usher in the coming spring.

Wildlife watchers will also enjoy Red Lodge, since the Meeteetse Wildlife Trail is found southeast of town. On this 19-mile nature drive through arid sagebrush plains, river bottoms, and rolling foothills you may spot moose, deer, pronghorns, beavers, hawks, golden eagles, coyotes, and foxes. If you are really lucky, you may see a badger. You can get out and walk just about anywhere or go for a spin on your mountain bike. For more information ask at the nearby ranger station.

You will find a barrier-free day-use area with trails and fishing docks at Wild Bill Lake southwest of Red Lodge. Follow the paved Forest Road 71 (West Fork Rock Creek Road) toward Red Lodge Mountain Ski Area, bypassing the road to the ski hill. Follow signs to Wild Bill Lake, about 3.5 miles farther. There's also good mountain biking up the West Fork Rd. Ask at Wacky's Spoke and Hackle about places to mountain bike.

The Beartooth Mountains fringe the upland range northwest of Red Lodge.

When you have exhausted yourself in Red Lodge, follow signs for MT 78, leading northwest out of town. The sinuous road billows over hilly grain fields and rangeland. The Beartooth Mountains, to the southwest, seem to rise up out of the plateau as if they had been carelessly set down and forgotten in the middle of flat farmland. A network of braided willows along the route laces the thousands of stream channels trickling their way out of the mountains.

When you get to the wide spot in the road called Roscoe, named for the favorite horse of the town's first postmaster, you can take a bumpy but spectacular side trip to East Rosebud Lake. It is easy to miss the turnoff from Roscoe to the west, so watch carefully for the signs. Go through the one-street town, then take the main gravel road south. After about 4 miles you will come to a fishhook turn. Just after the hook, take a right and follow the gravel road through ranchland dotted with summer homes. The road winds and is bumpy and rough for several miles, so take it slowly. After 5 or 6 miles from the second turnoff, the road changes to pavement, for 6 miles, then turns back to gravel for the last leg into East Rosebud Lake. A four-wheel-drive is not necessary, but if your car sits low to the ground be mindful of rocks in the road.

The road takes you deeper into the Beartooth Mountains the closer you get to the lake. The surrounding spruce and fir forest makes excellent cover for all kinds of wildlife. Watch for mule deer. There are a couple of campgrounds along the paved stretch of road if you decide to spend more time here. At Jimmy Joe Campground, get out and look for butterflies. An interpretive sign details the species you might find fluttering about in the wildflowers. Some species seen here include angle wing, blue butterflies, lesser fritillaries, and Weidemeyer's admiral.

East Rosebud sits in a deep chasm and has a small community of summer cabins on a bit of private lakeshore. There is a public boat launch and campground. Signs mark the few hiking trails, one of which takes you up and over the peaks to Mystic Lake, to the west. You can also drive to Mystic Lake from the West Rosebud Road; check a Custer National Forest map for directions. From Mystic Lake, only the most experienced mountain hikers attempt the 12,799-foot summit of Granite Peak, Montana's highest mountain. Moderately skilled hikers can take Trail 15 from East Rosebud Lake to Elk Lake. Along the 3-mile trail, you will see a waterfall and wonderful views of both lakes.

Once you've seen East Rosebud, you can either go back to Roscoe and take MT 78 again north to Absarokee (pronounced the same as the mountain range, ab-SOR-kee, but spelled differently), or take a cutoff gravel road just before you reach Roscoe again on the way out. This is Ingersoll Creek Road, and it heads northwest through private ranchland. Take this until it dead-ends at West Rosebud Road, then turn left. After about 4 miles the road turns into Fiddler Creek Road and dead-ends at Nye Road.

At Nye Rd. you can turn left, going to the community of Dean and on to Buffalo Jump Campground near the town of Nye. This is a primitive campground administered by the State of Montana. There is no water, but there are toilets, picnic tables, fire rings, and fishing access to the Stillwater

East Rosebud Creek flows from the Beartooth Mountains.

River. You can follow Nye Rd. (County Road 419) east through Fishtail and back to MT 78, just south of Absarokee.

Between Roscoe and Columbus, MT 78 passes through private ranchland bisected by coulees. There are a few fishing access points along the Stillwater River. Cooney Reservoir State Park, to the east, is accessible from two major roads. One takes off east about 9 miles south of Absarokee; the other heads south from near the Fireman's Point fishing access, 4 miles south of Columbus. Both are marked.

The town of Columbus was named for that illustrious explorer rumored to have discovered America. Residents changed its name about as often they would a pair of socks—from Eagle's Nest to Sheep Dip (supposedly a type of whiskey sold there) to Stillwater before finally settling on Columbus. Rocks from a quarry near here were used to build the state capitol in Helena. Columbus is now a railroad shipping depot for harvest from ranches in the surrounding region.

From Columbus, you can drive east on I-90 to Scenic Drive 15, which begins 35 miles south of Billings, or west to Scenic Drives 11 and 12 near Big Timber and Livingston.

15 CROW COUNTRY

Crow Reservation Road, BIA Roads 91, 193, and 73

General description: This little-traveled route takes you through 70 miles of the Crow Reservation. The landscape seems to roll on forever here, punctuated by coulees, pine-covered knobs, and multicolored rock formations. To the south lies Bighorn Canyon and Yellowtail Reservoir.
Special attractions: Chief Plenty Coups State Park, Bighorn Canyon National Recreation Area, Pryor Mountains National Wild Horse Range, Crow Fair; boating, fishing, mountain biking, camping, hiking, backpacking.
Location: Southeastern Montana, on the Crow Reservation. The drive begins in Pryor, 35 miles south of Billings. It heads east to Interstate 90 and ends at Lodge Grass, 35 miles south of Hardin.
Drive route number: Crow Reservation Road, Bureau of Indian Affairs (BIA) Road 91, BIA 193, BIA 73.
Travel season: Year-round. Snow and ice conditions make winter travel hazardous. During severe conditions the road is not maintained.
Camping: There are campgrounds at Bighorn Canyon, and north along the Bighorn River. Just south of the reservation boundary are a few campgrounds in Custer National Forest.
Services: Full services at Fort Smith and Hardin. Limited services it Pryor and at Ok-A-Beh boat ramp.
For more information: Bighorn Canyon National Recreation Area; Custer

15

CROW COUNTRY

Crow Reservation Road, BIA Roads 91, 193, and 73

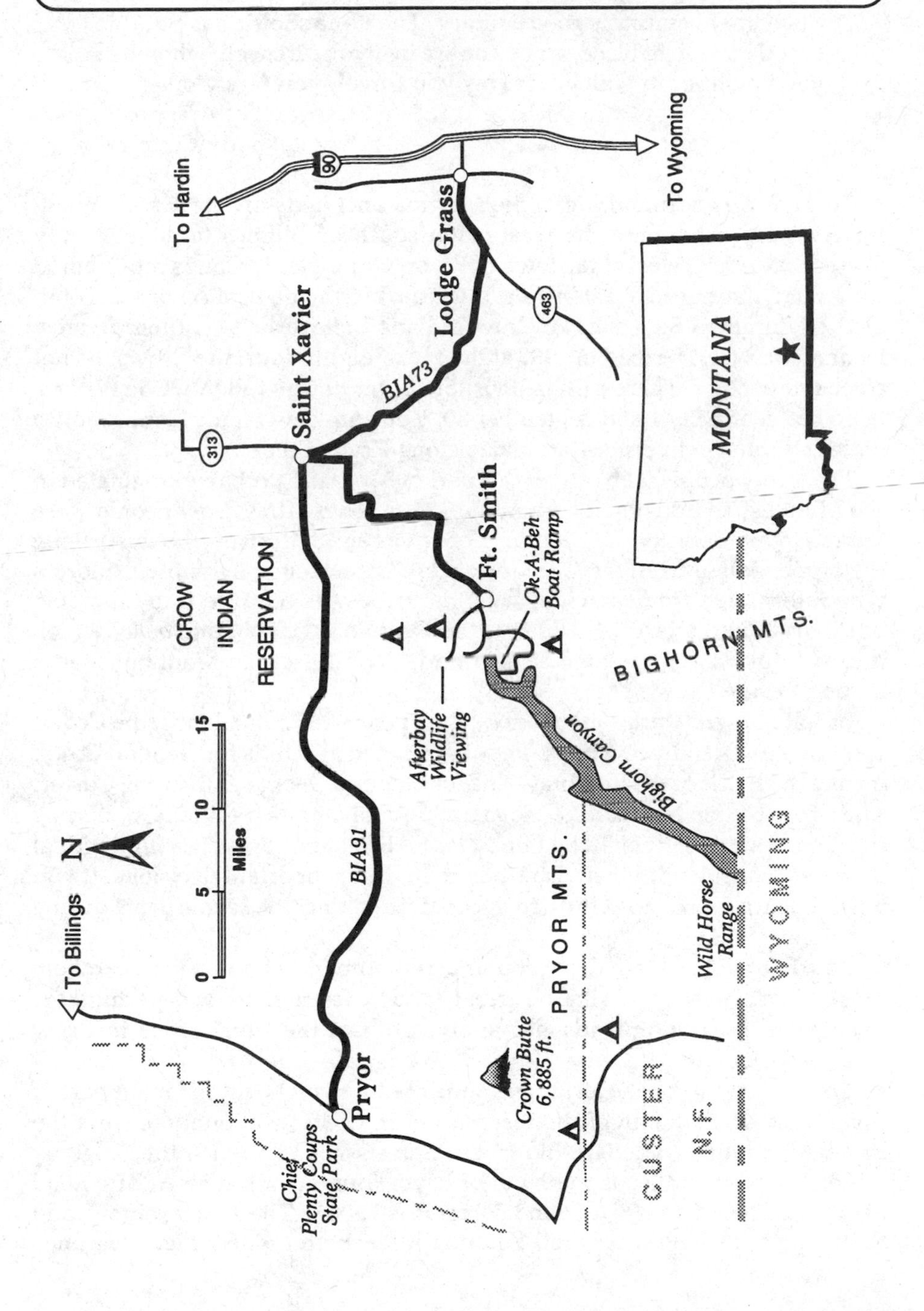

National Forest, Beartooth Ranger District; Fort Smith Visitor Center; Chief Plenty Coups State Park; Crow Reservation (see Appendix).

The drive:

> The Crow country is good country. The Great Spirit has put it in exactly the right place; while you are in it you fare well; whenever you go out of it, whichever way you travel, you fare worse.
>
> - Crow chief Arapooish,
> "My Country"

To take this scenic drive, which begins and ends on the Crow Indian Reservation, drive onto the reservation south of Billings to Chief Plenty Coups State Park, west of the town of Pryor. Chief Plenty Coups represented the Indian nations in Washington, D.C., during the dedication of the Tomb of the Unknown Soldier. The Crow Indians believe he was their greatest leader, and when he died in 1933 at the age of eighty-four, the Crows did not elect a new chief. There's a small visitor center at Chief Plenty Coups park, open between May 1 and September 30. You can view Plenty Coups' house and read interpretive signs, or picnic along Pryor Creek.

The Crow people who settled this part of Montana probably originated in the Midwest and migrated here in the 1300s. These first Crow people were related to members of the Hidatsa tribe, river agriculturists who lived along the Upper Missouri River. The Crow were named such by white explorers who interpreted from sign language; the tribe was referred to by flapping one's arms like a bird. In Hidatsa, the Crow are called *Apsalooke*, which means "children of the large-beaked bird." The Absaroka Mountains were named for the Crow people.

In spite of westward settlement by Europeans on Indian lands, the Crows were mostly friendly to whites. They even acted as scouts for General Crook during the Battle of the Rosebud—and for General George Armstrong Custer. The Crow Nation has managed to maintain many of its traditions, including the clan system, in which the family is the basic unit of society. Individual members consult with their clans before making important decisions. If you wish to learn more about the Crow, consider taking this scenic drive during Crow Fair, in August.

As you travel through Crow country, remember that non-tribal members must have a permit to hike on tribal lands. Restrictions and permits for fishing on reservation lands also apply. Contact the tribal office in Crow Agency for details.

You may wish to take a side trip south before you begin the main part of this scenic drive. South of the reservation in Custer National Forest is the Pryor Mountains National Wild Horse Range. You can reach the range by taking the road that leads south out of Pryor (Bureau of Indian Affairs Road 5) to Sage Creek Road (BIA 11 and Forest Road 3085). The area is remote, and the road impassable when wet. You might feel better with a high-clearance vehicle as well. You are not guaranteed a view of the wild horses, but you have about a fifty-fifty chance.

There are many other opportunities to see wildlife in this area. Near Big Ice Cave you can see bats roosting in the limestone cliffs. Towhees, rock wrens, kinglets, hummingbirds, kestrels, and golden eagles haunt the lonely hills. There are many opportunities for mountain biking. If you go this route, bring food, water, and a Custer National Forest map—and watch the weather.

To begin the main scenic drive route, take BIA 91 due east of Pryor and head toward Saint Xavier, a mission town founded by a Jesuit priest who sought to convert the Crows to Christianity. Directly to the south are the Pryor Mountains, named for a member of the Lewis and Clark Expedition. Castle Rocks, where medicine men once fasted, are also to the south, and are now penetrated by a railroad tunnel.

The road is in good shape and dips in and out of shallow coulees. You will drive through open range, so watch for cattle on the road. Even though the cattle can pose a threat if they wander by the road, it is nice not to see miles and miles of fencing sectioning off the prairie. To the north, the landscape is open and mostly flat with low buttes. Western meadowlarks flit about or pose on mile posts. The unobstructed views of expansive plains here make you feel alone in the world, or at least in this corner of it.

Where it is safe to pull over, stop and look at the interesting geology along the road as it dips into one of the many coulees flowing like veins through the earth. This area is considered "badlands," although whoever came up with

The Bighorn River winds through the Crow Indian Reservation below Yellowtail Dam at Bighorn Canyon.

Yellowtail Dam at Bighorn Canyon.

the name obviously never appreciated the rich beauty of exposed black, red, and yellow gashes in crumbly grassland soil. And although it may seem like no animal with a brain would choose to live in this open and harsh habitat, many of the coulees harbor mule deer, antelope, snakes, lizards, and birds.

At Saint Xavier turn south and follow signs to Bighorn Canyon, about 20 miles. You will pass through fields of sugar beets, harvested in early October. Bighorn Canyon National Recreation Area is a fine place for boating, fishing, and camping. There is a visitor center at Yellowtail Dam and a smaller visitor center in Fort Smith, just below the dam, with a short nature trail.

Fort Smith was Montana's second U.S. military post, established in 1866 to protect settlers and other immigrants traveling the Bozeman Trail. Blackfeet, Sioux, and Cheyenne Indians, attempting to keep possession of their favored hunting grounds, often attacked settlers near here. The Indians won the battle for this country (if not the war against settlement), and the fort was abandoned two years later when a treaty was signed ceding the land to the Indians. The Bozeman Trail became too dangerous for settlers and was little used after the closing of Fort Smith.

During winter you can view thousands of waterfowl in the afterbay below Yellowtail Dam. In addition to Canada geese are mallards, teals, goldeneyes, and ringnecked ducks, as well as mergansers, grebes, and cormorants. Bald eagles find the smorgasbord of birds here delectable. During migration you can see tundra swans, white pelicans, common loons, and sandhill cranes.

The 520-foot Yellowtail Dam is the highest in the Missouri River system. The Bighorn River carved 50-mile-long Bighorn Canyon, now mostly filled by water. The Bighorn Mountains, to the south, stretch for 150 miles from southern Montana into Wyoming. The mountains are largely composed of sedimentary rock, having originated in a marine environment between 600 million and 65 million years ago. The river slowly sliced through these limestone deposits to create the high bluffs of Bighorn Canyon. Some of the Bighorn Mountain peaks in Wyoming reach 13,000 feet elevation.

The only way to really see the red canyon cliffs of 71-mile-long Bighorn Lake is by boat. Rentals are available at the lake. You can see a portion of the bluffs from an overlook area near Ok-A-Beh boat ramp, south of Yellowtail Dam. The 10-mile drive to Ok-A-Beh (complete with marina and store) is a wonderful little scenic drive in itself. At one point you can look across the rangeland on top to the west and glimpse some of the cliffs that enclose Bighorn Lake.

To continue the main scenic drive, go north from the lake back toward Saint Xavier, then continue east to Lodge Grass. You must watch carefully for the turn to Lodge Grass, since the road is not marked. If you are heading north from Bighorn Canyon, you should turn east at mile marker 25 on BIA 73, just south of Saint Xavier. Again this is open range and cattle will wander into the road, so be alert.

This part of the drive passes through more coulees and grass range weaving along Rotten Grass Creek. The road is narrow with no shoulder, but the surface is in good shape. Notice the American kestrels perched on fence posts and telephone lines. These are the smallest and most common of our falcons, which hover low above the ground before dive-bombing their prey.

After 19 miles on this road you will come to a stop sign. Turn left to go to Lodge Grass. This tiny village was once a summer gathering place for the Crow. It was actually called "greasy grass" because the nutrient-rich grasses that grew here made animals fat. The Crow words for "grease" and "lodge" are very similar, thus greasy grass was mis-translated. You will not find much entertainment in Lodge Grass, but Scenic Drive 16, on the Northern Cheyenne Reservation, is not far to the east. Begin that drive at the Little Bighorn Battlefield, 20 miles north.

16 TONGUE RIVER LOOP

U.S. Highway 212, County Road 314

General description: The 147-mile Tongue River loop, on mostly gravel roads, crosses badlands country with rock spires, arid plateaus, river bottoms, and rangeland. The northern part of the loop winds around knobby hills on the Northern Cheyenne and Crow reservations.
Special attractions: Little Bighorn Battlefield, Rosebud Battlefield, Tongue River Reservoir, Saint Labre Mission; fishing, boating, hiking, mountain biking, camping, wildlife viewing.
Location: Southeastern Montana. The drive begins at the Little Bighorn

16 TONGUE RIVER LOOP
U.S. Highway 212, County Road 314

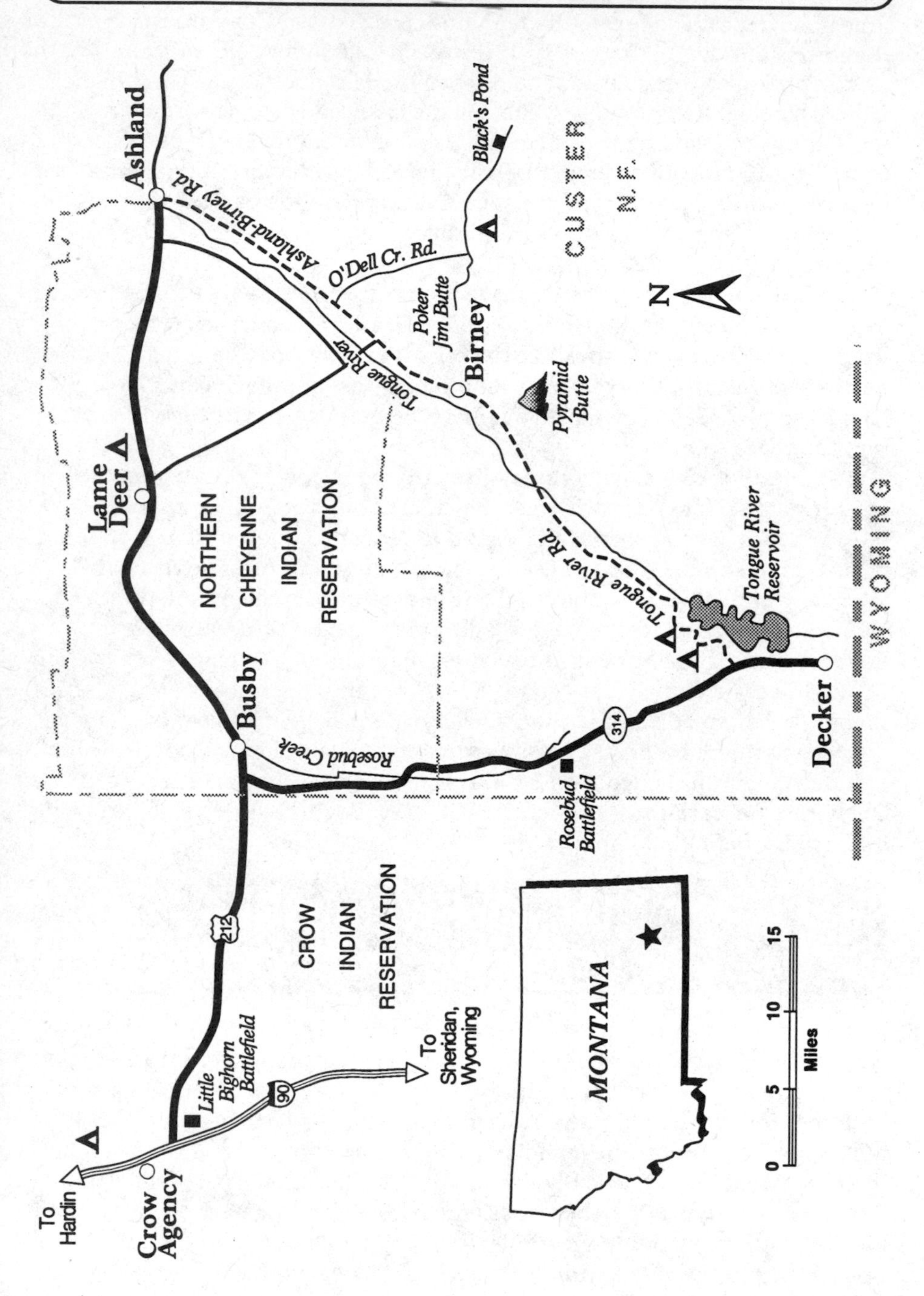

Battlefield, just off Interstate 90, 15 miles south of Hardin. It continues east on U.S. Highway 212 to Busby, then heads south to Tongue River Reservoir near the Wyoming border before turning north again to US 212 and back to I-90.
Drive route numbers: US 212, Rosebud Creek Road, Tongue River Road, Ashland–Birney Road.
Travel season: Year-round. During severe winter weather conditions, portions of the gravel road may be closed.
Camping: Tongue River Reservoir has several campgrounds with many individual sites. You can camp in undeveloped sites in Custer National Forest and on a developed site in Lame Deer. There are private campgrounds, none in good shape, near the Little Bighorn Battlefield. You can also camp in Hardin.
Services: Full services at Crow Agency, Lame Deer, Hardin, and Ashland. Limited services at Tongue River Reservoir. There is a small store in Decker, but no gasoline.
For more information: Little Bighorn National Battlefield; Custer National Forest, Ashland Ranger District; Northern Cheyenne Chamber of Commerce; Hardin Chamber of Commerce (see Appendix).

The drive:

> When I got near my lodge, I looked up the Little Horn towards Sitting Bull's camp. I saw a great dust rising. It looked like a whirlwind. Soon [a] Sioux horseman came rushing into camp shouting: "Soldiers come! Plenty white soldiers." I ran into my lodge, and said to my brother-in-law, "Get your horses; the white man is coming. Everybody run for horses."
>
> — Northern Cheyenne Chief Two Moon,
> from his account of the Battle of the
> Little Bighorn, 1898

This drive begins at Crow Agency, headquarters for the Crow Indian tribe and reservation. The third weekend in August, Crow Agency becomes one giant tepee town during the annual Crow Fair and Powwow. But Crow Agency is perhaps more well known as the site of the Battle of the Little Bighorn, which took place on June 25, 1876. The battlefield is a must-see; it is not over-developed, and the car tour along the ridge is a short and wonderful scenic drive in itself. As you drive it, you get a feel for this sorrowful place where many U.S. and Native American soldiers died.

A condensed version of the battle goes something like this: Following the Civil War, the U.S. Army was charged with forcing Indians onto reservations in order to open up lands for white settlement. The Cheyenne and Sioux nations were warned that if they did not comply by a certain date, they would be rounded up like stubborn cattle and forced onto their allotted pieces of ground. The allied tribes resisted, troops were dispatched. But due to various

The hill where Custer's men fell at Little Bighorn Battlefield.

twists of fate, the Sioux and Cheyenne forces managed to defeat General George Armstrong Custer and his accompanying cavalry. The bloody incident on the Little Bighorn River was only a temporary victory for the tribes. The battle marked the beginning of the end of traditional Indian lifestyles in this country.

In all about 270 U.S. soldiers were killed in the battle compared to about 100 Indian warriors. Archeological digs on the battlefield have yielded hundreds of artifacts, some of which are on display in the visitor center. A 1983 grass fire removed much of the vegetation on the battlefield, making investigations of the site easier. Many of the soldiers were buried where they fell. Although a stone marks the place where Custer likely fell, his remains were interred at West Point one year after the battle. Among the people buried in the Custer National Cemetery at the battlefield is a woman with the dubious honor of having been the first woman to be shot by her husband in Montana. Here lies also an army corporal whose wife, a laundress at the Yellowstone Depot, was discovered, upon her death, to be a man.

Incidentally, the visitor center, as well as the Stone Lodge by the cemetery, are supposedly haunted. Employees of the national monument over the years have reported strange noises, apparitions, and unexplained lights going on and off, as well as objects being mysteriously moved. Is it any wonder the spirits are restless?

The battle is re-enacted (in part) every year with a cast of 300 that includes descendants of both whites and Indians who participated in the original battle. The hour-long affair ends in a skirmish near the battle site. Tickets and more information are available from the Hardin Chamber of Commerce.

To continue on this scenic drive, follow US 212 east from the battlefield site. The road rolls over grass-covered coulees for 23 miles before reaching the Tongue River Road turnoff, just west of Busby. The landscape probably looks much the same today as it did when Native Americans hunted bison on these plains. This country is a land of extremes. The heat of summer can sear right through you, and winter blasts of snow make you think you were in the Arctic. Watch for signs for County Road 314 directing you south to Decker, Montana, and Sheridan, Wyoming. The right-hand turnoff is just before the town of Busby, which you can see on the return trip.

The road is a single lane with little or no shoulder. It is paved until the turnoff to Tongue River Reservoir. It traverses the bottomlands along Rosebud Creek, rarely rising to the plateaus above, and crosses scattered forest and rangeland. The stream bottoms are brilliant gold and red in autumn, especially when the cottonwoods and dogwoods begin to turn. To the west are the low Wolf Mountains, ribbed with shallow coulees. The road is in fair shape, but watch for potholes. Also watch for cattle and antelope crossing.

About 23 miles south of the turnoff, look for signs to Rosebud Battlefield State Park. Thus far the park's 5,000 acres have only a few interpretive signs, but there are plans to build a picnic area, a trail through the grass hills, and maybe a small visitor center here. The Rosebud Battle was another significant event in U.S. Army-Indian relations. The battle here, one of the largest Indian-White battles waged in the West, occurred just days before Custer's "last stand" at the Little Bighorn; had the Rosebud battle never happened, Custer's forces may not have been killed.

In 1876 General George Crook led more than one thousand men north from Wyoming to aid Colonel John Gibbon and General Alfred Terry in bringing the Sioux and Cheyenne "under control." Crook intended to meet up with the others to converge on the Indians, but never made it. On June 17, 1876, fifteen hundred Sioux and Cheyenne warriors rode on horseback down the hill to ambush Crook and his company, which included Shoshoni and Crow scouts. The battle lasted most of the day. Chief Crazy Horse was among the warriors here. When the Sioux and Cheyenne finally withdrew, they left only nine of Crook's men dead; Indian loss counts were unknown. The U.S. Army appeared to have won the battle; however, the conflict turned Crook and his men away, so Custer (who split from Terry's group) never received his much-needed help a few weeks later.

From the Rosebud battlefield park, go back to CR 314 and follow signs south to Decker. The turnoff to Tongue River Reservoir State Park is 12 miles south, and Decker is a few miles south of that on the Montana–Wyoming border. This area is coal country, and you will see some processing plants near Decker and Tongue River Reservoir. If you go to Decker, you will also see signs of strip-mining. The Decker mine is one of the largest producers of bituminous coal in the state. This type of coal is high grade with low sulphur content, which means it burns cleaner and hotter than lower grade stuff. The coal seams here are from 12 to nearly 40 feet thick, and they are estimated

Badlands of the Tongue River.

to contain about 2 billion tons. Other than coal, Decker has a post office and store, with a home or two and small schoolhouse.

Just north of Decker is the Tongue River Reservoir. This region holds more "badlands," rich in scenery. Red, brown, and yellow bluffs cut by the Tongue River and its tributaries are a wonderful contrast to Montana's mountains. The reservoir provides a playground for typical activities such as boating, fishing, and camping. You can ride mountain bikes here, too. There is a marina with gas, fishing supplies, and some food. Plenty of picnic sites and campgrounds along the shore are more than adequate to accommodate visitors.

The road around the reservoir is very curvy with some short, steep pitches as well. Rocky Mountain junipers, ponderosa pines, cottonwoods, sagebrush, and grasses blanket the shore and uplands. The road is in good shape when recently graded, but can quickly develop a washboard surface and potholes with summer traffic. As you head north past the earthen dam, you enter Tongue River Canyon, full of old-growth cottonwoods along the river bottom. Most of the land along the river is private with open cattle range, so watch for cows on the road. The Tongue River has the only small-mouthed bass population in the state able to support itself without stocking. The river is also home to the only rock bass population in Montana. Other fish that ripple and glide through the Tongue include walleye, channel catfish, shovelnose sturgeon, and northern pike.

The gravel road follows the snakelike Tongue River, becoming narrow in spots with no guardrail. Slow travel is recommended. In other places the road is wide and flat. Where ever you approach intersections in the road follow signs to Birney (when marked). At Fourmile Road, you will turn right. A couple of miles beyond that, bear left where the road splits again. A few miles beyond Deadman Gulch the road crosses the river and comes up on top of the plateau, where you get a good view of the red bluffs to the north. Pyramid Butte's pointy top is visible in front of you.

The little town of Birney is about a 0.5 mile or less long, but by now you likely have been choking on road dust, and Birney's short stretch of paved road is a nice breather. In 1877 Oglala Sioux, led by Crazy Horse, and Cheyenne Indians, led by Two Moon, were attacked by General Nelson A. Miles here. Just north of town you should bear left up the hill at the fork in the road. Here the route name changes from the Tongue River Road to the Ashland–Birney Road.

North of Birney the road rises above the river bottom and courses through expansive badlands. If you are unsure about driving out too far in this country, now is the time to choose a shorter route. About 6.5 miles north of Birney you can take a cutoff to the left at the first major "Y" in the road, crossing the river and heading north to Lame Deer. This is Bureau of Indian Affairs Road 4, which is paved. You can also take another paved road, Bureau of Indian Affairs Road 11, which follows the Tongue River's west bank. To do so, take the same left-hand turnoff as you would for BIA 4, then go right about 1 mile after crossing the river. This road meets up with US 212 about 1.5 miles west of Ashland.

For hearty souls, the main part of this scenic drive goes onward, taking the gravel road along the east bank of the Tongue River. The road is in fairly good shape, so travel is not all that slow under good conditions. Watch for golden eagles soaring in the skies or perched on telephone poles. This is no longer reservation land, so you are more free to explore some of the side roads that take off into Custer National Forest or slice through bluffs and buttes. O'Dell Creek Road, to the southeast, offers camping and wildlife viewing at Black's Pond. Look for bats in the evening, and wild turkeys. Poker Jim Butte has a picnic area and a scenic overview of the landscape.

North of O'Dell Creek, the Ashland–Birney Road passes through several dry washes reminiscent of desert. You may have been wondering what the white, frostlike patches of ground are along the road. These are saline seeps. They occur in areas where irrigated crops have replaced natural grasses. Since crops cannot always take up all the water that comes from irrigation, the excess water accumulates just below the surface, absorbing salts and minerals in the ground. As the water rises to the ground surface, it evaporates, leaving behind white, crusty salts.

When you get to a high spot north of King Creek Road, stop and look behind you. Here are more sweeping views of the badlands. Farther north, the road dips down to the Otter Creek lowlands and arrives at US 212 in downtown Ashland.

Ashland is home to Saint Labre Mission, an Indian school that has a small museum with wonderful artifacts; there are Native American crafts for sale here. You can also get a tour of the mission. The church itself is conical-shaped. The cross on top falls to near a 45-degree angle, giving the intended appearance of a tepee. To finish the Tongue River loop, head west on US 212 from Ashland toward Lame Deer. The road is hilly and winds in spots as it passes through burned forest; black snags accentuate the green ground cover.

Lame Deer was named for an Indian chief who was killed by U.S. soldiers here. After a broiling battle that took place near the present town site, soldiers under the command of General Miles looted and burned Lame Deer's camp. Today, it is a meeting place for the Northern Cheyenne people. The Tribal Museum here depicts Northern Cheyenne culture. In the cemetery are buried Dull Knife and Little Wolf, two chiefs who fought in the Battle of the Little Bighorn and led their people out of exile in Oklahoma. The town of Lame Deer's Fourth of July Powwow has dance contests, drumming, and a parade.

West of Lame Deer is the little hamlet of Busby, near the border of the Northern Cheyenne and Crow reservations. Custer supposedly made his last camp where Busby now sits. Busby was also the site of the 1993 reburial of seventeen Indians who died more than a century ago in one of the many clashes with white settlers. The remains, which had been in the possession of the Smithsonian Institution, the National Museum of Health and Medicine, and Harvard University's Peabody Museum, were those of Indians killed in nineteenth-century battles and then collected for study. They are now buried near Chief Two Moon Monument.

From Busby you can head back to I-90 and pick up Scenic Drive 15 to the south, or go back to Ashland and head northeast to Scenic Drive 17, which begins in Miles City.

17 POWDER RIVER COUNTRY

U.S. Highway 12

General description: This 77-mile drive on the eastern fringe of Montana is a pleasant alternative to Interstate 94. Miles City rides high with cowboy events and art museums. The Yellowstone River rolls by badlands, cultivated plains, and Medicine Rocks State Park's bizarre sandstone landscape.
Special attractions: Range Riders Museum, Miles City Bucking Horse Sale, South Sandstone Recreation Area, Medicine Rocks State Park; art museums, history museums; camping, fishing, boating, wildlife watching.
Location: East-central Montana. The drive begins in Miles City and heads east to Baker, near the North Dakota border.
Drive route number: U.S. Highway 12.
Travel season: Year-round.
Camping: There is some camping in and around Miles City, at Medicine Rocks State Park, and in Ekalaka. There are two campgrounds in Baker.
Services: Full services in Miles City, Baker, and Ekalaka. Limited services in Plevna.
For more information: Custer National Forest, Grand River Ranger District; Medicine Rocks State Park; Miles City Chamber of Commerce; Baker Chamber of Commerce; Ekalaka Chamber of Commerce (see Appendix).

17 POWDER RIVER COUNTRY

U.S. Highway 12

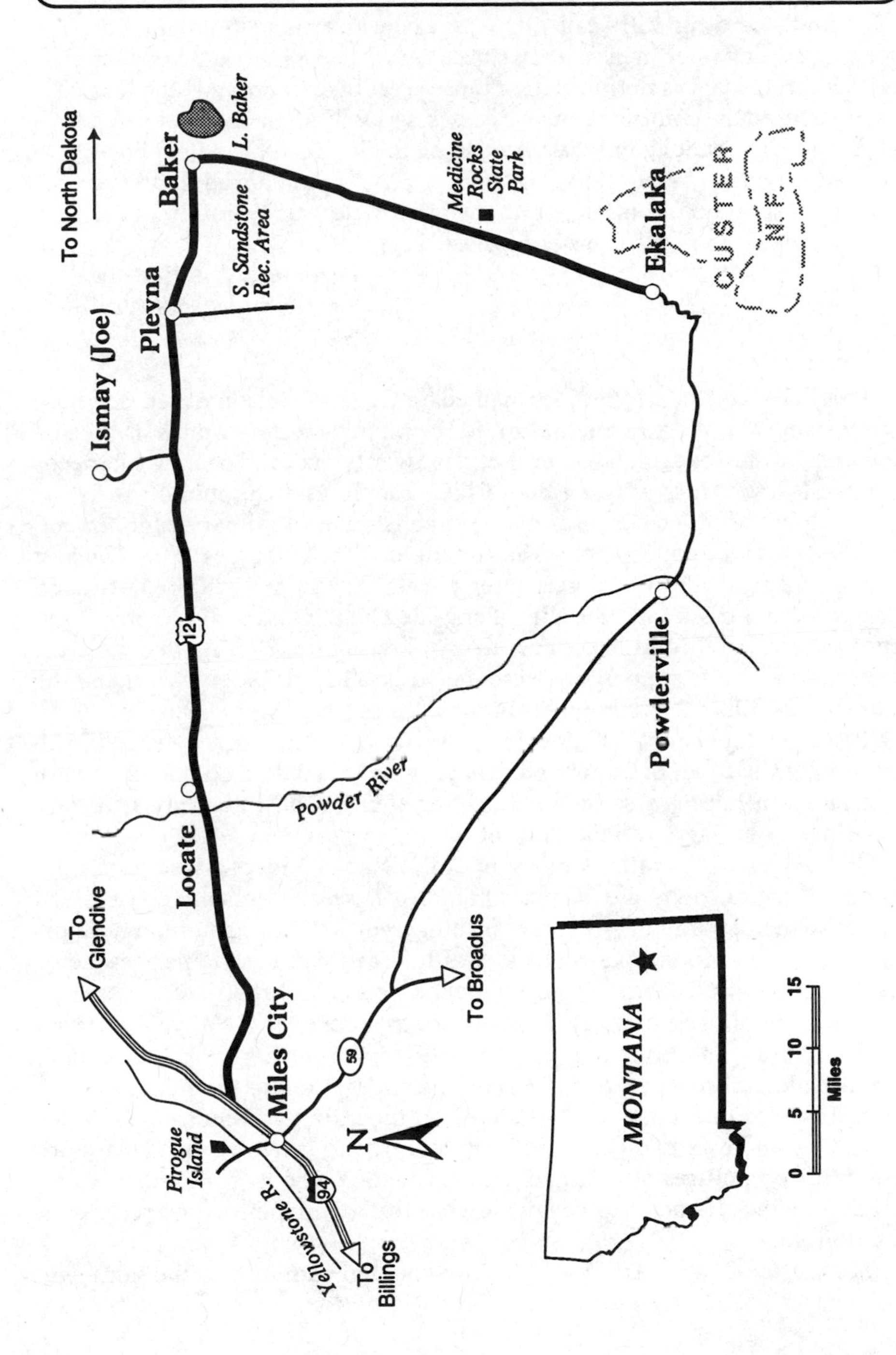

The drive:

> That year the buffalo were still so thick that Mrs. Lays had only to say: "Mr. Alderson, we're out of meat"; and he would go out and find a herd and kill a calf, all just as easily as a man would butcher a yearling steer in his own pasture. Yet when I came out, one year later, there was nothing left of those great bison herds, which had covered the continent, but carcasses. I saw them on my first drive out to the ranch, and they were lying thick all over the flat above our house, in all stages of decay. . . . I am afraid that the conservation of buffalo, or of any other wild game, simply never occurred to the westerner of those days.
>
> — Nannie T. Alderson,
> *A Bride Goes West*

This drive begins in Miles City, named for General Nelson A. Miles, whose army swept the West in attempt to rid the plains and mountains of "hostile Indians." Miles became a general at age twenty-six, and among his deeds defeated Crazy Horse, Sitting Bull, Chief Joseph, and Geronimo.

The town of Miles City was really established as a military cantonment, Fort Keogh, at the confluence of the Tongue and Yellowstone rivers. The post was established in 1877, a year after the Battle of the Little Bighorn, and named for an Irishman who died alongside Custer. Many Northern Cheyenne surrendered to Miles at Fort Keogh, joining the U.S. Army as scouts. These same scouts supposedly were the ones to locate Chief Joseph and the Nez Perce in the Bears Paw Mountains. Today the 55,000-acre fort is an agricultural experiment station for research on crops and livestock. The Miles City Chamber of Commerce will provide you with a booklet if you are interested in taking a self-guided driving tour to view the city's historic buildings or taking a walking tour of town.

While you are in Miles City, stop at the Range Riders Museum on the eastern edge of town, a collector's paradise for every imaginable western object. Among some of the fanciful things you will find there are chaps, saddles, spurs, guns, plates, hats, waffle irons, knives, tools, seashells, Charles M. Russell prints, all varieties of barbed wire, broad axes, telephone pole insulators, iron brands, dinosaur bones, rocks, and Native American artifacts. You can also tour the original officers' quarters from Fort Keogh. Small-scale dioramas with audio-taped narrations relate the history of the area. Life-size dioramas recreate nineteenth-century Main Street in Miles City. One room is dedicated to the riders of the range themselves, with hundreds of pictures of weathered and rugged cowboys, some surly, some gentle-looking characters. Each picture has the brand the cowboy rode for at the bottom.

The Custer County Art Center is off the beaten path, but on the same side of town as the Range Riders Museum. It is housed in the old Miles City waterworks plant—you have to walk through a giant culvert to enter the gallery. In 1979 the center won an award for its adaptation of the facilities, and it is now listed on the National Register of Historic Places. A gift shop sells jewelry, pottery, woven items, and art by Montana and regional artists. The Wool House Gallery is another unique gallery, with antiques, railroad artifacts, and art in many forms. The Wool House handled more than 2 million pounds of sheep fleece in the 1880s. It is located near Montana Highway 59 and Seventh Street, north of town.

Miles City is home to the world-famous Bucking Horse Sale, an auction held the weekend before Memorial Day every year. As many as 200 horses are auctioned each year; these horses appear in some of the top rodeos nationwide—including the Eastern Montana Fair and Rodeo here in Miles City in August. The bucking horse event also features quarter horse and thoroughbred racing.

The rich grasslands surrounding Miles City were once the final destination of cattle drives from as far away as Texas. At Miles City the cattle could be fattened up, then put on the rails and sent to slaughterhouses in Chicago. In eastern Montana today you may still get a chance to witness a cattle drive or overland travel by horse-drawn wagon. Originally organized to celebrate our country's bicentennial, the Southeastern Montana Wagon Train still rolls across the prairie every June. Starting points and destinations vary from year to year, so if you are in this part of the state during that month, do not be surprised to see wagons bouncing along the prairie hillocks.

North of Miles City, on the other side of the Yellowstone River, Pirogue Island is a large park area of tall cottonwoods and grassy meadows. To get to the island, go about 1 mile north of town on MT 59 and turn east onto Kinsey Road. After another 1.5 miles, turn south at the signs marking Pirogue Island. Here you can look for birds and waterfowl such as warblers, kingbirds, downy and hairy woodpeckers, flickers, white pelicans, teals, wood ducks, and great blue herons. During winter bald eagles are more common. A few miles of rutted dirt roads through the park might best be traveled on foot or mountain bike. Park your car near the undeveloped campsite at the entrance.

Once you have exhausted Miles City and environs, head east on I-94 and exit at the signs for US 12 (Exit 141). This scenic drive is a short one, and will not bear lengthy description. It can be used as an alternate route to I-94 if you are coming from or going to North Dakota. At Baker you can take Montana Highway 7 north and meet up again with I-94 in Wibaux, or vice versa.

Just east of Miles City, US 12 slices through badlands with buttes, coulees, and bluffs of crumbly black deposits laid down by an ancient inland sea. The road passes through some sharply defined, pine-covered hills, unlike the rolling pine ridges in other parts of the state. It appears as if giant piles of dirt were dumped here at random, their steeply sloping sides and knobby tops giving them an unpolished look. The road then climbs up a plateau scattered with pine and ribbed with coulees. US 12 dips every so often as the terrain begins to soften farther east. At the small town called Locate, the road crosses the Powder River, where the landscape opens up even more.

The Powder River east of Miles City makes its way to the Yellowstone River.

The Powder River country was once a favored bison hunting ground for Sioux and Cheyenne peoples, the first rulers of these Montana plains. More rough-cut hills and buttes dot the landscape for another 16 miles before the country turns into open grass prairie west of Plevna. This town was named for a city in Bulgaria where Russians and Turks engaged in a great battle. Many Bulgarian immigrants built the railroad through here. As you near Plevna, the landscape flattens, and the prairies are converted for hay and grain. You can take the Plevna Road about 7 miles south of town to the South Sandstone Recreation Area for boating and fishing. With the exception of a few buttes, the rest of the main route to Baker is all farmland.

The town of Ismay, 13 miles east of Plevna and north of US 12, was renamed Joe, Montana, in 1993 in honor of the football player of the same name. To celebrate their new name, Ismay's twenty-two residents hosted a rodeo and other activities to raise money for their volunteer fire department. The event was such a success they are considering making it an annual celebration.

In Baker, the endpoint of this drive, you can swim, boat, and fish on Lake Baker. The town also is home to the Baker Recreation Center, with an indoor pool, exercise classes, racquetball courts, and a weight room, which you can use if you are passing through during winter. The O'Fallon Historical Museum here has Native American, pioneer, and explorer relics from Montana's early days. Museum personnel can direct you to tepee rings and wagon ruts on the nearby prairie. Baker has a county fair in August and a rodeo in March.

You will see a few oil wells in the grain fields outside of Baker. Natural gas was discovered here in 1915, as oil was later. Baker was a favorite site for wagon trains because of its abundant grasses for horses and other livestock, and its many springs. Wagon trains passed through north of the present townsite, and some of these ruts are still visible. To see them, follow MT 7 to mile marker 44. An interpretive sign will direct your gaze to ruts on the southwest ridge.

About 25 miles south of Baker on MT 7, you will find Medicine Rocks State Park. You can camp and picnic among the unique sandstone formations here, where once Indian hunting parties gathered to pray to spirits. With its pockmarked sandstone buttes, the park is home to a variety of raptors. You can drive the road around the park or go for a walk near Eagle and Castle rocks. Look for golden eagles, merlins, ferruginous hawks, prairie falcons, and kestrels, as well as sharp-tailed grouse, nuthatches, bluebirds, and meadowlarks. Mule deer, pronghorns, coyotes, and red foxes also live here. The strange Swiss cheese-like monoliths and arches at Medicine Rocks may have been sand dunes millions of years ago. The holes were created by wind erosion over time. Sioux Indians called the place *inyan oka lo ka*, or "rock with hole in it."

About 10 miles south of Medicine Rocks lies the town of Ekalaka. In Sioux *Ijkalaka* means "swift one" and was the name given to a niece of Sitting Bull. The town was founded originally as a watering hole for thirsty cowboys. As legend has it, a bison hunter named Claude Carter decided he could make more money mining "liquid gold." When his load of logs bogged down in mud at the present site of Ekalaka, he allegedly exclaimed, "Hell, any place in Montana is a good place to build a saloon!" Mr. Carter, it seems, was not the only one to have subscribed to that philosophy.

When visiting Ekalaka be sure to see the Carter County Museum. It has specimens of ancient marine life unearthed in this county. Most of southeastern Montana was a sea bed more than 50 million years ago. In the ancient sea deposits lie the remains of marine fossils. The most complete skeleton at the museum is a duck-billed dinosaur called *Anatosaurus*. The building also houses remains of a *Tyrannosaurus rex*, a *Mosasaurus*, and a *triceratops*. Museum curator Marshall Lambert discovered the only *Pachycephalosaurus* remains in the world, which now reside in New York. You can see a plaster cast of the original here.

If you want to head back to Miles City a different way, you can take a back road through Powderville, to the west of Ekalaka. However, much of the road is gravel and should only be traveled in good weather. From Ekalaka, take Chalk Buttes Road south about 9 miles to Spring Creek Road. Turn west and follow the road to Powderville. From Powderville, continue on Spring Creek Rd. (County Road 203) northwest to MT 59. About 6 miles beyond Powderville, the road becomes Beebe Road. If you head north on MT 59, it will bring you back to I-94 near Miles City. From there you can head north to Scenic Drive 18, or south to Scenic Drive 16.

18 FORT PECK DAM

Montana Highway 24, U.S. Highway 2

General description: This 147-mile drive begins seemingly in the middle of nowhere at the junction of Montana Highways 200 and 24. It heads north through scrubland along the eastern fringe of Fort Peck Lake, then crosses the Milk River a half-dozen times on the way to Malta.
Special attractions: Charles M. Russell National Wildlife Refuge, Fort Peck Dam and Lake, Pioneer Museum, Sleeping Buffalo Hot Springs, Bowdoin National Wildlife Refuge; summer theater; camping, fishing, boating, swimming, wildlife viewing.
Location: Northeastern Montana. The drive begins at the junction of MT 200 and MT 24, east of Jordan, and heads north around Fort Peck Lake to Glasgow. It ends in Malta.
Drive route number: MT 24, U.S. Highway 2.
Travel season: Year-round. Blowing and drifting snow can make winter travel hazardous.
Camping: Dozens of campgrounds are situated on the shores of Fort Peck Lake. There are commercial campsites at Sleeping Buffalo Hot Springs as well.
Services: Full services at Fort Peck, Glasgow, Saco, and Malta. Limited services at marinas around Fort Peck Lake.
For more information: Charles M. Russell National Wildlife Refuge; Bowdoin National Wildlife Refuge; Fort Peck Museum at the Powerhouse; Glasgow Chamber of Commerce; Malta Chamber of Commerce (see Appendix).

The drive:

> "Does the wind blow this way here all the time?" asked the eastern visitor. "No, Mister," replied the cowboy, "it'll maybe blow this way for a week or ten days, and then it'll take a change and blow like hell for a while."
>
> — K. Ross Toole,
> *Montana, An Uncommon Land*

If you can find your way to the junction of MT 200 and MT 24, about 19 miles west of Brockway and 36 miles east of Jordan, you will enjoy this scenic drive through the Missouri River breaks and past Fort Peck Dam. The first part of the drive begins in range scattered with sagebrush and cut by shallow coulees with many dry washes. The road dips in and out of deeper coulees like a roller coaster through landscape furrowed with badlands and bluffs. Erosion is at work here, and the flat rocks perched atop giant mounds of dirt look like they are straight out of a book by Dr. Seuss.

18 FORT PECK DAM

Montana Highway 24, U.S. Highway 2

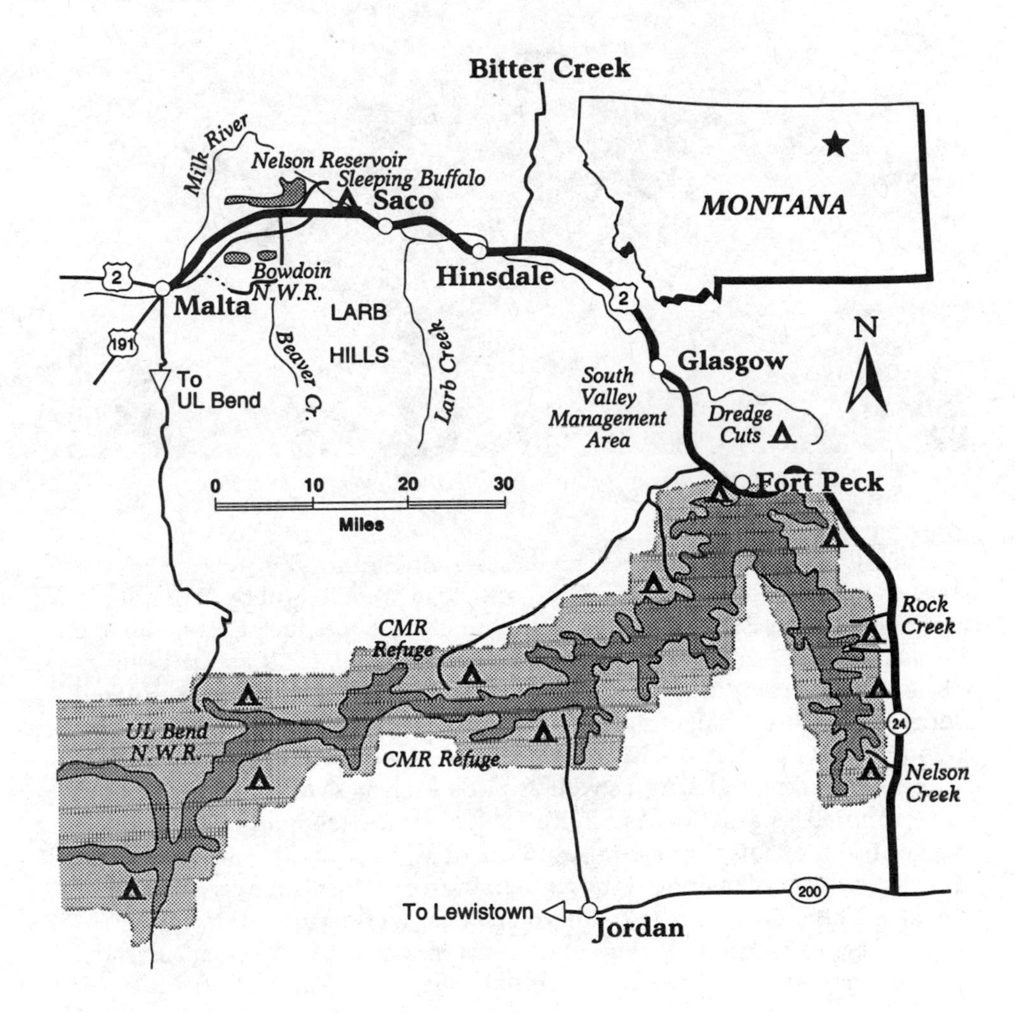

The Missouri River trickles out of Fort Peck Lake through the spillway.

If you want to experience this landscape a little more closely, turn off the main route at the Nelson Creek Road and head west to Stubby Point at the south end of Fort Peck Reservoir. You cannot miss the turnoff; it is the one with a phone booth on the corner. You will see a sign for it about 14 miles into the drive. This detour is part of the 1.2 million-acre Charles M. Russell National Wildlife Refuge that encompasses 1,600 miles of shoreline surrounding Fort Peck Lake. The refuge began as a game range in 1936 for elk, mule deer, and pronghorns, as well as birds such as sage grouse. In 1976 it was classified as a national wildlife refuge. It now supports hundreds of species of mammals, birds, and reptiles. At Nelson Creek you can camp, launch a boat, or hike around the endless buttes of the refuge on this arm of the lake. There are also side roads you can explore on mountain bike.

This region warrants some cautions as to driving conditions. Eastern Montana has what are known as "gumbo" soils, which turn slicker than you could ever imagine with the slightest amount of moisture. Most, if not all, unpaved roads in this region are impassable under wet conditions, and many roads bear signs indicating so. TAKE THESE SIGNS SERIOUSLY.

It is a wonder how pioneers ever managed to cross this part of the state, so deeply gouged with bluffs and coulees. But perhaps its desolate appearance and sometimes wicked climate will save it from development. Driving through this lonely country with nothing but sky between you and the road ahead can be amazing. Miles of barbed-wire fencing seem out of place, almost intrusive, since you begin to expect pronghorn and bison herds to roam unhindered across the plateaus here. There are no bison left here, though, and pronghorn and mule deer compete with cattle for grasses and forbs.

The main scenic drive route is in good shape for most of the way, but narrows in places. Slight shoulders and steep drop-offs with no guardrails warrant cautious driving. About 12 and 15 miles north of Nelson Creek, the south and north forks of Rock Creek cut to the eastern shore of the lake. There are boat ramps, campgrounds, picnic sites, restaurant, bar, cabins, and fuel here. The town of Fort Peck and the dam site are another 29 miles north.

The scenery near Rock Creek resembles a moonscape. This land is unapologetic. Eastern Montana does not whisper gently to your senses like a flowery prairie; it shouts, "Here I am!" You either love this labyrinthine land for its endless barrens, fickle weather patterns, and loneliness, or you hate it for the same reasons. North of Rock Creek the landscape loses this badlands look and turns to grass-covered hills and coulees.

The Fort Peck area is well developed, with beautiful picnic grounds, beaches, campgrounds, and fishing access sites. Take some time to look at the spillway (3 miles east of the dam), an engineering marvel with sixteen gates, each 25 feet high by 40 feet wide and weighing 80 tons. The entire structure is 100 feet high and 1,000 feet long. The dam itself is 250 feet high and creates a lake that is 220 feet deep and 130 miles long. Construction of the dam began in 1933 and took a decade to complete. Today it is one of the three largest earth-filled dams in the world.

Fort Peck Lake is a popular fishing destination. The four-day Montana Governor's Cup Walleye Tournament each July awards $40,000 in cash and prizes. Home to walleye, smallmouth bass, catfish, chinook salmon, and northern pike, the lake also holds funny-looking paddlefish, a species that is only found here, in the Yellowstone River, and in the Yangtze River in China. Paddlefish feed on plankton that are filtered from the water with the aid of comblike "gill rakers." These behemoths can grow to 100 pounds or more and have shown up in fossils dated as 70 million years old. The reservoir is also home to one of Montana's endangered species, the pallid sturgeon.

The scenic drive route crosses over the earthen dam of Fort Peck. The view across the lake from here is so vast it looks like an inland sea. A museum at the powerhouse relates the history of Fort Peck Dam and its construction. The museum has prehistoric fossils and Native American artifacts on display. Follow the signs for the museum and for the Downstream Recreation Area, where you will find picnic grounds, beaches, and boat launches. The picnic grounds have horseshoe pits, playgrounds for the kids, and a nature trail.

Winter is the best time to see bald eagles at Fort Peck. During early spring you might see sharp-tailed grouse vying for mates near Flat Lake. South of the dredge cuts and north of Fort Peck Lake (on Montana Highway 117) you can see bison, elk, and pronghorns in a 250-acre wildlife pasture. For more information on wildlife viewing sites in the vicinity, stop at the information kiosk on MT 24 near Wheeler, a few miles west of Fort Peck.

The town of Fort Peck has a summer theater; show information is available from the Glasgow Chamber of Commerce. Performances run June through August. Before the show you can view artworks by regional and local artists in the gallery.

Old Fort Peck was established in 1867 by Campbell Peck and E. H. Durfee as a trading post for Indians, trappers, and rivermen. The site where the 300-square-foot stockade with 12-foot-high walls stood was flooded when Fort Peck Lake was created, taking all its secrets down under. But that was not the first time the fort was flooded. In 1877 a wall of ice formed about where the dam now stands. In 20 minutes the Missouri River rose 20 feet, flooding the grounds with about 10 feet of water. Most of the fort buildings were dismantled for firewood to fuel riverboats by 1887.

Just northeast of Fort Peck is the Fort Peck Indian Reservation, Montana's largest at more than 2 million acres. It is home to Assiniboine and to Yanktonai and Sisseton Wahpeton Sioux.

To continue this scenic drive, go north of Fort Peck on MT 24. The terrain changes to gently rolling hills and grain fields as you approach the city of Glasgow. About 3 miles southeast of Glasgow you will come to a junction where MT 24 heads north to meet up with US 2. Bypass this turnoff and stay on the main road, which is now MT 24W, and head into Glasgow.

Glasgow was named for the city of the same name in Scotland, due to the proliferation of Scots who came to this town (one of the oldest eastern Montana settlements) to build the railroad. The first establishments here were—you guessed it—saloons, and a restaurant. Glasgow's first Sunday school was held in a boxcar. South of town, you can take a 65-mile auto tour through the coulees on the north shore of Fort Peck Lake. This South Valley route passes reservoirs, where you can fish and view wildlife. Ask at the chamber of commerce for more details on this side trip.

The Pioneer Museum in Glasgow exhibits Western artifacts, wildlife mounts, and information on historic events. Dioramas of the Lewis and Clark Expedition, fossils and dinosaur bones, and Indian and pioneer stories will interest and entertain you. Wild West fans might be interested in the Buffalo Bill Cody bar, complete with bullet and lead slug.

From Glasgow take US 2 west to Malta. The gentle hills here once supported shortgrass prairie, which bison devoured on their great movements across the plains. The same hills now support cattle. Some crops are grown here as well, including wheat, alfalfa, and barely. This is one of the best places to see weather moving across the land since there are no mountains to stop it. As quickly as thunderheads roll in they disappear again, leaving the air full of the scent of wet hay.

West of Vandalia the Larb Hills break up the flat terrain south of the highway. About 20 miles west of Glasgow, explore what has been termed a "pint-sized Grand Canyon with an Old West atmosphere," more of Montana's badlands at the Bitter Creek wildlife viewing area. Follow Britsch Road north about 9.6 miles until it becomes a dirt track. Continue for another 5 miles or so, staying to the right. Veer left and look for signs for Bitter Creek study area. Four-wheel-drives are recommended, but if you have any doubts about your vehicle or weather conditions, call the Bureau of Land Management in Glasgow. You can hike or mountain bike just about anywhere as long as you stick to the roads, but keep in mind that these roads are impassable when wet.

A swimmer takes a dip at Sleeping Buffalo Hot Springs.

Keep your eyes toward the ground for sharp-tailed and sage grouse. Mule and white-tailed deer and pronghorns haunt the coulees and uplands, while ferruginous hawks and prairie falcons hunt and play in the sky.

In the tiny town of Saco, farther along US 2, a rock in a small grassy spot by the railroad tracks memorializes the cowboy artist Charles M. Russell. The names of several area ranchers, indebted to Russell for his contributions to their profession, are engraved on a plaque. Russell is not the only famous person to have passed through Saco. Chet Huntley, television commentator, attended school here.

Just west of Saco you will see signs announcing Sleeping Buffalo Hot Springs to the north. This little oasis, which you can see from the highway before you get to it, looks a bit odd in the middle of the dry plains. It is a great place to stop if you feel like a soak and can tolerate the somewhat murky water of the pools. An interpretive sign at the Sleeping Buffalo turnoff explains about the sleeping buffalo rock, now under shelter here, where many people have left offerings of tobacco. The rock was moved from an area near where the Cree Indians regularly crossed the Milk River. From a distance, the boulders supposedly resembled a herd of sleeping bison. The Sleeping Buffalo Hot Springs area has a campground, motel, bar, store, restaurant, golf course, and indoor and outdoor pools. The outdoor pool has two waterslides. Right across from the hot springs is Nelson Reservoir, which offers opportunities for boating and fishing.

Just west of Sleeping Buffalo Hot Springs is Bowdoin National Wildlife Refuge. This 15,551-acre refuge, established in 1936 along the central migratory flyway, is ripe with eared grebes, white pelicans, cormorants, pintails, teals, gulls, sandpipers, godwits, pheasants, and grouse. Pronghorn like the lavish shortgrass prairie surrounding the lakes. If you are lucky, you may catch a glimpse of rare peregrine falcons hunting for a meal.

Lake Bowdoin was formed before glacial times, when it was part of the Missouri River. A self-guided auto tour takes you on a 15-mile loop, beginning and ending at refuge headquarters. The auto tour is on a well-maintained gravel road that circles Lake Bowdoin. A pamphlet is numbered corresponding to stops along the way. You can hike on parts of the refuge or boat on the lake. Ask at headquarters for information. To get to the refuge turn south off US 2 at the signs just west of Sleeping Buffalo Hot Springs and make a right at the first big intersection you come to. Signs will guide you to the refuge headquarters, about 9 miles down the road. The road is paved but rough, potholed, and narrow. Watch for deer and pronghorn crossings.

When you leave the refuge headquarters, continue on the same rough road to Malta, 7 miles west, or backtrack to US 2. From Malta (described in Scenic Drive 21), you can pick up Scenic Drive 19 or Scenic Drive 20. Scenic Drive 21 also continues from Malta and heads west to Havre.

19 LEWISTOWN AND THE LITTLE ROCKIES

U.S. Highway 191

General description: This 133-mile excursion begins in Lewistown, the geographic center of Montana. It is one of the more diverse drives, with mountains, badlands river breaks, and flat prairies. Some of Montana's gold camp history comes alive in the not-so-ghostly towns of Zortman and Landusky.
Special attractions: Charles M. Russell National Wildlife Refuge, Mission Canyon, the Missouri River Breaks; boating, fishing, wildlife viewing, camping, hiking, mountain biking.
Location: Central Montana. The drive begins in Lewistown, and follows U.S. Highway 191 north to Malta.
Drive route number: US 191.
Travel season: Year-round. Blowing and drifting snow can make winter travel hazardous.
Camping: There are a few developed campgrounds along the Missouri River and in the Little Rockies just south of the Fort Belknap Reservation.
Services: Lewistown and Malta have full services. Limited services in Hays, Zortman, and other small towns along the route.
For more information: Charles M. Russell National Wildlife Refuge; Lewistown Chamber of Commerce; Malta Chamber of Commerce (see Appendix).

19 LEWISTOWN AND THE LITTLE ROCKIES

U.S. Highway 191

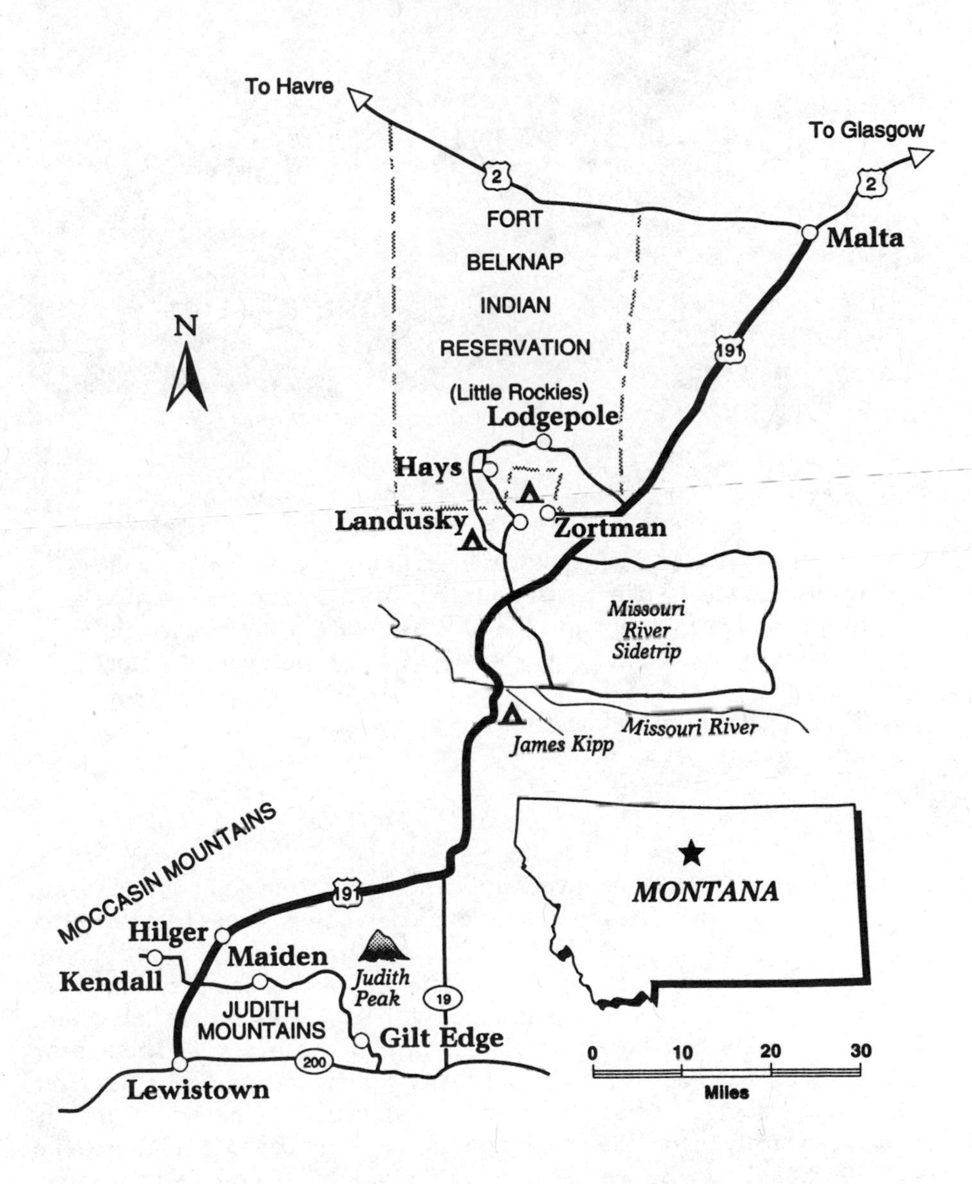

St. Paul's Mission in Hays on the Fort Belknap Reservation.

The drive:

> Owen and "Rattle Snake Jake" arrived in town about 1 p.m., rode up to Crowley's saloon, dismounted, went in and had several drinks and then rode on to the race track. Here they joined the throng around the track but took no part in the betting until almost the last race when they bet quite heavily and lost their money. This, together with a few drinks of bad whiskey, put them in an ugly mood.
>
> — Granville Stuart,
> *Forty Years on the Frontier*

Lewistown, the seat of Fergus County and the starting point of this scenic drive, is a pretty town that got off to a rough beginning. It was first a trading post for trappers and hunters, then later became an agricultural center. Cattle rustlers wrought havoc on local ranchers in the 1880s, until ranchers retaliated and dispatched two suspected villains, "Rattlesnake Jake" and "Longhair" Owen. A photographer sold pictures of the men's dead bodies for profit. Lewistown was also the site of many Indian and settler battles over bison. Reed's Fort, a trading post east of town, was a stopping point for the Nez Perce shortly before their surrender in the Bears Paw Mountains to the north. Although Lewistown has quieted down a bit since its wilder days, there are many things to do here, and you might want to plan on staying a day or two.

Many of Lewistown's buildings are listed on the National Register of Historic Places, and the chamber of commerce has a pamphlet-led walking tour of town. Lewistown has a museum and an art center that features the work of local artists. The Central Montana Fair is here in July, and the Cowboy Poetry Gathering, as well as an arts-and-crafts show, are held in August. In September, the one-day Chokecherry Festival draws crowds from all over the state to sample fare from various Lewistown restaurants and buy or eat anything that has to do with chokecherries. The fair also highlights a parade, fun run, children's bike rodeo, and a pit-spitting contest. During winter, enjoy music and dance concerts sponsored by the Community Concert Association.

The Big Springs Trout Hatchery, southeast of town, is open to visitors year-round. Brown, rainbow, and cutthroat trout, as well as kokanee salmon, raised here are supplied to rivers, lakes, and streams all over the state. To get to the hatchery, head south on First Avenue for about 7 miles, watching for hatchery signs. Lewistown's water supply comes from Spring Creek, one of the purest municipal water supplies in the country; the water is so clean it needs no treatment. If you go to the fish hatchery, be sure to pick up the "Upper Spring Creek Day Trip Guide" from the chamber of commerce. The pamphlet has a map listing points of interest along the way, including a mini scenic drive along Castle Butte Road.

Head north from Lewistown on US 191, which skirts the Judith Mountains. The mountains—along with a river, a town, and a county—were named by Meriwether Lewis for his cousin in Virginia. Some contend her name was Julia, and that the explorer got it wrong. But mountains by any other name would be just as beautiful. The Judiths arose as magma oozing up through sedimentary lakebed deposits about 50 million years ago. The crystallized rock yielded placer gold, found by prospectors in the 1880s. The find led to the birth of the camps of Maiden and Gilt Edge, now ghost towns.

To explore these ghost towns and the Judith Mountains, turn east on Warm Spring Canyon Road. You will pass the now closed Lewistown Air Force Base, built on the former townsite of Andersonville. Maiden is just under 9 miles up the road. Its peak population of twelve hundred people had no problem keeping seven saloons alive. If you continue up the road, turning north at a fork 1 mile past Maiden, you can access Judith Peak, a recreation area managed by the Bureau of Land Management. In winter, telemark skiers practice their skills on the south face of Judith Peak, also called Big Grassy. From the top you get spectacular views of central Montana.

Back on the main gravel road, southeast of Judith Peak, lies the ghost town of Gilt Edge. Not much remains of this town that Calamity Jane called home from time to time. From Gilt Edge you can either head back the same way or continue on the road heading east, bearing right at the fork, then make your way south to Montana Highway 200 (U.S. Highway 87), where you will come out about 12 miles east of Lewistown. If you have not had your fill of ghost towns yet, take Montana Highway 84 to Brooks and Kendall, about 2 miles west of the Warm Spring Creek Rd. turnoff. A few buildings remain, along with several foundations, a cemetery, and mine ruins. There is a small active mine near Kendall, which offers 1-hour tours during the summer.

To continue the main scenic drive, head north on US 191. At Hilger, you can turn off and follow County Road 236 north to Scenic Drive 20 if you so desire. To complete the drive to Malta, stay on US 191 north as it flows around the base of the Judith Mountains, now to the south.

When you get to the junction with Montana Highway 19 east of Roy, turn north to continue on US 191. As you approach the Missouri River here, the terrain quickly changes to "breaks." The term, applied only to the Missouri River, refers to the abrupt change in landscape from plateau and grasslands to high cliffs and bluffs cut by the river over millennia.

As you approach the river, you will be on the Charles M. Russell National Wildlife Refuge, which encompasses the entire shoreline of Fort Peck Lake as well as this part of the Missouri River. South of the river is a small information center about the refuge, on the east side of the road. Also on the river's south bank is the James Kipp Recreation Area, with a boat ramp and campground nestled among a grove of large cottonwood trees. Kipp and a party of forty-four men traveled up the Missouri River in 1831 and opened a fort at the mouth of the Marias River, where they traded furs with the Blackfeet Indians.

Just after you cross the bridge you will see a sign for an auto tour of the refuge, heading to the east. This 20-mile, well-maintained gravel road will take you along the river and through coulees covered with sagebrush, ponderosa pines, and grasses, then bring you back out to US 191 about 10.5 miles north of where you started. I recommend this side trip as a shorter alternative to Scenic Drive 20 if you are uncertain about rough roads but still want to experience some of the Missouri River country. You can hike anywhere along the way except for a section along the river where a remnant population of prairie elk thrive, as indicated on the refuge map. The CMR refuge drive is about 2 hours long, if you do not get out and do any exploring on foot. Follow Refuge Road 101. When you get to the intersection at White Bottoms, you can continue straight along the river for about 6 miles then will have to turn around again and head north at the intersection to get to US 191. Just before you reach the main road, you will find a campground and fishing access at Bell Ridge Recreation Site.

The area to the east of US 191 and north of the Missouri River is loaded with backroads, many very primitive and unmaintained, also impassable when wet. Explore this area with a detailed BLM map or the *Montana Atlas and Gazetteer*.

If you continue north on US 191 (whether or not you take the side loop through the refuge) you will come to a junction with Montana Highway 66. You can take this road north to the Fort Belknap Indian Reservation, and the little towns of Landusky and Hays. Landusky, once considered a ghost town, is now thriving again. The one-block-long town receives regular traffic from a nearby gold mining operation—which is in the process of tearing down the Little Rocky Mountains, a sacred place for the Indians. There is a wooded campground near Landusky, but you are warned not to drink the water there.

Contamination from the mine upstream has poisoned the water.

The mine that has revived the two towns of Zortman and Landusky is Montana's largest open-pit gold mine. It mines gold by dumping cyanide solution over tons of rock to leach out minute specks of the metal. The process extracts about an ounce of gold per 60 tons of rock. Cyanide has polluted the waters here; bighorn sheep and seagulls have died after drinking from ponds near the mine. The Canadian-owned mine has leveled portions of the Little Rockies, including Spirit Mountain, a sacred area for the Indians of Fort Belknap. A group of Native Americans now monitors mining activities and water quality in the area.

The Fort Belknap reservation is home to Assiniboine and Gros Ventre people. The Assiniboines tend to live in the northern reaches of the reservation (see Scenic Drive 21), while the Gros Ventre live in the Hays and Lodgepole areas. *Gros ventre* is French for "big belly." The Indian people with this name are thought to be the northernmost group of Arapahos.

If you look at a road map for this region, you will notice a small notch (7 miles by 4 miles) at the southern tip of the reservation. The mined areas you just passed are located in this notch; they were negotiated for by white representatives of the U.S. government in 1895. The government had known about the gold deposits there and sent three delegates to bargain with the Indians for cash in exchange for the gold-rich land that they claimed the Indians were not using anyway. One of the delegates, Audubon Society founder George Bird Grinnell, summed up the anti-Indian sentiment of the day with suspect concern:

> The only thing you have to sell is this little piece of land that you do not use. I should like to see you sell that, because if you don't, I cannot tell how after two years have gone by you are going to live.

Today the mine owners take in millions of dollars annually; the Indians here benefit little, if at all.

The town of Landusky was named for Pike Landusky, who discovered gold here in the early 1890s. According to historian Donald Miller in *Ghost Towns of Montana*, the town "soon became a favorite hangout for gunmen, claim jumpers, murderers, robbers, rustlers, and assorted unsavory characters." Landusky the man was a cantankerous sort said to have single-handedly fought off a small war party of Indians (who had kidnapped him) with a frying pan. He also regularly hit people with a gold-headed, weighted cane, whether they deserved it or not. He was beaten and shot to death by the outlaw Kid Curry (Harvey Logan) in his own bar.

Kid Curry was another cantankerous sort, ranking up there with Billy the Kid and Jesse James. Curry and his brothers were ranch cowboys in this area. Following the murder of Landusky, the Kid fled, becoming a thief, cattle rustler, and train robber. Curry even kept company with Butch Cassidy, killing a few more people until he was caught and jailed in Knoxville, Tennessee. By that time he had become a folk hero, and people were allowed to chat with him while he was incarcerated. He eventually escaped from Knoxville, and it is unclear what became of him. One story put him in Alaska where he supposedly died a poor prospector; another sent him to South America. You can see Kid Curry's hideout on Bull Creek Road, which is about 2 miles north of the junction of US 191 and MT 66. Turn west on Bull Creek Rd. and drive for about 11.5 miles until you come to a pair of dirt tracks heading south. Take the second track. The hideout is about 1 mile south.

If you continue on MT 66 north to Hays you can visit Saint Paul's Mission, established by Jesuits in 1886 and also used as a school. The stone building was constructed by gold prospectors from the nearby mines on a volunteer basis. Father Eberschweiler, a Prussian Jesuit priest here, was loved and respected by the Assiniboine because he translated sermons into their own language.

Nearby, a tiny shrine built in 1931 to the Virgin Mary houses a replica of a carved wooden statue of the Mother of God. Mass is conducted here some Saturdays.

Farther up the road is Mission Canyon, with several tiny picnic areas that have interesting names: Bad Road, Lame Bull, The Boy, Lone Fly, and Isa Hoo are some along Peoples Creek. At the head of the canyon is a natural stone bridge. A gravel road cuts through the narrow 50- to 60-foot high bluffs and leads toward Mission Peak, near the mine site. You will not be allowed to explore mining lands.

From Hays you can either go back out to US 191 or continue north on MT 66, turning east on Bureau of Indian Affairs Road 11 toward Lodgepole. BIA 11 will take you through rolling hills and buttes, around the Little Rockies, and back to US 191, 17 miles northeast of MT 66. About 2 or 3 miles past Lodgepole take a right at the first paved road and follow it back to US 191. You do not need a permit to hike on the Fort Belknap reservation, but you must have one to hunt or fish. Permits can be purchased at just about any store in Hays or Lodgepole.

If you skip the side trip to Hays or if you backtrack to US 191, you will pass some interesting forested knobs, buttes, and plateaus along the southern fringe of the Little Rockies. This is Missouri River Breaks country with trees, strange against the desertlike plains. But the trees' presence here means a greater number of wildlife species due to a more diverse habitat.

The Dry Fork Road, 7 miles east of the junction with MT 66, will take you to UL Bend National Wildlife Refuge within the CMR Refuge complex. It was in this area where nearly forty captively bred and raised endangered black-footed ferrets were released in October 1994. The UL Bend area should provide the ferrets with ample amounts of their favored prey: prairie dogs, whose active burrows number more than ten thousand in the area. The ferrets, which were thought to be extinct in the 1960s, are being monitored with radio collars to determine their success.

Also at the Dry Fork Junction you can follow signs north to Zortman. Zortman has a small motel, a supply store with gasoline, and a campground. A local cave may soon be open to experienced spelunkers; contact the BLM for more information. Bighorn sheep can be seen on the south side of Saddle Butte during winter.

Back on US 191 and continuing toward Malta, you will find rangeland with some crops folded over coulees. Keep your eyes open for pronghorns in the draws and crossing the road. For a description of the town of Malta, see Scenic Drive 21, which you can pick up from there. Alternately, you can head west toward Glasgow on Scenic Drive 18.

20 THE MISSOURI BREAKS

Missouri Breaks National Back Country Byway

General description: This spectacular but extremely rough 73-mile loop is for four-wheel-drive or high-clearance vehicles only. It bumps and scrapes through the Montana outback and its wheat fields, bluff country, and arid plains. Stand on 1,000-foot cliffs overlooking the wild and scenic Missouri River, or hike among scrubby ponderosa pines.
Special attractions: Missouri River; wildlife viewing, hiking, mountain biking.
Location: North-central Montana. The drive begins and ends near Winifred, 37 miles north of Lewistown.
Drive route number: Missouri Breaks National Back Country Byway.
Travel season: Late spring until snow season.
Camping: There is one campground with toilets at Woodhawk Creek, near the Missouri River. Primitive camping is allowed on public land anywhere along the route. The nearby James Kipp Recreation Area campground is located where U.S. Highway 191 crosses the Missouri.
Services: Limited services (gas and a small store) in Winifred. For full services you will have to go to Lewistown.
For more information: Bureau of Land Management, Lewistown (see Appendix).

The drive:

> The situation of man gliding over a beautiful river in a boat always has something magical about it, in that the country traversed seems to be moving by on either side. But on certain parts of the Missouri the charm is increased by reason of the real or fictitious beauty displayed on its shores. By fictitious beauty I mean the great landslides created by the depth of its bed, the adjacent land, and the subsiding of its high water. When seen close by they are, it is true, only hideous ravines, obscure holes, hanging ruins or trunks of uprooted trees—in a word, the picture of desolation.
>
> — Nicolas Point, S.J.,
> *A Journey on a Barge*
> *Down the Missouri*, 1845

20 THE MISSOURI BREAKS
Missouri Breaks National Back Country Byway

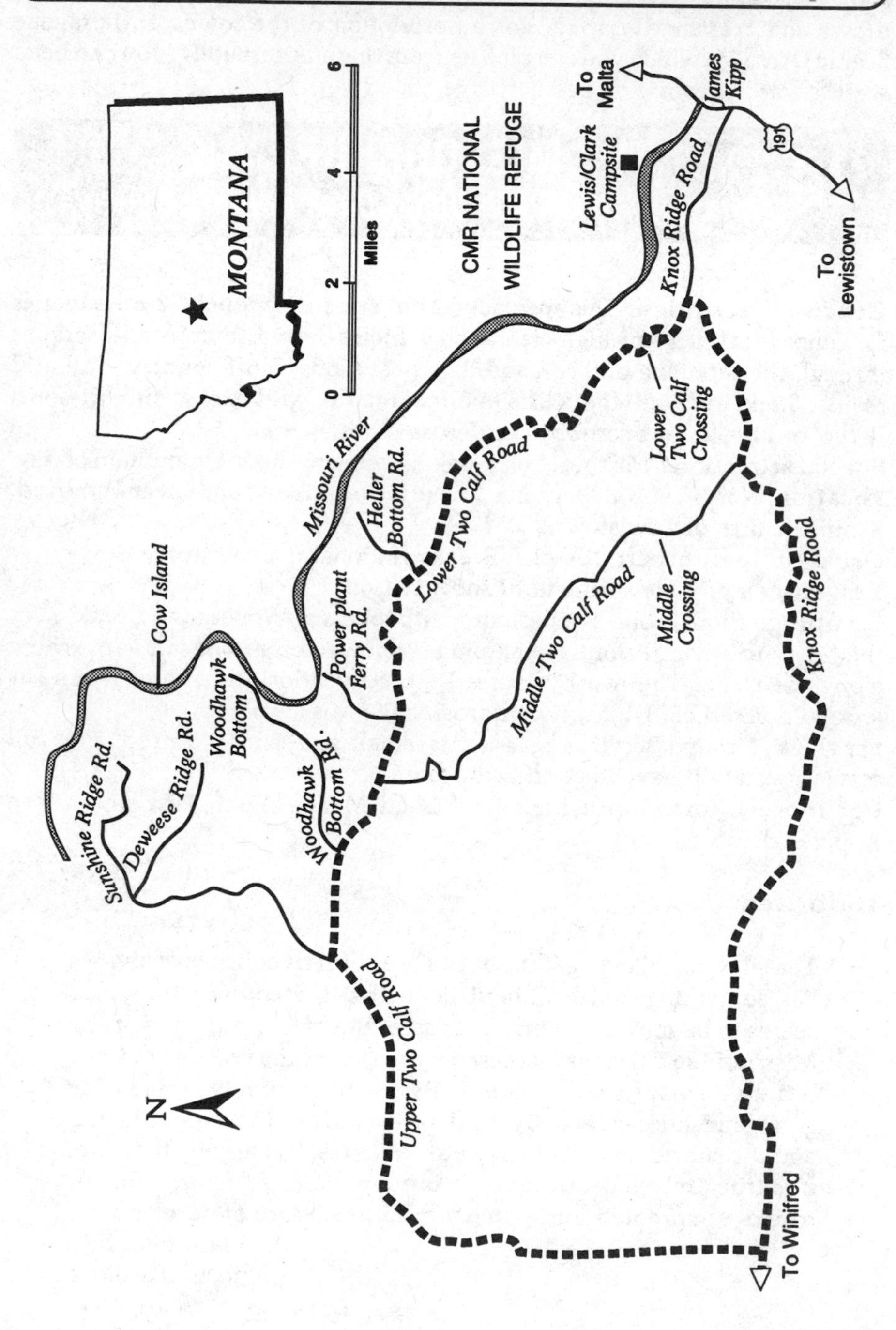

This off-road drive will leave you either exhilarated or cursing. It begins about 10 miles east of Winifred in the middle of wheat fields and rangeland. To get to Winifred, take US 191 north from Lewistown, going 14 miles to Hilger. At Hilger take County Road 236 for 23 miles to Winifred. Once there, you will see a sign indicating the Missouri Breaks National Back Country Byway route and Knox Ridge Road. Turn right on this gravel road, near the gas station, just before you head down the main road through Winifred. You will pass some grain elevators just after you turn; bear right beyond there, and go over a little bridge. The road passes through wheat fields for about 10 miles before arriving at the starting point of the scenic byway, where a large map is posted.

Follow signs for Knox Ridge Rd. if you do not see back country byway markers. I highly recommend getting the Bureau of Land Management's small and useful booklet about the Missouri River drive, with a map that provides historical anecdotes of the area. You can also use BLM maps of the Zortman/Winnett and Winifred/Lewistown quadrangles. These will prove useful, since some of the roads on this drive are not marked with signs.

This National Back Country Byway loop is 73 miles' worth of gravel and "gumbo," a term used to describe the soils in this part of the state. This roadbed here can become unbelievably slick with only a slight amount of moisture. Please take all warnings and precautions seriously. If you attempt to drive in the rain or get caught in wet weather while on this drive, make sure your legs are in good shape; it is a long walk home. Large RVs, motor homes, and vehicles longer than 20 feet should not attempt the Lower Two

The pine-studded flats of the Missouri Breaks Back Country Byway.

Overlooking the Missouri River with the Little Rocky Mountains in the background. This stretch of the Missouri once saw much steamboat traffic during Montana's settlement.

Calf Crossing, nor any of the side roads. Other drivers should use caution. You can always go as far as your vehicle will take you or as far as you dare, then backtrack.

A four-wheel-drive would be best for this trip, but I did it in a two-wheel-drive van with about 18 inches of clearance. At the Lower Two Calf Crossing, I was glad I had those 18 inches. Parts of the road get very rough and washed out. There are also spots where the road takes quite steep grades into and out of deep coulees. If you are not an experienced off-road driver, you may want to do only the Knox Ridge Rd. part of this loop, which takes you through rolling wheat fields. It is in good shape and mostly flat until you near its other end at US 191 across from James Kipp Recreation Area.

All warnings heeded, read the interpretive sign at the starting point, get a good look at the map and side trips, and begin the drive by following signs to Lower Two Calf Road and the National Back Country Byway symbol. There will be several side roads along the way, so continue on Lower Two Calf Road until further notice.

The first part of the drive takes you through wheat fields and open range. Watch for cattle in the road. A few buttes and ranch homes lay scattered about the plateau. You will notice missile silos tucked away in the grain fields; they are the strange, square, fenced-in areas. As you come up over the first ridge you can see the Little Rocky Mountains on the northeast horizon. Meriwether Lewis stood on high bluffs near here and viewed the Little

Rockies. Thinking they were part of the Rocky Mountain chain, he wrote about them in his journal.

> These points of the Rocky Mountains were covered with snow and the sun shone on it in such manner as to give me the most plain and satisfactory view. while I viewed these mountains I felt a secret pleasure in finding myself so near the head of the heretofore conceived boundless Missouri.

This region was covered with an inland sea between 135 and 65 million years ago, as evidenced by shale deposits exposed through downcutting by streams that flow through here. Where you see darker deposits in the bluffs, deep waters once flowed. You may find fossils and dinosaur bones while exploring parts of this Back Country Byway. You are permitted to keep plant and shellfish fossils, but are asked to leave dinosaur bones in place and report your findings to the BLM.

The road will make a major curve to the right, then continue due east for about 5.5 miles. It will begin heading slightly north a mile or so before curving right again. Just after this second bend, you will see a sign at an intersection with a dirt track heading north.

This side road cuts across the edge of a grain field and begins a descent into Woodhawk Creek Crossing. It is one of the longer side trips to the river, and the road can get steep and rough. If you do not have a four-wheel-drive or reliable front-wheel-drive, you may want to skip it. You can ride mountain bikes here, but it can be a grunt-filled trip because of soft ground. The road will take you to Sunshine Ridge and DeWeese Ridge, providing spectacular overlooks of the Missouri River. Consider driving the sometimes-harrowing road to the end of Sunshine Ridge, about 9 miles. This is part of the Nee-Me-Poo Trail, following the 1,170-mile journey of Chief Joseph and the Nez Perce Indians from Idaho to the Bears Paw Mountains.

As you look out over the Missouri from Sunshine Ridge, you might be surprised to know that where the river now flows is a relatively new channel, about 12,000 years old. Before glacial times, the Missouri flowed much farther north in what is now the Milk River drainage. As glaciers advanced south, they pushed the river south to where it now cuts through millions of years of marine deposits. The glaciers would have had to have been as thick as 1,500 or 2,000 feet to move the mighty Missouri.

Back on the main route, the road passes through more grain and hay fields. The vista is expansive. As the road nears the edge of the plateau that drops in the river channel, there are more opportunities to take shorter side trips to the river. If you do not want to drive out on the steep side roads, you can always try it on a bike or get out and walk.

You can camp at the Woodhawk Bottom area, the next side trip 2 miles east of Sunshine Ridge turnoff. Woodhawk Bottom has toilets but no water source. From here you can walk along the southwest bank of the Missouri and explore a small homestead, built by a man named Gus Nelson. The road to the river is 5 miles. You can also hike along the bank to Cow Island, the big island north of Woodhawk. Steamboats began making journeys to this part of the Missouri River in 1859, and often stopped at Cow Island to refuel. On their flight north in 1877, the Nez Perce demanded supplies from soldiers guarding steamboat freight on Cow Island. A small skirmish ensued, and the Indians continued up Cow Creek to the west of the river.

Not quite 2 miles east of the Woodhawk turnoff, you will come to a fork in the road. Signs point to Middle Two Calf Road. This is the bailout point for those who do not want to attempt the Lower Two Calf Crossing or for those who want to shorten this scenic drive. You will still have to drive across a creek on the Middle Two Calf Rd.—or turn around at that point. This route is less scenic, but the road is in much better shape and picks up with the Knox Ridge Rd. to the south.

The main, and rougher, scenic drive route continues along Lower Two Calf Road. From the Middle Two Calf junction, Lower Two Calf Rd. can be brain-rattling if not freshly graded. Hang in there or turn around; it will likely get a worse before it gets better. The road passes through a small area of pines and junipers, in contrast to the open plateau. Beyond this point, the road narrows to single dirt track with cobbles and a washboard surface. There are a few steep descents and ascents into and out of coulees before you dip down to Two Calf Crossing. Another side road to the river takes you to Powerplant Ferry, but do not let the name fool you: The ferry has long since disappeared.

At some road intersections the National Back Country Byway signs are missing. If you are attempting Two Calf Crossing, stay on Refuge Road 307. If you have gotten this far you are probably close to crossing Two Calf Creek. You have gone up and down a few very steep pitches on your way down to the creek bottom and you are wondering why you ever thought you could do this. Unfortunately, it may be too late to turn around. I hope you brought plenty of food and water! Just kidding. If you decide at this point that you cannot make the crossing, you can find a place to turn around. The crossing will have water in it during a normal or wet year; it can be completely dry during a drought. The crossing itself, with concrete slabs placed at angles in the water like a "V," might be hard without high clearance. The ascent back up to the plateau is steep and rugged, so excellent traction is essential.

Once you have made it to the top of the ridge, you may be cursing me to no end for sending you on this trip. But from here on out, the drive is a cakewalk along the Knox Ridge Rd. Take a sharp right at the "Y" intersection and head west, exactly the opposite direction from which you just came. You probably will not see the sign until after you have missed the turn.

Knox Ridge Rd. winds and dips through sagebrush and grain fields with a few buttes. It is regularly graded and a wonderful drive, should you decide to do just this part of it from the starting point near Winifred. If you have not had enough adventure yet, you can continue east on Knox Ridge Rd. (skipping the right-hand turnaround at the "Y") toward James Kipp Recreation Area, where US 191 crosses the Missouri River. It is only another 4 miles, but the steep, narrow road might be a little too exciting for some. From this route you can take another short side road to Knox Bottoms, where Lewis and Clark camped on May 24, 1805.

At US 191, you can pick up Scenic Drive 19 and head north to Scenic Drives 18 and 21. Or you can go back to Lewistown and take Scenic Drive 19.

21 THE HIGH-LINE
U.S. Highway 2

General description: This 88-mile drive follows Montana's High-Line, the name given the railroad (and U.S. Highway 2) in this part of the state. You will pass hay fields and prairie, and are more likely to see trains along the old Great Northern Railway tracks than cars on the road. Hundreds of pothole lakes host migrating waterfowl and shorebirds.
Special attractions: Black Coulee National Wildlife Refuge, Bears Paw Battleground, Fort Assiniboine, Wahkpa Chu'gn Archeological Site, Havre Beneath the Streets, Montana State University–Havre campus; hiking, mountain biking, fishing, camping.
Location: North-central Montana, just south of the Canadian border. The drive begins in Malta on US 2 and heads west to Havre.
Drive route number: US 2.
Travel season: Year-round. Blowing and drifting snow can make winter travel hazardous.
Camping: There are a limited number of commercial campgrounds in and around Havre.
Services: Full services in Malta, Chinook, and Havre. Limited services in Fort Belknap Agency, Zurich, Harlem, and Dodson.
For more information: Fort Belknap Tourism Office; Montana Department of Fish, Wildlife and Parks; Malta Chamber of Commerce; Chinook Chamber of Commerce; Havre Chamber of Commerce (see Appendix).

The drive:

> I thought of my wife and children, who were now surrounded by soldiers, and I resolved to go to them or die. With a prayer in my mouth to the Great Spirit Chief who rules above, I dashed unarmed through the line of soldiers.
>
> — Thunder-Rolling-in-the-Mountains
> (Chief Joseph), 1877

During the building of the Great Northern Railway, officials from the railroad named several towns along the line by spinning a globe and stopping it with the point of a finger. Malta was so named, after the Mediterranean island. From the 1870s to the turn of this century, Malta was the center of a great cattle empire stretching from Canada to the Missouri River and from Glasgow to Havre. Malta was also the entertainment capital for cowboys coming in from the range.

21 THE HIGH-LINE

U.S. Highway 2

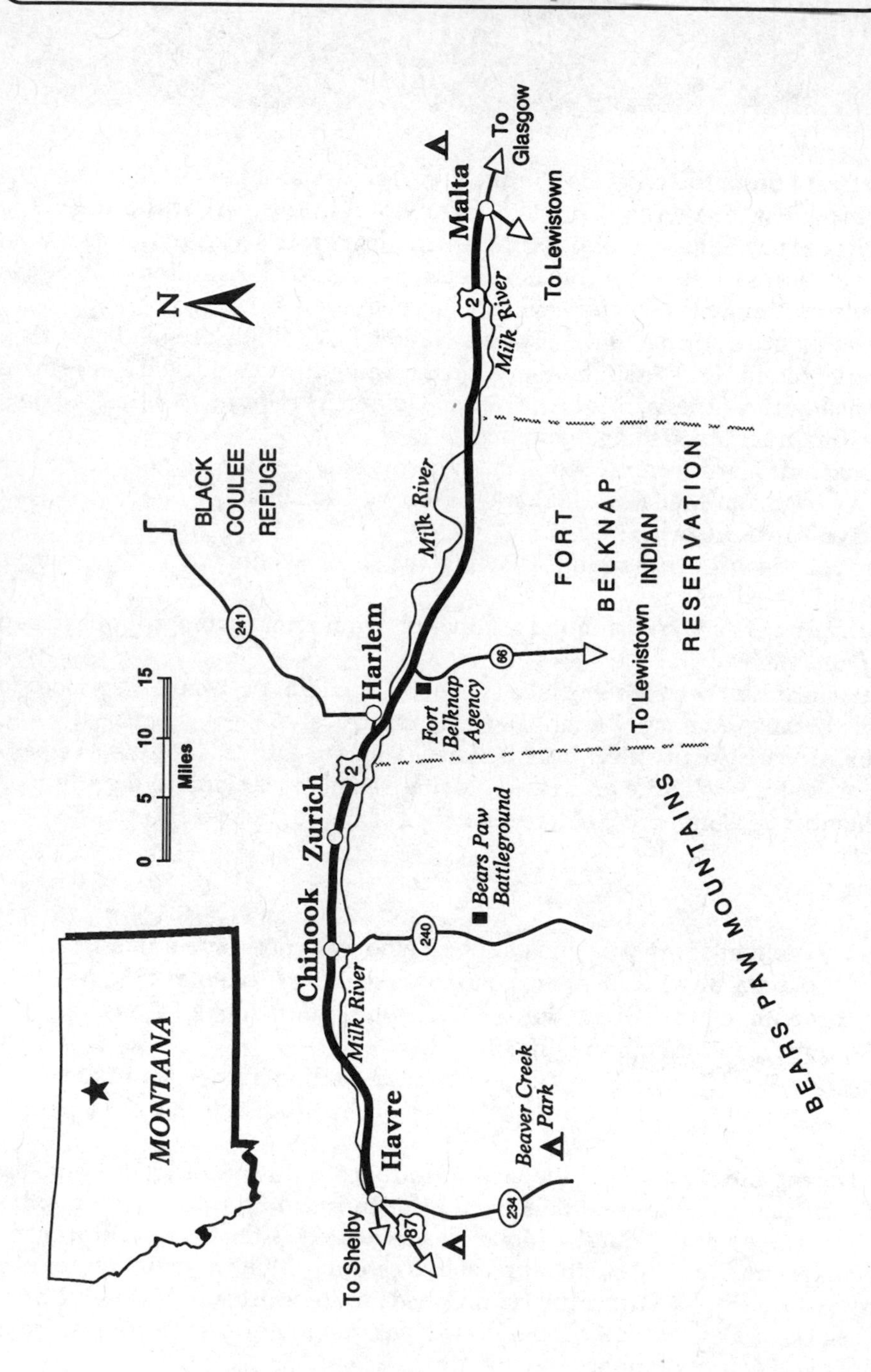

Every Labor Day weekend, the pioneer spirit lives on in this area during the annual gathering of the Milk River Wagon Train. Horse-drawn wagons and buggies take a 60-mile route over the plains and end their five-day trek in town, with a parade and other festivities. Contact the Malta Chamber of Commerce for information on joining the wagons or four-day cattle drives here in June and September. Malta history is on the go. There are plans to move the Phillips County Museum here to a new location and open a new dinosaur display, including a *Hadrosaurus*, a rare duck-billed dinosaur. The museum now features historical exhibits on homesteaders, Native Americans, and outlaws.

Bowdoin National Wildlife Refuge east of Malta is a beautiful spot complete with its own scenic drive (see Scenic Drive 18). There is quite a large area north of Malta saturated with potholes and marshes ideal for migrating waterfowl and shorebirds. From Malta take County Road 242 north to Loring or Whitewater to explore this pothole country.

This scenic drive heads west from Malta on US 2 and follows the Milk River all the way to Havre. The river was named by Lewis and Clark because the water's color was similar to a cup of tea mixed with a tablespoon of milk. The Indians called it the "river that scolds all others." The Milk River flows in the old channel left by the Missouri River after glaciers pushed the Missouri south to its present channel (see Scenic Drive 20). The old Great Northern tracks, now used by the Burlington Northern Railroad, also follow the highway.

The town of Wagner was the site of a great train robbery in 1901. A gang of hoodlums led by Kid Curry, a famous Montana outlaw (see Scenic Drive 19) held up a Great Northern train, grabbing a satchel they thought was full of cash. Some reports say the bag was full of worthless papers; others say the gang made off with $80,000 in cash.

US 2 flows over flat prairies and around minor hills and coulees of Montana's High-Line. Most of eastern Montana was shortgrass prairie before European settlement. Much of it now supports cattle and a smattering of crops, although the premier part of the state for growing dryland wheat is west of Havre. The wind blows fiercely up here, and if you are used to mountains, this area can seem desolate and lonely. But there is true beauty along the High-Line, even without mountains.

The terrain is mostly flat, dissected with shallow coulees and topped with low buttes. This country sees lots of waterfowl as they make their migrations north and south along the flyway. Northeast of Harlem is Black Coulee National Wildlife Refuge, another place where waterfowl and shorebirds rest up on their long journeys south or north. (Harlem is another town name determined by the spin of the globe. This time the finger landed on Haarlem, in the Netherlands.) To get to Black Coulee take County Road 241 northeast from Harlem for 24 miles. Ignore the major left-hand bend in the road. Instead, continue on the gravel spur road due east. Turn right and head south on Country Road 128 for about 3 miles. Turn east and go for 1 mile, then south for 0.5 mile until you reach the gate. From here you can walk into the marshy area full of mule deer, pronghorns, ducks, geese, golden eagles, and other birdlife. Tundra swans pass through in October. On clear autumn days, a walk around the marsh is very enjoyable.

South of US 2 from Harlem is Fort Belknap Agency, on the northern border of the Fort Belknap Indian Reservation. The reservation is home to both Assiniboine and Gros Ventre Indians. The Assiniboine came from a division of Yanktonai Sioux, who originally lived near Lake Superior. They eventually split off to form their own nation, and moved westward, settling in eastern Montana by the early 1800s. The name Assiniboine, or *assnipwan*, is of Sioux origin, meaning "stone Sioux," and probably refers to a traditional cooking method using hot stones (see Scenic Drive 19).

Fort Belknap Indian Days, in late July, feature dances and games. The Information Center in Harlem features Native American arts and crafts. The staff will provide tours of ancient tepee ring sites, Snake Butte (a sacred area), tribal bison pasture, and the Old Mission. You do not need a permit to hike on the reservation, but must buy one to hunt or fish. Permits are available from just about any store on the reservation.

West of Fort Belknap is the larger town of Chinook. Be sure to check out the Blaine County Museum here, which displays fossils and dinosaur bones collected from the area. The name Chinook was adopted from a Indian word meaning "warm wind." Warm winds known as chinooks blow through the High-Line country in late winter. Many livestock owners, past and present, have been grateful for these winds that melt snows, making grass available to their animals when they need it most. Chinooks have been known to cause ambient temperatures to rise as much as 50 degrees in just minutes. Charles M. Russell's drawing of a lone cow, nearly a skeleton, standing in the hard winter wind is titled *Waiting For a Chinook*, or *The Last of the Five Thousand*. This small sketch, sent to the cow's owner in response to an inquiry about his herd's condition, won Russell notoriety as an artist.

To the south of US 2 are the Bears Paw Mountains, where Nez Perce Chief Joseph laid down his weapons and surrendered to General Nelson A. Miles. On October 5, 1877, Chief Joseph with 87 warriors and 147 women and children gave up trying to reach Canada. After leading his people 1,170 miles, the weary leader delivered a moving speech.

> Tell General Howard I know his heart. What he told me before I have in my heart. I am tired of fighting. Our chiefs are killed. Looking Glass is dead. The old men are all killed. It is the young men who say yes or no. He who led the young men is dead. It is cold and we have no blankets. The little children are freezing to death. My people, some of them, have run away to the hills and have no blankets, no food; no one knows where they are, perhaps freezing to death. I want time to look for my children and see how many of them I can find. Maybe I shall find them among the dead. Hear me, my chiefs, I am tired; my heart is sick and sad. From where the sun now stands, I will fight no more forever.

The Bears Paws were volcanoes that erupted a mere 50 million years ago. To get to Bears Paw Battlefield, head south from Chinook on County Road 240 and go for about 16 miles. The battlefield is on the east side of the road. If you are here during the first week of October, many Native Americans from Montana and Idaho journey here to remember the plight of the Nez Perce and their own people. The gathering usually falls on the weekend closest to October 5, the anniversary of the surrender.

On October 7, 1877, more than 400 Nez Perce were led across North Dakota, South Dakota, and Kansas, eventually brought to Indian Territory in Oklahoma. Generals Miles and Howard promised the Nez Perce they could return to their homeland, but were overruled by superior officers. Chief Joseph and Yellow Bull continued to work for their people's return to their homelands. In 1885, with the help of General Miles, about 100 Nez Perce were allowed to go back to Idaho. The remaining 150, including Chief Joseph, were sent to the Colville Reservation in what is now Washington State. Chief Joseph continued to fight for the freedom of his people until his death in 1904. After becoming familiar with the workings of the U.S. government, he once remarked, "White men have too many chiefs." It was said he died of a broken heart.

On a cool autumn day, with fat, grey clouds dancing about the sun, I joined a small group of Nez Perce and a tour guide on a short walk to relive the events of the battle. At the site of surrender, the last stop on the tour, a Nez Perce elder delivered some powerful words about culture, spirituality, tolerance, and forgiveness. Four men beat hand drums and chanted in their people's tongue. As the group dispersed and headed back to the parking lot, a bald eagle glided low over Snake Creek where we had been gathered.

Continue on US 2, following the Milk River and the railroad, until you reach the town of Havre. Havre is one of the bigger towns in Montana, boasting of the Montana State University–Havre campus (previously Northern Montana College) and much to see and do. The town was named for a city in France (Le Havre, only here it is pronounced HAV-er) since several Frenchmen settled in the area before the turn of this century. Havre was a trading center and refuge for range riders. In the recent past, cowboys fought for the right to tie their horses to parking meters downtown. It is not clear who won the skirmish.

A much earlier part of this region's history lies behind Havre's Holiday Village Mall, at the Wahkpa Chu'gn Archeological Site. For about two thousand years, until six hundred years ago, Native Americans used the site to corral and kill bison with spears, rocks, and arrows. The name Wahkpa Chu'gn was that given to the Milk River by the Assiniboine people. In a one-hour guided tour, visitors can see five archaeological sites with bison kill and campsite artifacts.

Fort Assiniboine, south of town, was once a U.S. military post. It was established in 1879 to protect settlers from possible Indian attacks following General George Armstrong Custer's defeat by the Sioux and Cheyenne at the Battle of the Little Bighorn. Following the battle, the U.S. government was afraid that one of the strongest chiefs who led the charge against Custer, Sitting Bull, would return from exile in Canada and cause trouble for white settlers in this northern region. No major attacks on settlers ever took place, however, following the construction of Fort Assiniboine. General John Pershing (then a lieutenant), of World War I fame, served at the fort under General Miles. "Black Jack" Pershing, as he was called, was head of the Tenth Cavalry here, an all-black unit, in 1896. Fort Assiniboine is now an agricultural research center. Check with its headquarters before visiting.

One tour I highly recommend is Havre Beneath the Streets. This unique guided tour takes place under parts of Havre's main streets, an underground commercial strip that was once full of thriving businesses, complete with bordello, opium den, speakeasy, barber shop, meat market, saloons, and pharmacy, among others. According to our tour guide, the opium dens in Havre were not illegal, but the Chinese who ran them were. When the railroad was completed, the Asian workers who had labored on it were not allowed to remain in this country legally.

Many of the underground passages and businesses that make up the Havre Beneath the Streets tour are original; others have been recreated. Many of the featured businesses were on the street level, and some have been restored at the underground location. No one is sure why some legitimate businesses chose to go underground, but it is possible that a 1904 fire, which destroyed much of downtown Havre, forced people to set up temporary shops beneath the burned out areas. Others theorize that this area's cold winters and hot summers may have been more tolerable underground.

Offerings to the memory of Chief Joseph at Bears Paw Battlefield.

North of Havre is the Rookery, a wildlife management area with tremendous birdlife. The old-growth cottonwoods and Milk River bottomlands here, combined with surrounding uplands and coulees, provide outstanding habitat for golden eagles, great horned owls, American kestrels, hawks, great blue herons, American avocets, and several species of ducks and geese. Deer also find a home here. Several trails along the river provide nice walking, and you can canoe a 4- or 5-mile stretch of river. There are boat launches at the upper and lower ends of the wildlife area. To get to the Rookery, take Seventh Avenue north out of town. Cross the tracks and the river, then turn west on River Road. The Rookery is about 5 miles farther.

Another outstanding natural area can be found south of Havre. Beaver Creek County Park, 17 miles long by 1 mile wide, is one of the largest county parks in the United States. It rests comfortably between slopes of the Bears Paw Mountains and is dotted with small lakes and ponds. Rolling, grassy hills give way to pine forests and aspen groves above. As the name suggests, this is a good place to see beavers, as well as much birdlife. Deer, elk, coyotes, and raccoons also frequent the park. To get to Beaver Creek, take Fifth Avenue to Beaver Creek Road and head south for 9 miles to the park. There is a user fee.

At the Hill County Fairgrounds in Havre you will find the H. Earl Clack Museum, which houses artifacts from Wahkpa Chu'gn Archaeological Site, as well as pioneer exhibits and horse-drawn farm equipment. In August, take in the Great Northern Fair and Rodeo. From Havre you can continue west on US 2 to Browning, where Scenic Drive 22 begins. Or you can head back to Malta and pick up Scenic Drives 18 and 19.

22 THE ROCKY MOUNTAIN FRONT

U.S. Highway 89, U.S. Highway 287

General description: Imagine a 200-mile wall of mountains butted up against coulee-cut plains rich in wildlife and history. This 136-mile drive along the Rocky Mountain Front allows views of such a gigantic spine. Plan to start in the morning when the sun is shining on the mountain crests.

Special attractions: Museum of the Plains Indian, North American Indian Days, Heart Butte, Freezeout Lake Wildlife Refuge, Sun River Game Range, Holter Lake Recreation Area; dinosaur digs, museums; hiking, backpacking, mountain biking, fishing, boating, camping, wildlife viewing.

Location: Northwest Montana. The drive begins in Browning and heads south to Interstate 15 and the Missouri River at Wolf Creek.

Drive route numbers: U.S. Highway 89, U.S. Highway 287.

Travel season: Year-round. Extreme winter weather can make travel hazardous and sometimes prohibitive.

Camping: There are several Forest Service campgrounds in Lewis and Clark National Forest along the Rocky Mountain Front. Holter Lake also has campgrounds.

22 THE ROCKY MOUNTAIN FRONT

U.S. Highway 89, U.S. Highway 287

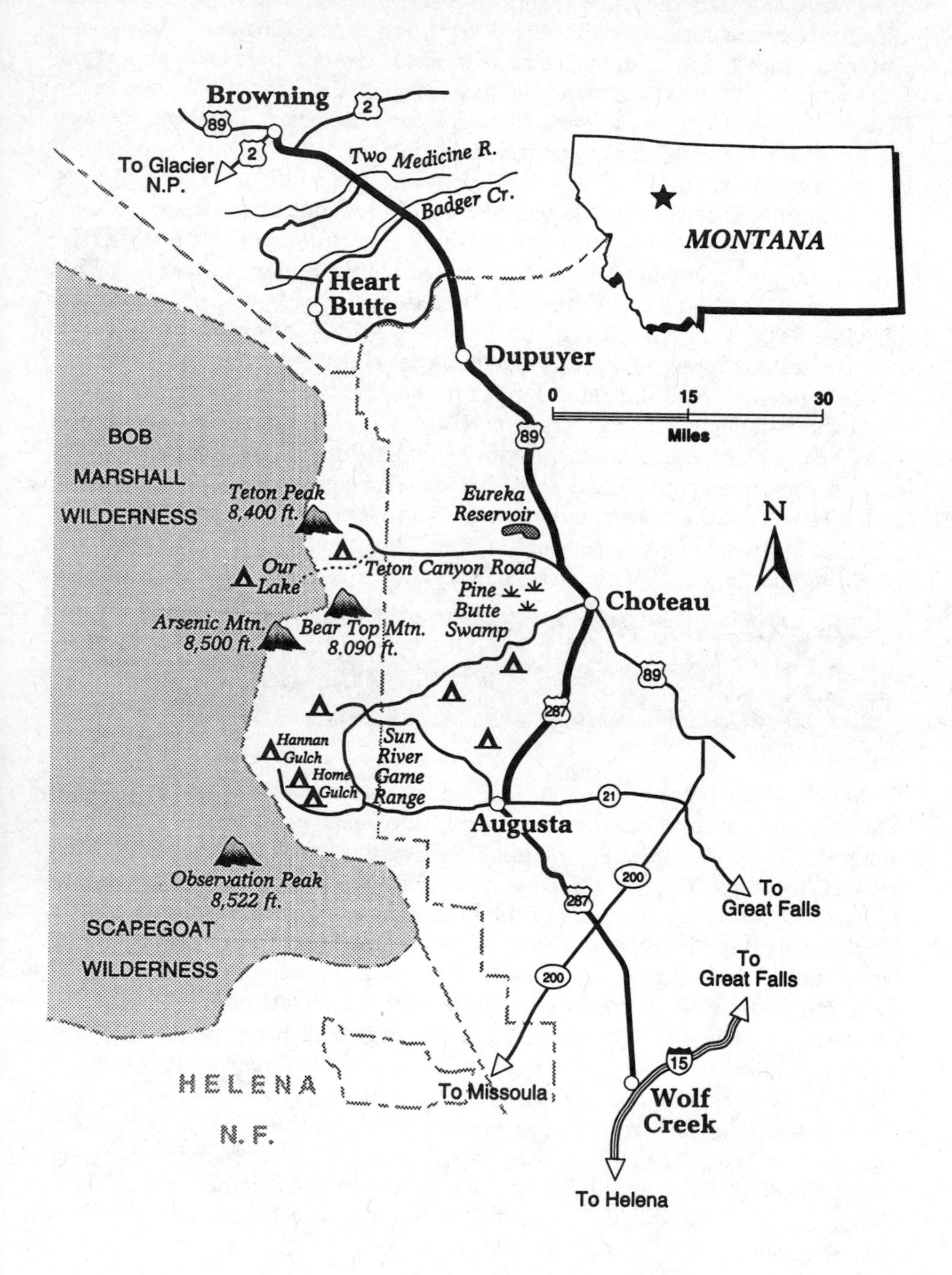

Services: Full services in Browning, Choteau, Augusta, and Wolf Creek. Limited services in other small towns along the way.
For more information: Lewis and Clark National Forest, Augusta Information Station and Rocky Mountain Ranger District; Montana Department of Fish, Wildlife, and Parks; Museum of the Plains Indian; Blackfeet Nation; Choteau Chamber of Commerce; Old Trail Museum; Pine Butte Guest Ranch (see Appendix).

The drive:

> February is the Moon of the Eagle, when the eagle returns from the winter migration. Also it is known as the Hatching Time of the Owl. The owl takes time to grow, he is awful slow. . . . February is also the moon of the dreaded northern blizzard. The natives call it Taking Orderly Position for the Attack.
>
> — Percy Bullchild,
> *"The Twelve Moons"*

Begin this drive in the town of Browning on the Blackfeet Indian Reservation east of Glacier National Park. Browning is home to the Museum of the Plains Indian on the west edge of town. This small museum is a great place to visit and does not take long to see. Native American clothing, toys, weapons, jewelry, arts, and crafts are wonderfully displayed in glass cases with excellent descriptions. Also on display are maps with interpretations of various American Indian nations and their homelands.

From Browning, the Blackfeet Nation offers full- or half-day tours of historical sites. Be sure to take in North American Indian Days if you are here during the second week in July. This Native American gathering is one of the largest, pulling visitors from both the States and Canada. Be sure to get permit information before hiking, hunting, or fishing on the reservation.

The Blackfeet have the largest membership of all Indian nations in Montana. There is uncertainty about the origins of the name, but "blackfeet" may have come from the blackened moccasins these Indians wore when they first met white explorers. Montana's Blackfeet are also known as Piegans, a name that refers to the southernmost of three tribes spread across Canada and Montana. The Blackfeet were probably the most feared of all Montana tribes by white settlers as well as other Native Americans for their ferocious bravery and the aggressiveness with which they raided other camps or defended their own.

The original Blackfeet Reservation encompassed roughly two-thirds of western Montana and had shrunk to a little less than 1.5 million acres by the turn of this century. In the late nineteenth century, the Blackfeet were pressured into selling a significant portion of their scenic and sacred lands, now part of Glacier National Park. Because of its proximity to the Front Range of the Rocky Mountains and the diversity of habitat, the Blackfeet Reservation and adjacent lands today are home to grizzlies, elk, bighorn sheep, mountain goats, and pronghorns.

The East Front of the Rocky Mountains near Pine Butte Swamp is home to grizzly bears that still live on the plains.

From Browning take US 89 south, following signs to Great Falls. Just south of Browning the road dips down into the Two Medicine River bottom, then into Badger Creek. Just east of here Meriwether Lewis had the first and only deadly encounter with Indians on the entire Lewis and Clark Expedition. The corps of discovery had camped for the night with eight or nine Blackfeet men whom Lewis had mistaken for Gros Ventres. Two Blackfeet were killed when caught stealing horses and guns the next morning. In fear of retribution, the exploring party made quick tracks for the Missouri River.

Southwest of Badger Creek is Ghost Ridge. During the winter of 1883-1884, more than 600 Blackfeet starved to death following the extermination of bison by commercial hunters. The dead were buried on Ghost Ridge.

The Badger–Two Medicine region, from which the Badger Creek waters flow, is forest land held sacred by the Blackfeet people. Along with the Blackfeet Nation, conservationists are trying to get the Badger–Two Medicine area federally designated as wilderness to protect wildlife habitat here. Oil and gas drilling interests have spurred strong opposition. The wild lands of the Rocky Mountain Front are vital to wildlife with large habitat needs, such as grizzly bears, that roam between Glacier National Park and the Bob Marshall Wilderness Area. To develop the Badger–Two Medicine lands would leave two wild areas with no bridge connecting them.

If you want to get a little closer to the Badger–Two Medicine area and hike its trails in Lewis and Clark National Forest, you can do so. About 11 miles south of Browning and just after you cross the Two Medicine River is Bureau of Indian Affairs Road 12, also called Joe Show West Road. Turn west on this road and take it until it dead-ends at Heart Butte Road. If you turn north here, you will end up in Browning again. If you turn south, you will follow the foothills of the mountains. You can access some trails from the Heart Butte Cutoff Road. The roads end at the reservation boundary, where the public trails begin. Please respect treaty rights and do your exploring on public lands only. Refer to a Lewis and Clark National Forest map for details.

If you continue on the main Heart Butte Rd. it will take you to Badger Creek Road and back out to US 89. Or you can continue south on Heart Butte Rd. and you will reach the small Blackfeet community called Heart Butte. From here you can continue on to Birch Creek Road, also called Arrowhead Road, back to US 89 at the southern boundary of the Blackfeet reservation.

You have probably noticed by now how the rolling, grassy hills and plateaus are the perfect medium for drawing your eyes to the western wall of mountains. Montanans call this the Rocky Mountain Front, or East Front, referring to the east side of the Continental Divide. The Front Range stretches all the way down to I-15. Coupled with the relatively flat plains to the east, this row of mountains is what makes this drive stellar.

The hummocky land here is glacial moraine: gravel and debris dumped by piedmont glaciers, which were fairly stagnant blocks of ice. Larger glaciers moved south from Canada and east from Glacier National Park, leaving remnant ice blocks and trails of boulders strewn about what eventually became the upland prairie.

About 11 miles south of the junction with Montana Highway 44 is the town of Dupuyer. The name comes from the French word *depouilles*, which refers to bison back fat, a delicacy for both Indians and white explorers. The writer Ivan Doig, whose novels about early settlers in Montana have made him a favorite of new and old Westerners alike, based his novel *English Creek* on old-timers' stories and the landscape surrounding Dupuyer. The town itself was settled in 1874 as cattle began replacing bison. Cowboy artist Charles M. Russell hung out near here at the Home Ranch.

South of Dupuyer the road curves through hilly country until you reach Pendroy. The road is narrow with no shoulder and no guardrail. Use caution here at any time of year, but particularly in winter. At the small community of Bynum, be sure to visit the rock shop; it is the old church building with dinosaurs painted on the sides. The shop also sells fossils found in the area. On the north end of town, Blackleaf Road will take you west to Bynum Reservoir for fishing and to Blackleaf Wildlife Management Area below Volcano Reef. Both grizzlies and black bears frequent the marshes and limber pine habitat of these ridges.

South of Bynum and just before you reach the town of Choteau, Teton Canyon Road heads west. This road will take you to Eureka Reservoir, the Nature Conservancy's Pine Butte Swamp Preserve, and numerous trails into the Bob Marshall Wilderness complex. Some trails you may want to explore here include Mill Falls, Green Gulch, and Our Lake, where you can hike a 3.5-mile trail to see mountain goats and view the Chinese Wall, a rock formation in the Bob Marshall Wilderness Area. Refer to a national forest map for details on roads and trails.

A travel companion of the Old Trail Museum in Choteau.

Pine Butte Swamp Preserve, now owned by the Nature Conservancy, was established in 1978. This 18,000-acre wetlands area was established primarily as a preserve for grizzly bears. The flatlands along the East Front are the only place where grizzlies still roam the prairies, once traditional habitat for the magnificent bears. The preserve also supports more than 150 bird species, deer, elk, beavers, and muskrats. Most of Pine Butte Swamp is off-limits to people, but you can use some areas with permission from the preserve manager. You do not need permission to hike along the ridge across from the information signs at the swamp. Contact the manager for information on guided nature walks given on Mondays during summer.

In Choteau, stop at the Old Trail Museum to learn a bit of area history. There is a unique fossil at the museum—*Trapper canadensis,* who appears to have gone extinct from a combination of lead poisoning of the brain and arrowhead affliction of the spine.

In the 1970s paleontologist Jack Horner discovered the first duckbilled dinosaur nesting colony in North America near Choteau, complete with fossilized eggs and embryos. The eggs belonged to a species of dinosaurs called *Maiasaura peeblesorum*, which is now Montana's state dinosaur. Ash from volcanoes in the Elkhorn Mountains to the south had buried the dinosaurs, preserving their nests and eggs so well that the find at the Willow Creek Anticline is considered among the most incredible dinosaur discoveries in the world. Horner further rocked the world of paleontology with his theory, now widely accepted, that some dinosaurs were caring beasts, raising and nurturing their babies much like birds do today. Other dinosaur finds along the East Front include a *Troodon*, which is a smaller version of the vicious velociraptor in the book and movie *Jurassic Park*. The Willow Creek site has also yielded dozens of other types of dinosaurs. If you dig dinosaurs, you can really dig them here. Full-day, half-day, and several-day tours are available. If you are interested in dinosaur tours of the Choteau area, contact the Museum of the Rockies in Bozeman for details (see Appendix).

Ten miles southeast of Choteau on US 89 is Freezeout Lake Wildlife Management Area. During peak times (spring and fall) the refuge supports up to one million birds on a migration stopover. Here you can see tundra swans and snow geese, sandhill cranes, curlews, stilts and black-crowned night herons. Upland game birds, raptors, and mammals are also abundant. There are hiking, boating, and hunting opportunities here, too.

South of Choteau, take US 287 for about 26 miles to the Old West town of Augusta. If you are not from Montana, this town might be what you imagine an old cowboy town to look like. Augusta has some wonderful characters. It was named for Augusta Hogan, the daughter of rancher J. D. Hogan, who managed extensive land holdings here for Conrad Kohrs, a Helena businessman. Augusta claims to be home to the "wildest show on Earth"—its annual rodeo, held the last weekend in June. It is also another of the gateways to the incredible Bob Marshall Wilderness complex to the west.

Northwest of Augusta in the foothills is the Sun River Game Range. From town, follow Willow Creek Road for about 4 miles over glacial moraine and bear right at Sun River Road. You will pass Willow Creek Reservoir, with fishing access. The Sun River was called the Medicine River by the Blackfeet; its bottoms provide winter range for one of Montana's largest elk herds. When Captain Meriwether Lewis passed through here on July 10, 1806, he

North of Wolf Creek on MT 287. Photo by Randall Green

noted vast herds of bison here in his journal, writing, "we hered them bellowing about us all night." Lewis also observed "vast assemblages of wolves" and "saw a large herd of Elk making down the river."

If you follow the road into Sun River Canyon, about 15 miles, you may see bighorn sheep, especially near Home Gulch Campground, or in Hannan Gulch across from it. Winter is the best time to see both sheep and elk from selected vantage points, since the game range itself is off-limits to hikers during winter. The road up Hannan Gulch is rough, so you may want to walk or ride your mountain bike.

To continue this scenic drive, go south of Augusta on US 287. After you cross Bowmans Corners, at an almost hidden intersection with Montana Highway 200, you leave the expansive plains and enter a landscape composed of more rugged, grass-covered hills and forested buttes topped with rocky ridges. The hills on the east side of the road are the Adel Mountains, the highest of which is called Birdtail Butte. These ancient volcanoes erupted 50 million years ago. To your southeast, the peaks of the Gates of the Mountains Wilderness pop over the horizon. These are part of the Big Belt Mountains, east of Helena.

You will hit I-15 just north of Wolf Creek. Go into Wolf Creek proper and you can follow signs to Holter Lake, a dammed portion of the Missouri River, for camping, fishing, and boating. Pelicans, loons, and a variety of ducks and geese can also be seen paddling around the lake. Keep your eyes peeled for peregrine falcons. These once-rare birds of prey are making a comeback in Montana after DDT almost wiped them out. The Beartooth Wildlife Management Area is just south of Departure Point, on the southeast end of Holter Lake. It is a good place to see elk and bighorn sheep, as well as a prairie dog town. You can hike or mountain bike on the dirt roads that cut through this wildlife area. To protect wildlife, the area is closed from December 1 until mid-May.

You can take a scenic wildlife viewing tour just south of here at Gates of the Mountains. Look for the Gates of the Mountains exit off I-15. From here you can take a boat tour on a portion of the Missouri River through which the Lewis and Clark Expedition passed, or you can launch your own boat. A Lewis and Clark journal entry dated July 19, 1805 tells of how the place got its name.

> This evening we entered much the most remarkable clifts that we have yet seen. These clifts rise from the waters edge on either side perpendicularly to the hight of 1,200 ft. . . . I called it the gates of the rocky mountains.

The 2-hour boat tour winds through bighorn sheep, mountain goat, and mule deer country. It also passes Mann Gulch, where in 1949, thirteen smokejumpers were killed while fighting a blaze that exploded up the mountainside. You can read about that incident in the book *Young Men and Fire*, by Norman Maclean.

From Gates of the Mountains, the closest scenic drive is Scenic Drive 23, to the northeast. You can also drive southwest through Helena to Anaconda, where you can begin Scenic Drive 5.

23 THE CRAZY AND LITTLE BELT MOUNTAINS

U.S. Highway 89

General description: This 140-mile drive begins in an arid river valley between the steep Bridger and Crazy mountains, then winds through Smith River country before climbing 7,000-foot-high Kings Hill in the Little Belt Mountains. The rounded, forested knolls of the Little Belts contrast with the sheerness of other Montana ranges.
Special attractions: Museums, hot springs, Castle ghost town; skiing, hiking, camping, fishing, swimming, floating.
Location: Central Montana. The drive begins just east of Livingston off Interstate 90 and heads north to Montana Highway 200.
Drive route number: U.S. Highway 89.
Travel season: Year-round. Blowing and drifting snow can make winter travel hazardous.
Camping: There are many Forest Service campgrounds in the Bridger and Crazy Mountains and in the Little Belt Mountains. You can also pitch a primitive camp just about anywhere in national forest.
Services: Full services in Livingston and White Sulphur Springs. Limited services in smaller towns along the route, such as Clyde Park, Wilsall, Neihart, and Monarch.
For more information: Lewis and Clark National Forest—Neihart Information, Judith Ranger District, and Kings Hill Ranger District; Montana Department of Fish, Wildlife, and Parks; White Sulphur Springs Chamber of Commerce (see Appendix).

The drive:

> As I looked across the rolling expanse of prairie, fired with the beauty of a Montana sunset, I sent up a little prayer of thanksgiving from my heart for this, our very first home. Only a rectangle of prairie sod, raw and untouched by the hand of man, but to us it was a kingdom.
>
> — Pearl Price Robertson
> *Homestead Days in Montana*

This drive begins in the Shields River valley, a long stretch of open, dry, scrubby ranchland with the Crazy Mountains to the east and the Bridger Range to the west. The Shields River was named by Captain William Clark in honor of John Shields, a member of the Lewis and Clark Expedition. Clark camped at the mouth of the river on July 15, 1806, while exploring Yellowstone River country.

23 THE CRAZY AND LITTLE BELT MOUNTAINS

U.S. Highway 89

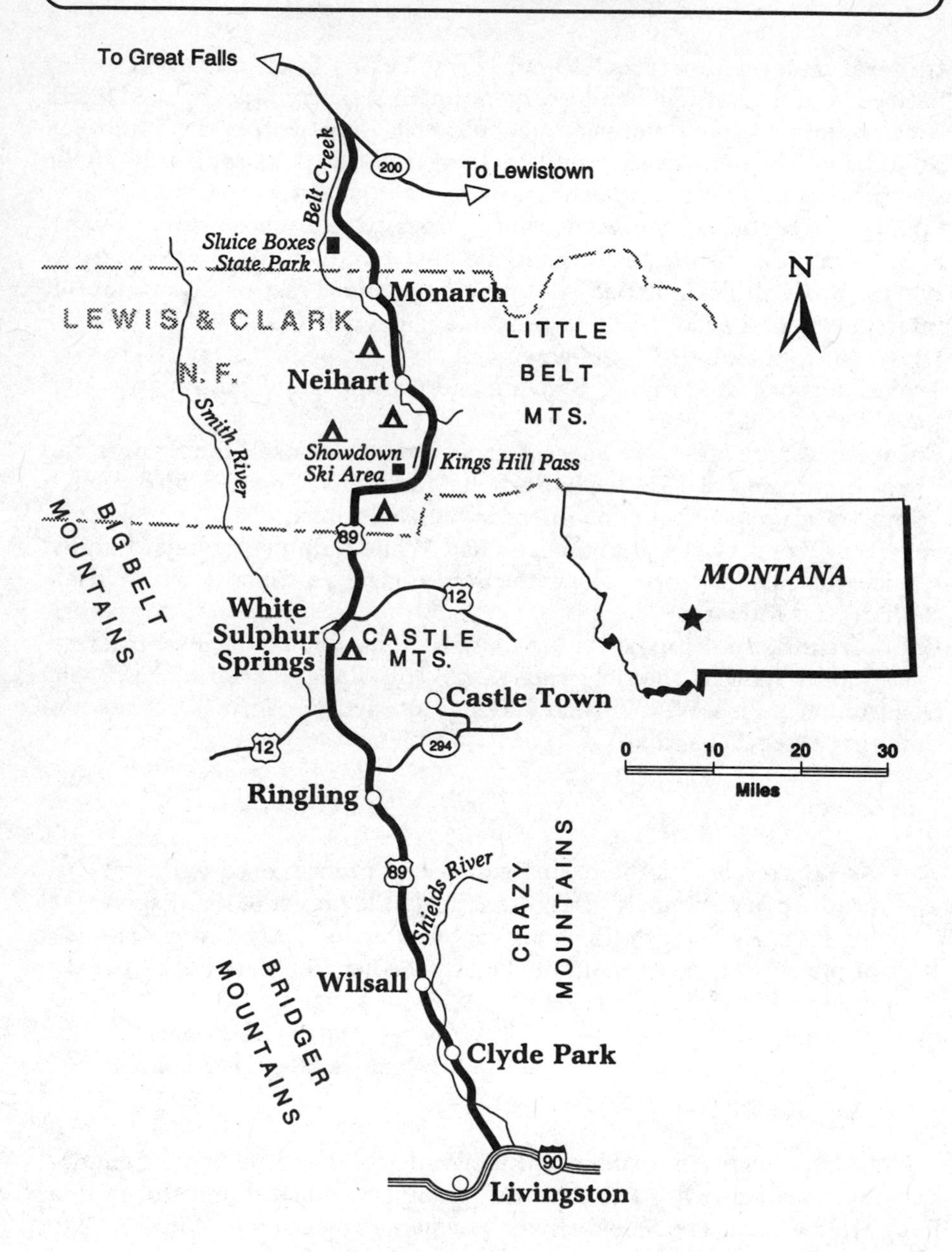

The Bridger Mountains are named for Jim Bridger, a trapper, trader, and scout who guided wagon trains from Fort Laramie to Virginia City in the 1860s. He often came up this valley from the Yellowstone River, crossing the mountains that bear his name to the west before heading into what is now Bozeman. The Crazy Mountains to the east, isolated and mysterious, were revered by the Crow Indians as sacred ground. They were originally called the Crazy Woman Mountains, after a pioneer woman who supposedly went mad and disappeared into these hills.

Driving north on US 89, you will soon pass the little town of Clyde Park, which was named for the Clydesdale horses that were bred on a ranch near here in the late nineteenth century. Old Settlers Days here in September feature games, dancing, barbecues, and a parade. Just 6 miles up the road is Wilsall, a combination of the names Will and Sally, son and daughter-in-law of the early settler who laid out the town. The annual Wilsall rodeo takes place in June. In recent years human bone fragments and stone tools have been unearthed on a private ranch near Wilsall. These finds are several thousand years old, indicators of some of the earliest inhabitants here.

The highway is mostly straight and flat north of Wilsall as it courses through hay fields and cattle range. To the east loom the Crazy Mountains, little-used by recreationists because of limited access, but nevertheless both eerie and spectacular. Geologists remain perplexed by the odd mix of igneous rocks that form these mountains. The higher southern end of the range was heavily glaciated, although glaciers left the lower northern end unscathed. A small piece of one of these glaciers remains as a snowfield; it holds grasshoppers frozen during the Ice Age. You can backpack in to this glacier from Cottonwood Creek, near Clyde Park. The Shields River Road, just north of Wilsall, provides one of the few access points into the Crazies' limited trails. Refer to Gallatin or Lewis and Clark national forest maps for details.

When you reach the small town of Ringling, you will see an abandoned church on a small hill above the highway, a clue that times were once better here. The Milwaukee Road railroad used to snake its way through this part of the state, but many of the former whistle stops, like Ringling, are quiet and lonely if they have survived at all. Ringling got its name from John Ringling, of circus fame, who also built a railroad that ran through here when this town was a big shipping depot for wheat and cattle. Contemporary singer Jimmy Buffet has described this small town, saying, "The streets are dusty and the bank has been torn down. It's a dying little town." A bar, post office, and ethanol fuel plant are about all that remain.

Just north of Ringling, the highway intersects with County Road 294, which heads east. Take this road 16 miles to the town of Lennep, made up of a few houses and a church, then head northwest on Forest Road 581 for about 7 miles to the ghostly remains of Castle Town, so named for the castlelike granitic spires in the Castle Mountains. At one time, Castle was one of the richest mining camps in the state, with about eighty homes, fourteen saloons, and seven brothels. It also had its own brass band. Smelters were built here between 1889 and 1891, and the Cumberland Mine was once the

A hiker and his companion at Memorial Falls along Belt Creek.

biggest producer of lead ore in Montana but by 1893 the town started to die. The last reported residents to live in Castle were two elderly gentlemen in the 1930s. For liability reasons, the owner of Castle Town requests that you ask permission before exploring. For details, call the Kings Hill Ranger District of the Lewis and Clark National Forest, listed in the appendix.

Once you have visited Castle, go back to US 89 and follow it north. South of White Sulphur Springs, the road is in fair shape although narrow, with a few potholes. The surrounding landscape is made of rolling hills, glacial moraines, and rangeland. Look for pronghorns on the range and great blue herons in the warm creek along the road, which is the South Fork of the Smith River. At White Sulphur Springs you can soak in mineral baths at a motel on the edge of town—hence the town's name, which describes the mineral deposits found in the local hot springs.

In White Sulphur Springs, visit the Castle Museum. (You cannot miss it; it looks just like a small castle.) It was built by B. R. Sherman, in 1892. Sherman grew wealthy from the livestock and mining industries, both booming here at the turn of the century. The house is full of antiques, most of which were donated by locals in memory of their pioneer ancestors. The cherry wood used for the staircase and entryway was imported from Europe. The stone used to build the Castle was hauled by oxen from 12 miles away. There is also a small room full of artifacts and newspaper clippings about Castle Town.

Several miles northwest of White Sulphur Springs you can get access to the gorgeous Smith River. Because of this river's popularity, you must apply for a permit in February if you wish to float it. This is practically the only way to enjoy the Smith; there are only a few fishing access points along its entire length. Much of the floatable portion of the river spirals through cliff-lined canyons.

To continue this scenic drive, take US 89 north of White Sulphur Springs into the Little Belt Mountains, which change the landscape dramatically. The main road through here is the Kings Hill National Scenic Byway. You enter the Little Belt foothills from the south, where the view of surrounding country narrows a bit. The curvy road traverses hilly rangeland scattered with homes. The hills are clad with Douglas-firs and pines. The road climbs a low pass, then heads down again before reaching Newlan Creek Reservoir, where you can fish. Newlan Creek, flowing along the west side of the road, is flanked with lush willow thickets.

The Little Belt Mountains are composed largely of sedimentary deposits laid down by a giant inland sea. Evidence of this exists in marine fossils found here dating from more than 200 million years ago. The Belts also contain igneous rocks, which form the round buttes found in the range. The buttes began as bubbles of magma punching their way through the sediment deposits. The rounded terrain indicates that the Little Belts escaped the ice-age carving tools called glaciers.

US 89 climbs north through open rolling hills that gently slope up to rounded tops. As the road makes a sharp east turn around the base of Green Mountain, 7,047 feet high, the rangeland opens up even more. There are four

Overlooking Sluice Boxes State Park along Belt Creek, to which residents of Great Falls once hopped the train to fish for the day.

or five Forest Service campgrounds along the way, all of which are wooded and close to the main road; the first one is a few miles east of the Green Mountain bend. The elevation at this point is about 6,000 feet.

Temperatures are cool here as evidenced by the spruce-fir forest that flanks the road. The area is heavily forested, with some clearcuts. The road begins its ascent up Kings Hill Pass, elevation 7,393 feet. Showdown Ski Area is at the top; you can go downhill skiing or rent snowmobiles here if you take this drive in winter. A fire tower near the top of the ski area on Porphyry Peak is occupied during summer. The road to it is narrow and rocky but passable. From the lookout you get a wonderful view of the Little Belts and the valley below.

Coming down from Kings Hill Pass on the north side, the road winds through a somewhat narrow canyon with rocky slopes. Again the land is heavily forested on both sides of the road. You can see the bald knob of Long Mountain in front of you. Just past Many Pines Campground, you will notice a large area of trees blown over and strewn about the hill. A tornado of sorts blew through here on the heels of a severe thunderstorm in spring 1994. Winds damaged trees in a 50- or 60-acre swath, and a solid 10 acres of trees were completely knocked down. Although no one was hurt, some people were trapped at the campground and had to be rescued. The Forest Service will eventually erect interpretive signs at Many Pines (they may even have to change the name), which will describe this windy event, called a "microburst."

A little more than 1 mile past Many Pines Campground, where the road crosses Belt Creek, is a short trail that leads to Memorial Falls. The trail is about 0.5 mile to the falls and is very rocky and ribbed with tree roots. Watch your footing carefully if you decide to walk up this trail. During high water, it may not be possible to cross the creek, which you must do to get to the falls. It is a nice little hike for stretching your legs, and the falls, only about 10 to 15 feet high, are pretty.

The tiny community called Neihart lies just north of Memorial Falls on US 89. It offers limited services, including a small grocery store with gas, and a bar and grill. The hills northeast of the townsite are loaded with private mining claims dating back to the 1880s. Silver and lead were mined here until the silver crash of 1893 put most mines out of business. Some mining was revived in the earlier part of this century, but nothing significant was found. Neihart is now a winter recreation hub for snowmobilers and skiers, especially those from Great Falls.

Just north of town is the Neihart cemetery, spread out at the foot of a forested hillside. Many of the headstones are so old they are unreadable; some were cut from wood instead of granite. Many markers were once encircled by picket and iron fencing (to keep livestock out), now rotted and collapsed. Some of the iron grates have ornate designs.

North of Neihart is the little town of Monarch. It also offers limited services, and includes a restaurant and small motel or two. Like its neighbor, Monarch was once a mining community that shipped ore to Great Falls by rail to be smelted.

Past Monarch, the road traverses more rangeland with coulees and foothills adding to the relief. Some of the country resembles badlands as you near Sluice Boxes State Park. There is a scenic turnout here, from which you can look down into the deep bottomland of Belt Creek. Access to the park is by Evans–Riceville Road, just beyond the scenic turnout. Sluice Boxes Park is considered a primitive state park, which means there are no camping sites or developed picnic areas with potable water. There is an outhouse at the parking lot, however. The single, 8-mile hiking trail that starts here is also not maintained, and the brush can grow high on both sides. The trail follows Belt Creek, then an abandoned railroad berm in a canyon with bluffs as high as 500 feet. The privately owned Montana Central Railroad (later part of the Great Northern Railway) laid tracks here in the 1880s to serve local mining communities. The railbed was blasted into the cliff in places, and needed forty trestles to cross Belt Creek and tributaries on its sinuous route. It was also considered a scenic route, and people from Great Falls often hopped the train to get to fishing and picnicking sites along Belt Creek. The tracks were abandoned in the late 1940s when the mines finally closed.

There is little shade at Sluice Boxes State Park, and walking the trails on hot summer days is not always pleasant. If you are brave enough, though, you can go for a dip in Belt Creek. It has some great swimming holes, but the water is quite cool, even on the hottest of days—heart-stopping cool. Trust me. One of those swimming holes is about 0.3 mile up the main trail. Take any one of the little paths through the brush to the creek. You can even jump off the 10-foot-high ledge.

Another mile or so up the trail you have to cross Belt Creek, which is about 50 feet wide at this point. During low water it is only a few inches deep and slow-moving. On the other side you can continue up the trail or stop to explore the abandoned buildings of Don Boscoe Camp, last operated in the 1970s by Boy Scouts and the Lions Club. The camp, which is privately owned, has been badly vandalized; do not add to the damage. In the main lodge, furniture and kitchenware are piled in one giant demolished heap. The state is hoping to buy the property and remove the buildings. Use caution if exploring.

From the camp the trail makes several more crossings of Belt Creek, impassable during high water. If you want to wet a line, rainbow, brook, cutthroat, and brown trout are the creek's main piscine residents. You might spot a mink hopping along the bank.

Just north of Sluice Boxes State Park, US 89 ends at an intersection with MT 200. From here you can head east on MT 200 to Scenic Drive 24, which starts on U.S. Highway 191 near Moore. Scenic Drive 19 begins in Lewistown, just east of Moore.

24 JUDITH BASIN

U.S. Highway 191

General description: This 83-mile scenic drive goes through the heart of Montana's wheat-growing region, scattered with buttes and coulees. Here you understand why Montana is called the Big Sky State, with vast blue heavens above thousands of acres of prairie.

Special attractions: Snowy Mountains, Crystal Lake, Judith River wildlife area, Crazy Mountains, Big Timber, Victorian Village Museum, Ackley Lake State Park; fishing, boating, wildlife viewing.

Location: Central Montana. The drive begins at Moore, where Montana Highway 200 intersects with U.S. Highway 191. It follows US 191 south and ends in Big Timber, on Interstate 90.

Drive route number: US 191.

Travel season: Year-round. Blowing and drifting snow can make winter travel hazardous.

Camping: There is limited camping in the Little Belt, Snowy, and Crazy mountains, as well as at Ackley Lake State Park.

Services: Full services in Harlowton and Big Timber. Limited services in Moore, Judith Gap, and Melville.

For more information: Lewis and Clark National Forest, Musselshell Ranger District; Gallatin National Forest, Big Timber Ranger District; Montana Department of Fish, Wildlife, and Parks; Harlowton Chamber of Commerce; Big Timber Chamber of Commerce (see Appendix).

24 JUDITH BASIN
U.S. Highway 191

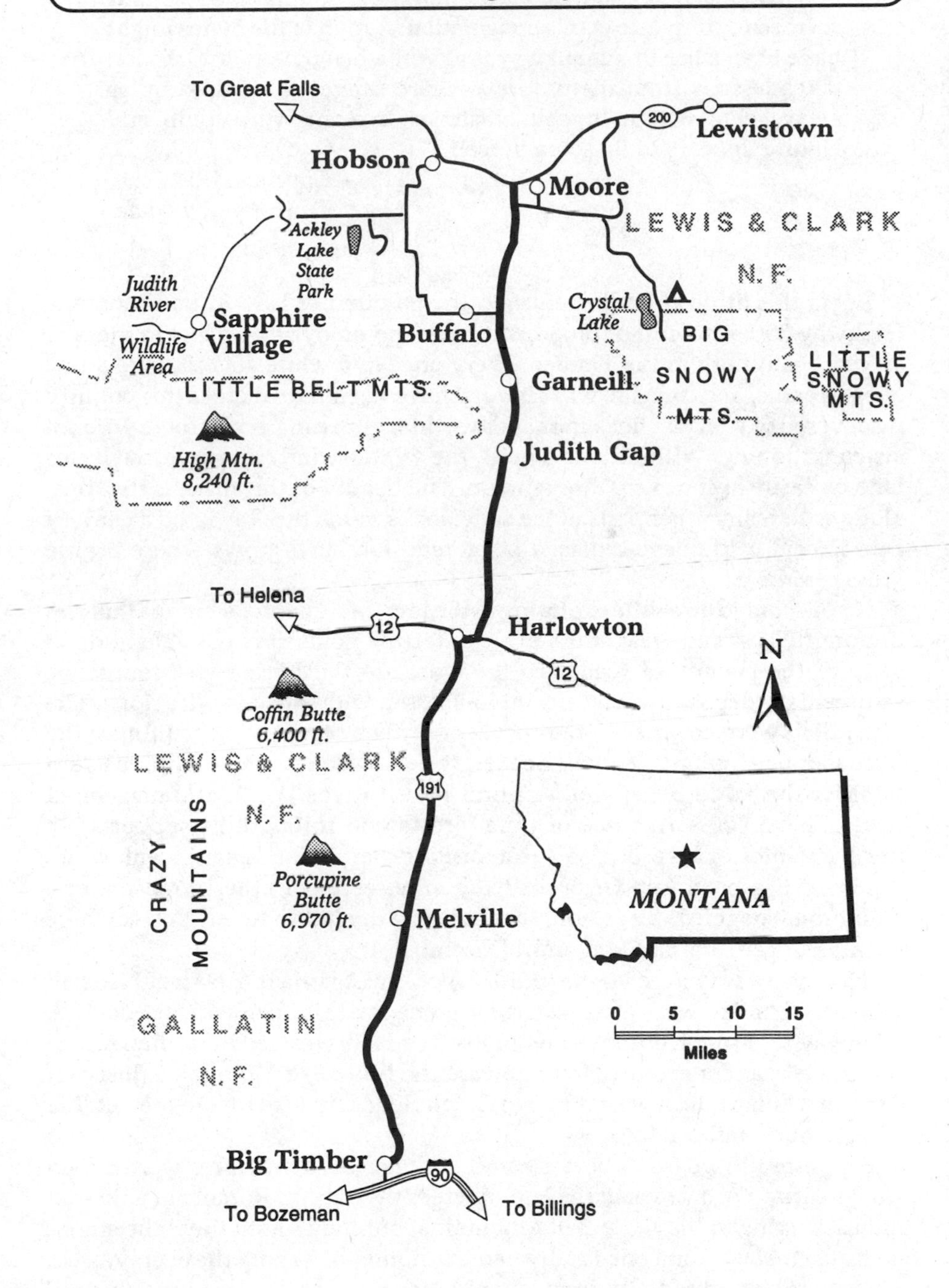

The drive:

> Speakin' of liars, the Old West could put in its claim for more of 'em than any other land under the sun. The mountains and plains seemed to stimulate man's imagination. A man in the States might have been a liar in a small way, but when he comes west he soon takes lessons from the prairies, where ranges a hundred miles away seem within touchin' distance, streams run uphill and Nature appears to lie some herself.
>
> — Charles M. Russell,
> *Trails Plowed Under*

Begin this drive at Eddie's Corner, the junction of US 191 and Montana Highway 200, just west of Moore. Sit back and enjoy getting lost in thought as you head south to Big Timber. Every once in a while get out, take a few deep breaths, and imagine what it must have been like to cross this country by covered wagon. On hot summer days, this route can be miserable without air-conditioning. With little to stop it, the winter wind can rip through this land as easily as it can rip through you. The beauty of this drive is that this, along with many other parts of the state, looks much the way it did a century ago. Except cattle have replaced bison, and hay now grows where prairie grasses did.

If you want to do a little exploring in the low, mountainous bumps that rim the prairie east and west of the drive's starting point, it is possible to do in spite of the paucity of roads. To the west are the Little Belt Mountains, sedimentary deposits left by a giant inland sea with igneous intrusions. The Little Belts were never glaciated because they were too low to accumulate the tremendous amounts of snow needed to feed glaciers. On the mideastern flank of the Little Belts, you will find Judith River Wildlife Management Area. This 5,000-acre space of pine forests and rolling hills supports elk during winter. There is also great birding here. The magnificent white goshawk has been known to visit the area, as have other large raptors. Numerous songbirds flit around shrubs lining the Judith River. You can hike in this refuge from mid-May until December 1.

The easiest way to get to the Judith River WMA is via the town of Hobson, which is 6 miles west of the starting point for this scenic drive, on U.S. Highway 87. From Hobson, take County Road 239 west to Utica, then follow the gravel road for about 12 miles toward the Little Belt Mountains. Just past Sapphire Village, turn west on Yogo Creek Road and take that to the wildlife area, about 1 mile farther.

Sapphire Village exists because brilliant deep blue sapphires were mined from nearby Yogo Creek in the late-nineteenth century. Rumors of gold sent men scurrying to the Little Belt Mountains, but they found tiny blue stones instead. In 1894, someone finally had the notion of having these appraised. They were recognized as unique sapphires, and were mined extensively until about 1929, and are still picked sporadically today. The Crown Jewels of England may contain Yogo sapphires. At one time sapphire mines in the Little Belts had greater earnings than many Montana gold mines. Lots in the community of Sapphire Village were sold along with partial claims to the sapphire mines. Buyers complained that the mining claims they received were worthless and in past years won a lawsuit that gave them rights to productive sapphire claims.

On your way back to Hobson you can stop at Ackley Lake State Park, southwest of town, for boating, fishing, and camping. From Ackley Lake you can weave through farm country east to US 191, picking up the main scenic drive from the hamlet of Buffalo. Without a detailed national forest map or the *Montana Atlas and Gazetteer*, the roads may be a bit too labyrinthine. The easiest way is to go back to US 87 at Hobson and pick up the drive from Eddie's Corner.

The Snowy Mountains are the tiny range you see to the east, just one of several "island," or isolated, mountain ranges in Montana. There is a designated Forest Service campground and several hiking trails near Crystal Lake, a popular and easily accessed recreation site in this range. There are trails to Crystal Cascades and some caves. The lake itself, set in a glacier-carved basin, bubbles from natural springs beneath its surface. The ridges, rocky outcrops, and cone-shaped hills above it are a wonderful setting for picnics. Pick up a pamphlet at the campground for a self-guided tour around the lake. The lake is only about 13 feet deep in spring after runoff, and by autumn it is only knee- to waist-deep. The national recreation trail here passes through subalpine forest and meadow ecosystems. Look to the cliffs above the lake to spot foot-sure mountain goats, introduced here in 1954. If you do not see them hopping about the cliffs, take a hike up Grandview Trail, northwest of the campground.

To get to the Snowy Mountains from US 191 you have to follow a maze of roads. The easiest route might be to head east from Sipple, 4 miles south of Eddie's Corner. Take the gravel road east for just more than 6 miles and turn south. Go 1 mile more, then turn east again for 2.25 miles. Turn south and follow the winding road along Rock Creek to Crystal Lake. The Snowies, which cradle the lake, are almost in the shape of a dome. Most of the range was deposited by an inland sea that covered this region about 300 million years ago. Like the Little Belts, the Snowies escaped scouring by glaciers.

To go on with the scenic drive, go back to US 191 and head south to the town of Garneill, which has an interesting "sculpture" of granite rock with a concrete base in which objects of various origin are imbedded. The monument honors early pioneers and Native Americans. Judith Gap is the next town south. It sits in the "gap" between the Little Belt and Snowy mountains. The area surrounding here was prime hunting ground for Native Americans until pioneers arrived and turned Judith Gap into a bustling shipping depot for wheat.

The country all around you, and through which many of the eastern scenic drives in the book traverse, is shortgrass prairie, the most northwesterly of

The Crazy Mountains rise seemingly out of nowhere on the flat plains of central Montana.

the Great Plains. Standing water is scarce here, rainfall even more so, and the growing season short. In the rain shadow of the mountains to the west, grasses here must be adept at sending out roots to capture the sparse soil moisture. To thrive, plants must be able to survive sometimes months without rain and be able to take quick advantage of rain when it does fall. It is hard to imagine how beasts as great and hairy as bison scattered across these plains with no shade from the fierce sun and nothing to block the wind, except other bison, during Arctic-like winters here.

Harlowton is the only major town on this scenic drive and therefore seems like a bit of oasis on the arid range. Here you will find a museum and city park with a playground and picnic areas. In the center of town is a rail car from the last electric railroad, the Milwaukee Road, which ended its run in Harlowton in 1974. The town was named for Richard Harlow, who built a branch line of the Milwaukee Road to Lewistown called the Jaw Bone. This track was the longest stretch of electrified railroad in the country. Much earlier in Harlowton history, dinosaurs roamed the once-tropical landscape. They left their legacy in bone fragments found throughout the area. The Upper Musselshell Museum displays some of these finds, along with pioneer exhibits.

Southwest of Harlowton, the Crazy Mountains are visible in the distance. Chief Plenty Coups (see Scenic Drive 15) was said to have had a vision in the Crazies, following several days of fasting and praying. The vision revealed to him that in his lifetime bison would vanish and be replaced by "the bulls and the calves of the white men"—a prophesy that sadly has proved true.

US 191 continues south of Harlowton, whisking you through sweeping country. As you enter Sweet Grass County, another oasis of sorts arises on both sides of the road. These are the Cayuse Hills, their coulees scattered with pine trees. It may seem strange to see the pines, relatively lush growth on these desertlike plains. This area is mostly sandstone, and its porous structure holds water well enough to support the pines. The road drops into some more lush lowlands with benches and mesalike formations above. Several creeks meander through this land, all private, from the Crazy Mountains to the west and Glaston Lakes to the east. The road through here is narrow with little shoulder.

Big Timber Canyon Road turns off toward the Crazy Mountains 9 miles south of Melville and leads to a campground with hiking trails to several small lakes. This is a popular spot in summer.

Past this road, the highway winds down through some badlands-type landscape. The stream bottom is lush along Big Timber Creek, and you can fish at marked access sites. Big Timber Creek flows into the Yellowstone River just north of town. The Yellowstone, the longest undammed river in the United States, is a popular fishing and floating river, meeting up with the Missouri near the Montana–North Dakota border. The Bozeman Trail crosses the Yellowstone just west of Big Timber. The trail was more or less abandoned in 1868 after six years of bloody skirmishing between Native Americans, who began to envision the end of their traditional lives, and settlers who envisioned new lives and acres of land free for the taking.

US 191 ends at Big Timber, a town so-named by William Clark of the Lewis and Clark Expedition for a large stand of cottonwood trees at the point where either the Boulder River or Big Timber Creek flows into the Yellowstone River. Clark and his exploring party, on their way East from the Pacific Ocean, chopped down one of the trees here to make a pirogue.

Big Timber is a quaint town with a little park and tree-lined streets along which tidy houses are situated. The Victorian Village Museum here houses 5,000 square feet of antiques, all arranged in rooms respective of their function. Each year the museum features a new special exhibit. The Crazy Mountain Museum displays items reflecting the history of Sweet Grass County and the surrounding area, including fossils, dinosaur bones, and Indian artifacts. The Sweetgrass and Sage Gallery and Gift Shop showcases the works of local artists Jessica Zemsky and Jack Hines. Crazy Mountain Art and Antiques also features works of Montana artists, including hand-crafted gifts. If fishing is your bag, several guides are available in Big Timber to take you along the Yellowstone or Boulder rivers. Big Timber's rodeo is in June, and the county fair is held in August.

From here you can reach Scenic Drives 23 and 11 near Livingston, west of Big Timber, or take Scenic Drive 12 south from Big Timber into the Absaroka–Beartooth Wilderness Area. Scenic Drive 14 ends in Columbus, 38 miles east.

APPENDIX: SOURCES OF MORE INFORMATION

Before setting out on any of Montana's scenic drives, you want to get more information about the lands crossed by the drive routes and the events sponsored in the area by contacting the agencies listed below.

National Parks, Monuments, and Recreation Areas

Big Hole National Battlefield
P.O. Box 237
Wisdom, MT 59761
(406) 689-3155

Bighorn Canyon National Recreation Area
Visitor Center
Box 458
Fort Smith, MT 59035
(406) 666-2339

Glacier National Park
Park Headquarters
West Glacier, MT 59936
(406) 888-5441

Little Bighorn National Battlefield
P.O. Box 39
Crow Agency, MT 59022

Yellowstone National Park
Superintendent
Mammoth, WY 82190
(307) 344-7381

National Wildlife Refuges

Bowdoin National Wildlife Refuge
Refuge Manager
Malta, MT 59538
(406) 654-2863

Charles M. Russell National Wildlife Refuge
P.O. Box 110
Lewistown, MT 59457
(406) 538-8706

Red Rock Lakes National Wildlife Refuge
Monida Star Route, Box 15
Lima, MT 59739
(406) 276-3536

Bureau of Land Management Offices

Dillon Resource Area
1005 Selway Drive
Dillon, MT 59725
(406) 683-2337

Judith Resource Area
P.O. Box 1160
Lewistown, MT 59457
(406) 538-7462

USDA Forest Service Offices

Beaverhead National Forest
420 Barrett Street
Dillon, MT 59725
(406) 683-3900

Madison Ranger District
5 Forest Service Road
Ennis, MT 59729
(406) 682-4253

Wisdom Ranger District
P.O. Box 238
Wisdom, MT 59761
(406) 689-3243

Wise River Ranger District
Box 100
Wise River, MT 59762
(406) 832-3178

—

Bitterroot National Forest
1801 North First Street
Hamilton, MT 59840
(406) 363-3131

—

Custer National Forest
2602 First Avenue North
P.O. Box 2556
Billings, MT 59103
(406) 657-6361

Ashland Ranger District
P.O. Box 168
Ashland, MT 59003
(406) 784-2344

Beartooth Ranger District
HC 49, Box 3420
Red Lodge, MT 59068
(406) 446-2103

Grand River Ranger District
P.O. Box 390
Lemmon, SD 57638
(605) 374-3592

—

Deerlodge National Forest
P.O. Box 400
Butte, MT 59703
(406) 496-3400

Philipsburg Ranger District
P.O. Box H
Philipsburg, MT 59858
(406) 859-3211

—

Flathead National Forest
1935 Third Avenue East
Kalispell, MT 59901
(406) 755-5401

Swan Lake Ranger District
P.O. Box 370
Swan Lake, MT 59911
(406) 837-5081

—

Gallatin National Forest
P.O. Box 130
Bozeman, MT 59771
(406) 587-6701

Big Timber Ranger District
P.O. Box 196
Big Timber, MT 59011
(406) 932-5155

Bozeman Ranger District
3710 Fallon Street, Box C
Bozeman, MT 59715
(406) 587-6920

Gardiner Ranger District
P.O. Box 5
Gardiner, MT 59030
(406) 848-7375

Hebgen Lake Ranger District
P.O. Box 520
West Yellowstone, MT 59758
(406) 646-7369

Livingston Ranger District
Route 62, Box 3197
Livingston, MT 59047
(406) 222-1892

—

Kootenai National Forest
506 U.S. Highway 2 West
Libby, MT 59923
(406) 293-6211

—

Lewis and Clark National Forest
1101 15th Street
P.O. Box 869
Great Falls, MT 59403
(406) 791-7700

Augusta Information Station
405 Manix Street
P.O. Box 365
Augusta, MT 59410
(406) 562-3247

Belt Creek Information Station
U.S. Highway 89
Neihart, MT 59465
(406) 236-5511

Judith Ranger District
P.O. Box 484
Stanford, MT 59479
(406) 566-2292

Kings Hill Ranger District
204 West Folsom, Box A
White Sulphur Springs, MT 59645
(406) 547-3361

Musselshell Ranger District
809 2 NW, Box 1906
Harlowton, MT 59036
(406) 632-4391

Rocky Mountain Ranger District
1102 Main Avenue NW
P.O. Box 340
Choteau, MT 59422
(406) 466-5341

—

Lolo National Forest
Building 24, Fort Missoula
Missoula, MT 59801
(406) 329-3750

Seeley Lake Ranger District
HC 31, Box 3200
Seeley Lake, MT 59868
(406) 677-2233

—

Shoshone National Forest
P.O. Box 2140
Cody, WY 82414
(307) 587-6241

Clarks Fork Ranger District
P.O. Box 1023
Powell, WY 82435
(307) 754-2407

Indian Reservations

Blackfeet Nation
P.O. Box 850
Browning, MT 59417
(406) 338-7276

Confederated Salish and Kootenai Tribes
P.O. Box 278
Pablo, MT 59855
(406) 675-2700

Crow Reservation
Crow Agency, MT 59022
(406) 638-2601

Fort Belknap Tourism Office
Fort Belknap Agency
Rural Route 1, Box 66
Harlem, MT 59526
(406) 353-2205

Fort Peck Assiniboine and Sioux Tribes
P.O. Box 1027
Poplar, MT 59255
(406) 768-5155

Northern Cheyenne Chamber of Commerce
P.O. Box 328
Lame Deer, MT 59043
(406) 477-6253

State Parks

Montana Department of Fish, Wildlife & Parks
Parks Division
1420 East Sixth Avenue
Helena, MT 59620
(406) 444-3750

Region 1 (Placid Lake, Salmon Lake)
3201 Spurgin Road
Missoula, MT 59801
(406) 542-5500

Region 4 (Ackley Lake, Bears Paw Battlefield, Sluice Boxes)
4600 Giant Springs Road
P.O. Box 6610
Great Falls, MT 59406
(406) 454-3441

Region 5 (Chief Plenty Coups)
2300 Lake Elmo Drive
Billings, MT 59105
(406) 252-4654

Region 7 (Medicine Rocks, Rosebud Battlefield, Tongue River Reservoir)
Rural Route 1, Box 2004
Miles City, MT 59301
(406) 232-4365

Region 8 (Bannack, Holter Lake, Lewis & Clark Caverns, Missouri Headwaters)
1404 Eighth Avenue
Helena, MT 59620
(406) 444-4720

Chambers of Commerce

Anaconda
306 E. Park
Anaconda, MT 59711
(406) 563-2400

Baker
Box 849
Baker, MT 59313
(406) 778-2879; (406) 778-2883, Ext. 13

Bigfork
Box 237
Bigfork, MT 59911
(406) 837-5888

Big Timber
Box 1012
Big Timber, MT 59011
(406) 932-5131

Bitterroot Valley (Corvallis, Darby, Florence, Hamilton, Sula, Stevensville, Victor)
105 East Main
Hamilton, MT 59840
(406) 363-2400

Bozeman
Box B
Bozeman, MT 59715
(406) 586-5421; (800) 228-4224

Browning
Box 99
Browning, MT 59417
(406) 338-7911; (800) 775-1355

Chinook
Box 744
Chinook, MT 59523
(406) 357-2313

Choteau
Route 2, Box 256
Choteau, MT 59422
(406) 466-5332

Columbus
Box 783
Columbus, MT 59019
(406) 322-4505

Dillon
Box 425
Dillon, MT 59725
(406) 683-5511

Ekalaka
Box 297
Ekalaka, MT 59324
(406) 775-6658

Ennis
Box 291
Ennis, MT 59729
(406) 682-4388

Eureka
Box 186
Eureka, MT 59324

Gardiner
Box 81
Gardiner, MT 59030
(406) 848-7971

Glasgow
Box 832
Glasgow, MT 59230
(406) 228-2222

Hardin
200 North Center Avenue
Hardin, MT 59034
(406) 665-1672

Harlowton
Box 694
Harlowton, MT 59036
(406) 632-5523

Havre
Box 308
Havre, MT 59501
(406) 265-4383

Lewistown
Box 818
Lewistown, MT 59457
(406) 538-5436

Libby
Box 704
Libby, MT 59923
(406) 293-4167

Livingston
212 West Park
Livingston, MT 59047
(406) 222-0850

Malta
Drawer GG
Malta, MT 59538
(406) 654-1776

Miles City
901 Main Street
Miles City, MT 59301
(406) 232-2890

Missoula
Box 7577
Missoula, MT 59807
(406) 543-6623

Philipsburg
Box 661
Philipsburg, MT 59858
(406) 859-3388

Red Lodge
Box 988
Red Lodge, MT 59068
(406) 446-1718

Saco
Box 195
Saco, MT 59261
(406) 527-3361

Seeley Lake
Box 516
Seeley Lake, MT 59868
(406) 677-2880

Swan Lake
Stoney Creek Road
Swan Lake, MT 59911
(406) 886-2279

Troy
Box 3005
Troy, MT 59935
(406) 295-4216

Virginia City
Box 218
Virginia City, MT 59755
(406) 843-5345

West Yellowstone
Box 458
West Yellowstone, MT 59758
(406) 646-7701

White Sulphur Springs
Box 356
White Sulphur Springs, MT 59645
(406) 547-2223

Miscellaneous

Big Sky Ski & Summer Resort
P.O. Box 160001
Big Sky, MT 59716
(800) 548-4486

Chico Hot Springs Lodge
P.O. Drawer D
Pray, MT 59065
(406) 333-4933; (800) HOT-WADA

Museum of the Plains Indian
U.S. Highway 89
Browning, MT 59417
(406) 338-2230

Museum of the Rockies
Montana State University
Bozeman, MT 59717-0272
(406) 994-3466

Old Trail Museum
P.O. Box 919
Choteau, MT 59422
(406) 466-5332

Pine Butte Swamp Guest Ranch
HC 58, Box 34C
Choteau, MT 59422
(406) 466-2158

Red Lodge Mountain Ski Area
Box 750
Red Lodge, MT 59068
(800) 444-8977

BIBLIOGRAPHY

Alt, David, Donald W. Hyndman. *Roadside Geology of Montana.* Missoula, Mont.: Mountain Press, 1986.

Beal, Merrill D. *I Will Fight No More Forever: Chief Joseph and the Nez Perce War*. Seattle: University of Washington Press, 1963.

Bradshaw, Glenda Clay, comp. *Montana's Historical Highway Markers.* Helena, Mont.: Montana Historical Society, 1989.

Chadwick, Douglas H. *A Beast the Color of Winter*. San Francisco: Sierra Club Books, 1983.

Cheney, Roberta C. *Names on the Face of Montana.* Missoula, Mont.: Mountain Press, 1983.

DeVoto, Bernard, ed. *The Journals of Lewis and Clark*. Boston: Houghton Mifflin Company, 1953.

Doig, Ivan. *English Creek*. New York: Penguin Books, 1984.

Fischer, Carol, and Hank Fischer. *The Montana Wildlife Viewing Guide*. Rev. ed. Helena, Mont.: Falcon, 1995.

Fritz, Harry W. *Montana, Land of Contrasts*. Woodland Hills, Calif.: Windsor Publications, Inc., 1984.

Graves, F. Lee. *Bannack, Cradle of Montana.* Helena, Mont.: American World & Geographic Publishing, 1991.

Howard, Joseph Kinsey, ed. *Montana Margins: A State Anthology*. New Haven: Yale University Press, 1946.

Kipling, Rudyard. *From Sea to Sea: Part II, Letters of Travel*. New York: Doubleday & McClure Co., 1899.

Kittredge, William, Annick Smith, eds. *The Last Best Place: A Montana Anthology*. Helena, Mont.: Falcon, 1993.

Leopold, Aldo. *A Sand County Almanac and Sketches Here and There*. New York: Oxford University Press, 1949.

Lopez, Barry. *Arctic Dreams: Imagination and Desire in a Northern Landscape*. New York: Charles Scribner's Sons, 1986.

McEneaney, Terry. *The Uncommon Loon*. Flagstaff, Ariz.: Northland Publishing, 1991.

Miller, Donald C. *Ghost Towns of Montana*. Boulder, Colo.: Pruett Publishing Company, 1974.

Montana Atlas and Gazetteer. Freeport, Maine: DeLorme Mapping Co., 1994

Muir, John. *Wilderness Essays*. Salt Lake City: Peregrine Smith, Inc. 1980.

Schneider, Bill. *The Hiker's Guide to Montana*. Rev. ed. Helena, Mont.: Falcon, 1992.

Seibel, Roberta V. *Motorist's Guide to Glacer National Park*. West Glacier, Mont.: Glacier Natural History Association, Inc., no date.

Toole, K. Ross. *Montana, An Uncommon Land*. Norman: University of Oklahoma Press, 1959.

Weide, Bruce. *Trail of the Great Bear*. Helena, Mont.: Falcon Press, 1992.

ABOUT THE AUTHOR

S. A. Snyder came to Montana when she was nineteen. Like many other Montana transplants, she wanted to escape from somewhere else; she also tapped family roots. Her great-great-grandparents had homesteaded in the Bitterroot Valley in the 1870s, among the valley's first white settlers. They are buried in Florence, and their homestead still stands.

When she is not researching her ancestors' past, Snyder writes magazine articles, travel stories, poetry, essays, screenplays, and stageplays, or bags it all and heads for the hills on foot or mountain bike. She is an inveterate traveler, having visited forty-six states and a dozen foreign countries. The rest of her life will most likely be spent exploring the territory she hasn't yet seen.

Snyder has college degrees in Forestry Resources Management, Wildlife Biology, and Journalism.

Photo by Paul Dumond.